ISLANDICA

AN ANNUAL RELATING TO ICELAND

AND THE

FISKE ICELANDIC COLLECTION

IN

CORNELL UNIVERSITY LIBRARY

EDITED BY

GEORGE WILLIAM HARRIS

LIBRARIAN

VOLUME I.

BIBLIOGRAPHY OF THE ICELANDIC SAGAS
AND MINOR TALES

BY HALLDÓR HERMANNSSON

ISSUED BY CORNELL UNIVERSITY LIBRARY
ITHACA, NEW YORK
1908

INTRODUCTION.

Willard Fiske, the first Librarian of Cornell University, was not only a skilful bibliographer and scholarly librarian but also an indefatigable book-collector. When he resigned his librarianship in 1883, after fifteen years of service, and took up his residence in Italy, he was fortunate in being able to devote his leisure to bibliographical studies and to indulge his fondness for collecting books. How he was led, a few years later, to bring together and present to the University Library a collection of Rhæto-Romanic literature, numbering some fourteen hundred volumes, and a remarkably complete Dante collection, comprising over seven thousand volumes, he has charmingly told in the introductions to the printed catalogues of these collections. His visits to Egypt led him to make a collection of the literature of transcription which he also presented to the University Library, while to the National Library of Iceland he presented a collection of some twelve hundred volumes on the game of chess. and its history. At his death in 1904, he bequeathed to Cornell University his extensive Petrarch and Icelandic collections and not only made generous provision for their maintenance and increase, but bequeathed also to the University all his residuary estate as a fund for general library purposes, adding altogether about half a million dollars to the endowment of the University Library.

Of the collections given by him to the University Library the Icelandic collection is much the largest. It is also the oldest and perhaps the richest in rare books and editions. Its formation was the work of a lifetime, for its beginning was made by Mr. Fiske when a student in the University of Upsala more than fifty years ago. Here he became imbued with a deep and abiding love for the Old-Icelandic language and literature, and took advantage of the favorable opportunity offered by his residence in Scandinavia to collect books in this field. Upon his return to America in 1853, he became an assistant in the Astor Library, then just about to open its doors under the superintendence of that able and learned librarian J. G. Cogswell, from whom he received valuable training in bibliographical methods. At the same time he kept up his Icelandic studies and gradually added to his Icelandic collection. A description of the collection was given in 1860 in Wynne's "Private Libraries of New York," and it was then reputed to be the richest collection of Icelandic literature and history in the country. A later account of the collection is given by M. W. Plummer in the "Bulletin of Bibliography" for April, 1897; but the fullest description is that given by E. P. Evans in the "Beilage zur Allgemeinen Zeitung," 13, 14 Sept. 1896. Since then it has been largely increased and now contains about nine thousand volumes.

Some idea of the completeness of the collection in its special field may be gained from the four numbers of Mr. Fiske's privately printed "Bibliographical Notices" which contain supplements to the British Museum Catalogue of Books printed in Iceland, and from the Bibliography of the Icelandic Sagas here printed. But a clearer conception of the scope and extent of the collection will perhaps be obtained from the following general description of it, given by Mr. Fiske himself in No. V. of his "Bibliographical Notices."

"The collection includes nearly every publication enumerated by Möbius, besides all the archæological treatises, all the works on the scattered remains of runic literature and on Scandinavian mythology, all the annals, travels, natural histories, government documents, ecclesiastical writings, biographies and bibliographies, which can, in any way, throw light on the history, topography, indigenous products, commerce, language and letters of Iceland. It lacks very few of the editions and translations of the sagas, the ancient laws, the Eddas, and the skaldic lays, and very few of the treatises which illustrate them; it lacks still fewer of the strictly linguistic works—dictionaries grammars, anthologies—relating to either the Old-Icelandic or the New-Icelandic, possessing, to give a single instance, every edition and version of the numerous philological productions of Erasmus Rask. It includes most of the texts edited by Swedish scholars in the 17th and 18th centuries, and all of those edited by the remarkable group of Norwegian scholars in the 19th century, as well as every text, translation and tract issued by the Arna-Magnæan Commission, the Lærdómslistafèlag, the Royal Society of Northern Antiquaries, the Icelandic Literary Society, the Nordisk Literatur-Samfund, the Norsk Oldskrift-selskab, the Pjóðvinafèlag and the Samfund til Udgivelse af gammel nordisk Litteratur. It has all the impressions of the Icelandic Bible, or of its parts. Its series of Icelandic periodi-cals—whether printed in the island itself, in Denmark or in Canada—is absolutely complete ; and all but complete is its series of laws, ordinances and rescripts, regulating the island's affairs, promulgated by either the Danish or the Icelandic au-thorities. Of the geographical descriptions of Iceland, from those published in Hakluyt and Purchas and Ramusio to the voluminous work of the French expedition under Gaimard—from the earliest dubious notices of Thule in the mediæval chronicles to the recent and exact topographical reports of Thoroddsen—scarcely one is wanting, each and every published voyage being present not only in its various original editions but in all its translations. The cartography of Iceland is especially well represented, beginning with the charts compiled to accompany the voyages of the Zeni, the editions of Ptolemy and the works of Olaus Magnus, Ortelius and Münster, and coming down to the remarkable map of Björn Gunnlaugsson and the marine and coast surveys issued by the Danish, British and French governments. As to Greenland the collection possesses those writings which concern themselves with the early Euro-pean settlements in that icy region, and with the fugitive visits paid by navigators from the Icelandic commonwealth to the opposite northernmost shores of the American continent ; and as to the Færo archipelago it has brought together those which treat of the Icelandic dialect there spoken, or of the older history—the saga age—of the interesting insular group. In addition to its books and pamphlets and journals the collection includes a great number of ephemeral publications—broadsides of various sorts, placards, funeral inscriptions, *vers d'occasion*, prospectuses, circulars—and not a few engravings and photo-graphs of Icelandic persons and places.''

Besides making ample provision for the maintenance and in-crease of the Dante, Petrarch, and Icelandic collections, with which Mr. Fiske so greatly enriched the University Library, and which constitute such a splendid and permanent memorial of the bibliographical knowledge and skill of their collector, his will contained the following bequest :

" I give and bequeath to the said Cornell University . . . . the sum of Five Thousand (5000) Dollars, to have and to hold the same forever, in trust, nevertheless, to receive the income thereof, and to use and expend the said income for the purposes of the publication of an annual volume relating to Iceland and the said Icelandic collection in the library of the said University."

At the time the will was made, Mr. Fiske, in discussing its provisions with Professor Horatio S. White, whom he appointed his literary executor, suggested that this annual volume might contain an accession list of the collection, or papers, etc., on, *e. g.*, the discovery of America by the Norsemen, or on any topic connected with the history, philology, literature, etc., of Iceland, including, *e. g.*, the saga literature. In pursuance of these provisions and suggestions the first of the series of annual volumes is now issued, containing a bibliography of the sagas relating to Iceland, prepared by Mr. Halldór Hermannsson, who was associated with Mr. Fiske in his later bibliographical work and is now in charge of the Fiske Icelandic collection in Cornell University Library.

G. W. HARRIS.

CORNELL UNIVERSITY LIBRARY,
ITHACA, JUNE, 1908

BIBLIOGRAPHY

OF THE

ICELANDIC SAGAS

AND MINOR TALES

BY
HALLDÓR HERMANNSSON

PREFATORY NOTE.

Since 1880, when Theodor Möbius published his second catalogue, no bibliography covering the whole field of the Old-
Icelandic literature has appeared, although from year to year
bibliographies have been printed in various periodical publications. However desirable it might be to print a full catalogue
of the Fiske Icelandic Collection, which is one of the most complete in this field, the expense of so doing would far exceed any
sum now available for the purpose. It has therefore been de-
cided to publish from time to time, in the annual volume pro-
vided for in the will of Mr. Fiske, special bibliographies, of
which the present is the first. From a literary standpoint all
the sagas could be styled Icelandic, since with the exception of
a few Romantic sagas they were all written in Iceland or by
Icelanders. In this bibliography, however, are included only
the Icelandic sagas proper (Íslendínga sögur), that is, the sagas
and tales (þættir), historical and fictitious, the scene of which
is Iceland, or which treat of Icelandic persons at home or
abroad, from the settlement of Iceland in the ninth century
until the end of the Commonwealth in 1264, and which were
written before the end of the fourteenth century. Three sagas
dealing with events subsequent to 1264 and two composed later
than the fourteenth century have been included, because of
their close connection with the others.

The sagas and tales are here arranged in the order of the
English alphabet, the umlaut being neglected, and the letter þ
put at the end. The editions and extracts are given in chronological order, as are also the translations in each language. The
approximate date of events of each saga follows the main entry,
the date of composition being likewise given. For the earlier
sagas the date of events is chiefly in accordance with the chronology of Guðbr. Vigfússon in his essay " Um tímatal í Íslendinga sögum í fornöld," printed in " Safn til sögu Íslands,"
1855, II. pp. 185–502 ; but for the date of composition I have

in most cases followed Professor Finnur Jónsson's "Den old-norske og oldislandske Litteratur Historie," Köbenhavn 1894–1902, 3 vols. The principal manuscripts, especially vellum manuscripts, are also mentioned, and their dates given, mainly according to Dr. Kálund's catalogues of the Copenhagen collections. The abbreviations denoting the location of these manuscripts are the following: *AM.*, the Arna Magnæan Collection, Copenhagen; *Cod. Holm.*, codices of the Royal Library, Stockholm; *Gml. kgl. Saml.*, Gammel kongelig Samling in the Royal Library, Copenhagen; *Icel. Lit. Soc.*, the Icelandic Literary Society's manuscript collection, now in the National Library, Reykjavík. The dates of the Morkinskinna and the Flateyjarbók, the two codices most frequently mentioned, have not always been given, hence it may be proper to state here that the former (Gml. kgl. Saml. 1009 fol., a recension from circa 1220 of an older saga-work) is from c. 1300, while the latter (Gml. kgl. Saml. 1005 I.–II. fol.) was written between the years 1387 and 1394. The orthography of the titles is followed, the names of the editors are usually given, and those of translators always, when known to the compiler; the place of publication is given for books, but as a rule not for periodicals; it has been omitted for well-known series often quoted like the "Fornmanna sögur," "Oldnordiske Sagaer," "Scripta historica Islandorum," "Antiquités Russes," and usually for "Grönlands historiske Mindesmærker," all of which were printed at Copenhagen under the auspices of the Royal Society of Northern Antiquaries. Sizes are given with complete titles of books, otherwise only sizes other than octavo; but for periodicals mentioned in the notes generally no size is given. The abbreviations for titles of periodicals, I think, require no explanation.

Among critical works and commentaries on the sagas, reference is given to only two general works on the Old-Icelandic literature, viz. P. E. Müller's "Sagabibliothek," Kiöbenhavn 1817–1820, 3 vols., and Professor Finnur Jónsson's critical history mentioned above. These two works contain respectively the first and the latest lengthy account of the sagas in general.

The titles in the following pages are almost all in the Fiske Icelandic Collection or Cornell University Library; titles not found there are marked by a dagger. Of printed works which have been particularly useful to me in compiling this bibliography I might mention the two catalogues of Möbius, and the annual lists in "Germania," "Arkiv för nordisk filologi," and "Jahresbericht über die erscheinungen auf dem gebiete der germanischen philologie."

As an appendix to the present bibliography I have added a list of poetical writings and works of prose fiction based on these sagas. As is explained in another place, this list makes no pretence of exhaustiveness.

My best thanks are due to Mr. George W. Harris, Librarian of Cornell University Library, for the valuable help and numerous suggestions he has given me. I am indebted to my friend Mr. Sigfús Blöndal, of the Royal Library in Copenhagen, for the transcription of a few titles beyond my reach. Mr. R. Nisbet Bain, of the British Museum, has kindly given me information about the copy of the second edition of Ari's "Schedæ" in that library.

H. H.

CORNELL UNIVERSITY LIBRARY,
JUNE, 1908

CONTENTS.

BIBLIOGRAPHY

OF THE

ICELANDIC SAGAS.

Álptfirðinga saga. *See* Eyrbyggja saga.

Árna saga biskups Þorlákssonar.
> History of the life and the times of Árni Þorláksson (b. 1237, d. 1298), bishop of Skálholt 1269–1298. The saga stops abruptly at 1290–91 ; it exists in paper MSS., only two vellum fragments (AM. 122 B, fol. from c. 1400 ; AM. 220 VI. fol., from the 14th cent.). Written probably in the beginning of the 14th century, and presumably by Árni Helgason, bishop of Skálholt 1304–1320.

Saga Árna biskups Þorlákssunar. *In* Sturlunga-saga. Kaupmannahöfn 1820. 4°. II. 2. pp. 1–124.

> Extracts with notes in Grönlands historiske Mindesmærker. 1838. II. pp. 787–791, and Antiquités Russes. 1852. fol. II. pp. 361–367.

Árna biskups saga. *In* Biskupa sögur. Kaupmannahöfn 1858. I. pp. lxxii–lxxxi, 677–786.

> Edited (from Cod. Holm. 12, 4°) by Guðbr. Vigfússon.

Jónsson, Finnur (*bishop*). Historia Ecclesiastica Islandiæ. Havniæ 1774. 4°. II. pp. 1–55.
Jónsson, Finnur. Litteratur Historie. III. pp. 65–67.
Müller. P. E. Sagabibliothek. I. pp. 326–330.

Arnórs þáttr kerlingarnefs. *See* Svaða þáttr ok Arnórs kerlingarnefs.

Áróns saga Hjörleifssonar.
> C. 1220–1255. Written shortly after the middle of the 13th century (before 1280). Vellum fragment from c. 1400 (AM. 551 Dβ, 4°), paper MSS. of the 17th cent. (AM. 212 fol., 426 fol.).

Arons saga Hjörleifssonar. *In* Biskupa sögur. Kaupmannahöfn 1858. II. pp. lxvi–lxviii, 619–638.

> Edited by Guðbr. Vigfússon. Chap. 3–10 are omitted, but are found in the Guðmundar saga biskups hin elzta (chap. 74–90) in the same vol. pp. 515–540, the three following chapters of which (91–93) also treat of Árón, pp. 540–545.

Árons saga. *In* Sturlunga saga, ed. by Gudbr. Vigfusson. Oxford. 1878. II. pp. 312–347. (*Cf.* vol. I. pp. cxvi–cxvii).

> Extract (Árón's pilgrimage to Palestine) with notes in Antiquités Russes. 1852. fol. II. pp. 356–361.

DANISH. — Brudstykke af Aron Hiörleifssons Saga, om det
norske Hofliv i det trettende Aarhundrede, oversat af det
gamle Skandinaviske ved P. E. Müller. *In* Det skandinaviske
Litteraturselskabs Skrifter   1814. X. pp. 1–37.

Jónsson, Finnur. Litteratur Historie. II. pp. 768–769.
Muller, P. E.   Sagabibliothek. I. pp. 234–236.
Munch, P. A.   Aron Hjörleifsson i Norge.   Historisk Fortælling fra det
   13de Aarhundrede. *In* Norsk Folkekalender for 1849. Christiania.
   pp. 50–59.
Ólsen, Björn M.   Um Sturlungu. pp. 254–272.

Auðunar þáttr vestfirzka.

C. 1050.   In Haralds saga harðráða in the Morkinskinna (Gl. kgl. Sml.
   1009 fol., from the end of the 13th cent.) and slightly different in the
   Flateyjarbók (Gl. kgl. Sml. 1005 fol., from the end of the 14th cent).

Commentarium anecdotum de Auduno Regem Svenonem Astri-
thidam invisente islandice et latine edidit cum præfatiuncula
Birgerus Thorlacius.   Havniæ 1818. fol. pp. (4) + 10.
(*University program.*)

In Fornmanna sögur.   1831. VI. pp. 297–307.

Uddrag af Fortællingen om Audun den Vestfjordske. *In* Grönlands historiske Mindesmærker. 1838. II. pp. 630–653.

   The Flateyjarbók-text with introduction, notes and Danish version.

Audun den Vestfjordske. *In* Oldnorsk Læsebog af P. A. Munch
og C. R. Unger.   Christiania 1847. pp. 31–24.

Fra þvi er Auþun enn vestfirðzki færþe Sveine konvnge biarn-
dyre. *In* Morkinskinna.   Christiania 1867. pp. 61–65.

(Þattr Auðunar vestfirzka.)   *In* Flateyjarbók.   Christiania
1868. III. pp. 410–415.

Kong Harald og Islændingen. *In* Oldnordisk Læsebog af L. F.
A. Wimmer.   Kjöbenhavn 1870. pp. 54–59.

   The Morkinskinna-text. In all the subsequent editions: 1877, 1882,
   1889, 1896, 1903.

Audun. *In* An Icelandic Primer by H. Sweet.   Oxford 1886.
pp. 70–76. —2. edition. Oxford 1896.

Auðunar þáttr vestfirzka. *In* Fjörutíu Íslendinga þættir. Þórleifr
Jónsson gaf út.   Reykjavík 1904. pp. 1–11.

DANISH.—Om Audun den vestfjordske. En islandsk Fortælling
oversat udaf Thorlacii Program [ved K. L. Rahbek]. *In*
Dansk Minerva for Januarii 1818. pp. 83–93.

   Re-issued in Nordiske Fortællinger ved K. L. Rahbek. Kjöbenhavn
   1821. II. pp. 21–30 (Audun fra Vestfjord).

In Oldnordiske Sagaer. 1832. VI. pp. 242–251.

Ödun med Björnen. *In* Sagaer, fortalte af Brynjolf Snorrason og
Kristian Arentzen. Kjóbenhavn 1849. II. pp. 213–225.

GERMAN—†Audun aus Vestfjord. Eine Islandssage [deutsch
von F. W. F. Graf von Ahlefeldt-Laurvig]. *In* Winfrieds
(N. D. Hinsche's) Nordalbingische Blätter. 1820. I. 2. pp.
103–113.

LATIN.—Thorlacius's *version in the edition of* 1818 (*see above*).
Svb. Egilsson's *version in* Scripta historica Islandorum. 1835.
VI. pp. 274–282.

Cf. T. Torfæus's Historiæ rer. Norvegic. p. III. 1711. fol. pp. 329–332.

NORWEGIAN.—Audun Vestfjording, efter Morkinskinna. *In*
Fra By og Bygd. Björgvin 1875. V. 1. pp. 60–70.

SWEDISH.—Audun. *In* Isländsk och fornsvensk litteratur i
urval, af Richard Steffen. Stockholm 1905. pp. 134–140.

Jónsson, Finnur. Litteratur Historie. II. pp. 332–335, 549.
Müller, P. E. Sagabibliothek. I. pp. 345–346.

Bandamanna saga.

C. 1055. Written near the end of the 12th century. Vellum MSS.
(AM. 132 fol., Möðruvallabók, first half of the 14th cent.; Gl. kgl.
Sml 2845 4°, 15th cent.) In the Möðruvallabók the saga is called
Saga Ófeigs bandakalls (bragðakalls?), the name Bandamanna saga
occurs in Grettis saga (chap. xlv.). *Cf.* Odds þáttr Ófeigssonar, which
treats of the same person.

Bandamanna Saga. *In* Nockrer Marg-Frooder Sögu-Þætter
Islendinga, ad Forlage Biörns Marcussonar. Hólar 1756. 4°.
pp. 1–15.

Bandamanna saga udgivet af det nordiske Literatur-Samfund
ved H. Friðriksson. Kiöbenhavn 1850. (Nordiske Oldskrifter. X.) 8°. pp. (4)+90.

With Icelandic-Danish glossary. *Review:* Nÿ félagsrit. 1858. XVIII.
pp. 156–159, by Guðbr. Vigfússon (*cf.* Germania. 1867. XII. pp 481–482,
by K. Maurer).

Bandmanna saga, efter skinnboken no. 2845, 4to à kougl. bi-
blioteket i Köpenhamn. Akademisk afhandling af Gustaf J.
Chr. Cederschiöld. Lund 1874. 4°. pp. (2)+xiv+26, *facsim.*

Separate reprint from "Acta Universitatis Lundensis. X." The only
edition of this recension. *Review:* Germania. 1874. XIX. pp. 433–
448, by Konrad Maurer.

Zwei Isländer-Geschichte, die Hænsna-Þóres und die Bandamanna
saga mit Einleitung und Glossar herausgegeben von Andreas
Heusler. Berlin 1897. 8°. pp. xxix–lx, 27–59.

Reviews: Anz. f. deut. Altert. 1901. XXVII. pp. 230–234, by E.
Mogk;—Literaturbl. f. g. u. r. Philol. 1898. coll. 183–184, by W.
Golther;—Literar. Centralbl. 1897. col. 1531, by F. Detter (?);—Deut.
Lit. Zeit. 1899. col. 1064–66, by W. Ranisch;—Revue critique. 1898.
N. S. XLVI. pp. 14–15, by V. Henry;—Journ. of Germ. Philol. II. p.
547, by O. Brenner;—† Museum, maandbl. voor philol. 1897. pp. 364–
366, by R. C. Boer.

Bandamanna saga. Búið hefir til prentunar Vald. Ásmundarson. Reykjavík 1902. (Íslendinga sögur. 30.) 8°. pp. v+
52.

DANISH.—† De Sammensvorne. Dansk Gjengivelse af Banda-
manna saga ved Vilhelm Björg. Hillerod 1868. 4°. pp. 69.
(*Forms pt. ii.* of Oldnordisk Vinterlæsning for Danske ved V.
Björg. Kjöbenhavn 1868.)

De Sammensvornes Saga. *In* Billeder af Livet paa Island, ved
Fr. Winkel Horn. Kjöbenhavn 1876. III. pp. 63–99.

ENGLISH.—The Story of the Banded Men. *A paraphrase in*
Iceland, by Sabine Baring-Gould. London 1868. pp. 300–
316.

Bandamanna saga ; or The Story of the Confederates. *In* Summer Travelling in Iceland. By John Coles. London 1882.
pp. 205–229.

The Story of the Banded Men. *In* The Saga Library, by W.
Morris and E. Magnússon. London 1891. I. pp. xxiii–
xxviii, 71–121, *map.*

A facsimile of a page of Morris's MS. in "The Art Journal Extra
Number : Easter Art Journal. The Art of W. M." London 1899. 4°.
p. 30.—*Reviews.* The Academy. 1891. XL. p. 448, by C. Elton;—The
Nation (N. Y.). 1891. LIII. pp. 220–221 ;—Tímarit h. ísl. Bókmentafél.
1892. XIII. pp. 74–76, by V. Guðmundsson.

Cederschiöld, G.   Bidrag till kritiken af Bandamannasagas text. *In*
Arkiv f. nord. filol. 1889. V. pp. 150–154.

Jónsson, Finnur.   Litteratur Historie. II. pp. 471–474.

Müller. P. E.   Sagabibliothek. I. pp. 315–316.

Vigfússon, Guðbr.   Um tímatal í Íslendinga sögum. pp. 491–492.

Bárðar saga Snæfellsáss *or* Bárðar saga Snæfellsáss ok Gests.

A fictitious saga (c 900). It consists of two parts, probably by different
writers, viz. Bárðar saga (chap. 1–10) and Gests saga Bárðarsonar
(chap. 11–21), and dates from the first part of the 14th century. Paper
MSS., and late vellum MSS. (AM. 158 fol., and 489, 4°, from 16th and
17th century ; fragment AM. 564 A, 4°, c. 1400).

Sagann af Baarde Dumbssyne, er kalladur var Snæfells-as.—
Sagann af Gesti syne Baardar Snæfell-ass. *In* Nockrer Marg-

Frooder Sögu-Þætter Islendinga, ad Forlage Biörns Marcussonar. Hólar 1756. 4°. pp. 163–181.

Bárðarsaga Snæfellsáss, Víglundarsaga, Þórðarsaga, Draumvitranir, Völsaþáttr, ved Guðbrandr Vigfússon. Udgivet af det nordiske Literatur-Samfund. Kjöbenhavn 1860. (Nordiske Oldskrifter. XXVII.) 8°. pp. xvii+177.

The Icelandic text of Bárðar saga fills pp. 1–46, abstract in Danish, pp. 145-158.

Bárðar saga Snæfellsáss. Búið hefir til prentunar Vald. Ásmundarson. Reykjavík 1902. (Íslendinga sögur. 37.) 8°. pp. iv+64.

DANISH.—G. Vigfússon's *abstract* (1860), *see above*.

Gotzen, Joseph. Über die Bárðar saga Snæfellsáss. Inaugural-Dissertation. Berlin 1903. 8°. pp. (4)+67+(5).
Review · Arkiv f. nord. filol. 1905. XXI. pp. 386–392, by Heinz Hungerland.

Jónsson, Finnur. Litteratur Historie. III. pp. 24, 85-86.

Magnússon, Finnur. Grönlands og dets Nabolandes geographiske Forhold, fremstilte i Middelalderens forsætlig opdigtede Sagaer. *In* Grönlands historiske Mindesmærker. 1845. III. pp. 516–521.

Maurer, Konrad. Die Riesin Hít. *In* Germania. 1881. XXVI. pp. 505–506.

Müller, P. E. Sagabibliothek. I. pp. 359–361, 363.

Thorlacius, Árni. Skýringar yfir örnefni í Bárðar sögu og Víglundar. *In* Safn til sögu Íslands. 1876 III. pp. 299-303.

Bergbúa þáttr.

A legend, written in the 13th century.

Bergbúa þáttr. *In* Bárðarsaga Snæfellsáss. . .Draumvitranir. . . ved Guðbrandr Vigfússon. Kjöbenhavn 1860. pp. 123–128, 169.

Jónsson, Finnur. Litteratur Historie. II. p. 765.

Bjarnar saga Hítdælakappa.

1007-1024. Written about 1200. Vellum fragment of the 14th century (AM. 162 F fol.), paper-MSS. incomplete (AM. 551 Da 4°, 17th cent., etc.)

Sagan af Birni Hítdælakappa, besörget og oversat af H. Friðriksson, udgivet af det nordiske Literatur–Samfund. Kjöbenhavn 1847. ²(Nordiske Oldskrifter. IV.) 8°. pp. (4)+74+79.

Icelandic text, pp. 1–74; Danish version, pp. 1–79. *Review:* Ný félagsrit. 1858. XVIII. pp. 159-162, by Guðbr. Vigfússon.

Bjarnar saga Hítdælakappa herausgegeben von R. C. Boer. Halle a. S. 1893. 8°. pp. xliii+112.

Reviews: Literar Centralbl. 1894. col. 1893, by E. Mogk ;—Anz. f.
deut. Altert. 1896. XXII. pp. 36-40, by O. L. Jiriczek ;—† Museum,
maandbl. voor. philol. 1893. I., by W. Golther.

Bjarnar saga Hítdælakappa.   Búið hefir til prentunar Vald. Ásmundarson.   Reykjavík 1898.   (Íslendinga sögur. 24.)   8°.
pp. viii + 111.
Chap. IV. with introduction and notes in Antiquités Russes, 1852. fol II.
pp. 327-343.—For the verses see Corpus poet. boreale. II. pp. 105-
106, 108-109; and K. Gíslason's Udvalg af oldnord. Skjaldekvad. 1892.
pp. 29-31, 145-156.

DANISH.—† Hitdal-Kjæmpens Historie, tilligemed en Indledning
om Sagaskriftens Oprindelse, af Jacob Aall.   *In* Samlinger til
det norske Folks Sprog og Historie.   Christiania 1836.   4°.
IV. pp. 187-286, 387-437.

H. Kr. Friðriksson's *version in the edition of* 1847 (*see above*).

Björn Hitdalekjæmpes Saga.   *In* Billeder af Livet paa Island,
ved Fr. Winkel Horn.   Kjöbenhavn 1874.   II. pp. 213-272.

Jónsson, Finnur.   Litteratur Historie.   I. pp. 504-508, 573-577; II. pp.
425-429.
Jónsson, Jón (*of* Hlíð).   Örnefni í Snóksdalssókn.   *In* Safn til sögu Íslands.
1876.   II. pp. 319-324.
Müller, P. E   Sagabibliothek.   I. pp. 159-167.
Ólsen, Björn M.   Ströbemærkninger til norske og islandske skjaldedigte.
VI. Eyrb. 40. k., B. Hít. 21. k.   *In* Arkiv f. nord. filol. 1902. XVIII.
pp. 204-210.
Sigurðsson, Helgi.   Örnefni, einkum í sögu Bjarnar Hítdælakappa.   *In*
Safn til sögu Íslands.   1876.   II. pp. 307-318
For a few chorographical notes also see Árbók h. ísl. Fornleifafél. 1897.
pp. 10-11, by Bryn. Jónsson.
Vigfússon, Guðbr.   Um tímatal í Íslendinga sögum.   pp. 456-459.

Bjarnar þáttr Gullbrárskálds.   *See* Þorgríms þáttr Hallasonar ok
Bjarnar Gullbrárskálds.

Bolla þáttr Bollasonar.
An unhistoric tale probably penned in the latter part of the 13th century,
and afterwards added to the Laxdæla saga, a continuation of which it
was considered to be; it forms now chap. 79-88 of that saga (*q v.*).
Jónsson, Finnur.   Litteratur Historie II. pp 759-760.
Vigfússon, Guðbr.   Um tímatal Íslendinga sögum.   pp. 454-455.

Brandkrossa þáttr.
For the most part an unhistoric tale, intended as an introduction to the
Droplaugarsona saga (Fljótsdæla).   Written in the latter part of the
13th century.   Paper-MS. (AM. 164 K fol.)

Commentarium anecdotum, Brandkrossa þáttr dictum, islandice et latine edidit cum præfatiuncula Birgerus Thorlacius. ·Havniæ 1816. fol. pp. (4)+8. (*University program*).

Vápnfirðinga saga . . . Brandkrossa þáttr, besörget og oversat af G. Thordarson. Kjöbenhavn 1848. pp. 57–63, 62–70. Icelandic text with Danish version by S. P. Chr. Thorlacius.

Brandkrossa þáttr. *In* Austfirðinga sögur udg. ved Jakob Jakobsen. Kjöbenhavn 1903. pp. lxii–lxv, 181–191.

Helganna saga. I. *In* Origines Islandicæ, by G. Vigfusson and F. Y. Powell. Oxford 1905. II. pp. 533–536. Only the first part of the þáttr with English version. The title is that of the beginning: "Þar hefjom ver Helganna sogo."

DANISH.—Brandkrossathattr. Efter et Program af Thorlacius [ved K. L. Rahbek]. *In* Dansk Minerva for Julii Maaned 1817. pp. 47–58.

Thorlacius's *version in the edition of* 1848 (*see above*).

Et Billede fra Islands Landnamstid og Eventyret om Brandkrosse. Oversat fra Oldnorsk af O. A. Överland. Kristiania 1897. (Historiske Fortællinger 25 ; *forms also pt. iv. of* Överland's Norske historiske Fortællinger. Ny Serie. I. Bind). 8°. pp. 15. With an illustration by A. Bloch.

LATIN.—Thorlacius's *version in the edition of* 1816 (*see above*).

Jónsson, Finnur. Litteratur Historie. II. pp. 760–761.
Müller, P. E. Sagabibliothek. I. pp. 294–300.
A few chorographical remarks in Safn til sögu Íslands. 1876. II. p. 474, by Sig. Gunnarsson.

Brands þáttr örva.
C. 1050. Written in the 13th century or earlier. In the Morkinskinna (Gl. kgl. Sml 1009, fol).

Commentarium anecdotum de Brando, Liberali dicto, islandice et latine edidit cum præfatiuncula Birgerus Thorlacius. Havniæ 1819. fol. pp. 7. (*University program*).

In Fornmanna sögur. 1831. VI. pp. 348–350.

Brand den Gavmilde. *In* Oldnordisk Læsebog af P. A. Munch og C. R. Unger. Christiania 1847. p. 25.

Fra Haralldi konvngi oc Brandi orva. *In* Morkinskinna. Christiania 1867. pp. 69–70.

Brand the Open-handed. *In* An Icelandic Prose Reader by G. Vigfusson and F. Y. Powell. Oxford 1879. pp. 143–144.

Brands þáttr örva. *In* Fjörutíu Íslendinga þættir. Þórleifr Jónsson gaf út. Reykjavík 1904. pp. 12–14.

DANISH.—Brand den Gavmilde. En Fortælling. *In* Nordiske Fortællinger ved K. L. Rahbek. Kjöbenhavn 1821. II. pp. 18–20.

Translated from the Latin of Thorlacius. Was first published in †Tilskueren. 1819. No. 3. pp. 20 23.

In Oldnordiske Sagaer. 1832. VI. pp. 284–286.

Brandur hin gavmilde. *In* Udvalgte Sagastykker ved Grimur Thomsen. Kjöbenhavn 1846. pp. 6–7.

Brand den gavmilde. *In* Fortællinger og Sagaer af H. H. Lefolii. 3. Udg. Kjöbenhavn 1869. I. pp. 111–113.—†*1st ed.* 1859, †*2d ed.* 1862.

LATIN.—Thorlacius's *version in the edition of* 1819 (*see above*).

Svb. Egilsson's *version in* Scripta historica Islandorum. 1835. VI. pp. 323–325.

NORWEGIAN.—Harald hardraade og Brand den rauste. *In* Fra By og Bygd. Bjórgvin 1874. V. pp. 58–60.

Jónsson, Finnur. Litteratur Historie. II. pp. 548–549.

Müller, P. E. Sagabibliothek. III. pp. 371–375.

Brennu-Njáls saga. *See* Njáls saga.

Brodd-Helga saga. *See* Vápnfirðinga saga.

Búa saga Andríðarsonar. *See* Kjalnesinga saga.

Droplaugarsona saga, *or* Helga saga ok Gríms Droplaugarsona, *or* Helganna saga, *or* Fljótsdæla saga.

C. 965–1006. Of the earlier period of sagawriting (12th cent.) and found in the Möðruvallabók, a 14th century vellum-codex (AM. 132 fol.).—A much longer saga called Droplaugarsona saga hin lengri or Fljótsdæla hin meiri is a compilation, made in the first part of the 16th century, from the old saga and other sagas of the same districts (the Austfirðingasögur), and possibly also to some extent from oral tradition; the editions of it are given below under II.

I.

Sagan af Helga ok Grími Droplaugarsonum besörget og ledsaget med en Analyse og Ordsamling af Konrad Gislason, udgivet

af det nordiske Literatur-Samfund. Kjöbenhavn 1847. (Nordiske Oldskrifter. II.) 8°. pp. (2)+iv+38+141.
With Icelandic-Danish glossary.

Droplaugarsona saga. Þórleifr Jónsson gaf út. Reykjavík 1878. 8°. pp. vi+42.
Review: Skuld. 1879. III. coll. 220-221, by Jón Ólafsson.

Droplaugarsona-saga i den ved brudstykket AM. 162. fol. repræsenterede bearbeidelse. (Ved Kr. Kålund). *In* Arkiv f. nord. filol. 1886. III. pp. 159-176.

Droplaugarsona saga. *In* Oldnordiske Læsestykker udg. af. V. Levy. Köbenhavn 1887. I. pp. 1-36, 55-65.

Droplaugarsona saga. *In* Austfirðinga sögur udg. ved Jakob Jakobsen. Köbenhavn 1902-03. pp. liii-lxii, 139-180.
Text of the Moðruvallabók, followed by the fragment AM. 162 C. fol.

The Story of the two Helges. (Helganna saga II.). *In* Origines Islandicæ, by G. Vigfusson and F. Y. Powell. Oxford 1905. II. pp. 536-561.
Text with English version of chap. 9-14.

II.

Fljótsdæla hin meiri eller den længere Droplaugarsona saga efter håndskrifterne udg. af Kr. Kålund. Köbenhavn 1883. (Samf. t. udg. af gl. nord. litt. XI.) 8°. pp. (2)+xxxvii+139+(2).
Reviews Tímarit h. ísl. Bókmentafél. 1884. V. pp. 225-246, by Jón Jónsson ;—Literaturbl. f g u. r. Phil. 1884 coll. 379-382, by O. Brenner ; —†Deut. Lit. Zeit. 1884. no. 30, by J. Hoffory ; †Nord. Revy. 1883-4. pp. 311 ff., by E. H. Lind.

Fljótsdæla saga. Búið hefir til prentunar Vald. Ásmundarson. Reykjavík 1896. (Íslendinga sögur. 13.) 8°. pp. vii+168.
Text reprinted from the preceding edition followed by "Upphaf Droplaugarsona sögu," pp. 143-157.—*Cf.* Eimreiðin. III. p. 156.

DANISH.—† Droplögssönnerne. Fortælling fra Islands hedenske Tid. Bearbejdet til Læsning for Danske efter Sagan af Helga ok Grími Droplaugarsonum af Vilhelm Björg. Hilleröd 1868. 4°. pp. 68. (*Forms pt. i. of* Oldnordisk Vinterlæsning for Danske. Ved V. Björg. Kjöbenhavn 1868).

Sagan om Helge og Grim, Droplögs Sönner. *In* Billeder af Livet paa Island, ved Fr. Winkel Horn. Kjöbenhavn 1871. (I.) pp. 123-153.

ENGLISH.—Vigfússon *and* Powell's *version in* Orig. Island. II.
(*see above*).

A Legend of Shetland from Fljótsdæla saga, by W. G. Collingwood. *In*
Orkney and Shetland Old-Lore. 1907. I. pp 72-77, 96-105.

Gunnarsson, Sig.   Örnefni frá Jökulsá í Axarfirði austan að Skeiðará (3.
Sagan af Helga og Grími Droplaugarsonum.—13. Fljótsdæla hin meiri).
In Safn til sögu Íslands. 1876. II. pp. 458-468, 482-492.
Jónsson, Finnur.   Litteratur Historie. II. pp. 516-521.
Müller, P. E.   Sagabibliothek. I. pp. 86-94.
Thorlacius, Börge.   Undersögelse over en i det 12te Aarhundrede skreven
islandsk Historie, kaldet Fliotsdælernes, eller: Droplögs Sönners,
Helges og Grims Saga. 1816.   *In* Tritogenia. Sept. 1828. I. pp. 161-224.
Vigfússon, Guðbr.   Um tímatal í Íslendinga sögum. pp. 408-410.
Vigfússon, Sig.   Rannsókn í Austfirðingafjórðungi 1890.   *In* Árbók h. ísl.
Fornleifafél. 1893. pp. 28-60.

Egils saga Skallagrímssonar, *or* Eigla.

C. 825-982.   Written about 1200 and probably (according to Dr. Ólsen)
the work of Snorri Sturluson.   In the Möðruvallabók (AM. 132. fol.,
from c. 1350); several vellum fragments (AM. 162 A. fol, of the 13th
cent. *cf.* Kålund's Palæograf. Atlas. 1905. Nr. 14).

Eigils Saga Skalla-Grimssonar.   *At end*: Þryckt ad Hrappsey
1782 af Magnúsi Moberg. 4°. pp. 179.   (*No t.-p.*)

Egils-saga, sive Egilli Skallagrimii vita.   Ex manuscriptis Legati
Arna-Magnæani cum interpretatione latina, notis, chronologia
et tribus tabb. æneis. Havniæ 1809. (Sumptibus Legati Arna-
Magn.) 4°. pp. xx+772, 3 *facsims*.

Edited and translated by Guðmundur Magnússon; preface by Grímur
Thorkelin, who completed the edition.   The first 69 sheets were printed
in 1782 at the expense of P. F. Suhm; indices and vocabulary were
never printed, it is said, for lack of paper. *Review:* Kjobenh. lærde
Efterretn. for 1810, nos. 15-17, pp. 225-231, 241-254, 257-263, by P E.
Muller.—Selections from this edition in: E. S. Bring's Öfningsbok uti
fornnordiska språket, Lund 1848, pp. 2-65, with Swedish version;—
P. A. Munch and C. R. Unger's Oldnorsk Læsebog, Christiania 1847,
pp. 48-79; 2d ed. by Unger, ibid. 1863, pp. 22-57.

Extracts with notes in Antiquités Russés 1852. fol II pp. 248-260.

Sagan af Agli Skallagrímssyni.   Kostað hefir: Einar Þórðarson.
Reykjavík 1856. 8°. pp. viii+304.

Revised text of the 1809 ed., edited by Jón Þorkelsson; important for
the verses. *Review*. Þjóðólfur. 1856. VIII. p. 104.

Egils saga Skallagrímssonar tilligemed Egils större kvad udg.
for Samfund til udgivelse af gammel nordisk litteratur ved
Finnur Jónsson. Köbenhavn 1886-88. 8°. pp. (2)+xcv+465.

Critical edition. *Reviews* Literar. Centralbl. 1887. coll. 546–547, by
E. Mogk ;—Deut. Lit. Zeit. 1887. coll. 1403–05, by Fr. Burg ,—Literaturbl. f. g. u. r. Phil. 1889. coll. 253–254, by O. Brenner.

Egils saga Skallagrímssonar nebst den grösseren gedichten Egils
herausgg. von Finnur Jónsson. Halle a. S. 1894. (Altnordische
Saga-Bibliothek. 3.) 8°. pp. (8)+xxxix+334.

Annotated edition. *Review* · Zeitschr. f. deut. Philol 1897. XXIX.
pp. 228–235, by O. L. Jiriczek.

Egils saga Skallagrímssonar. Búið hefir til prentunar Vald. Ásmundarson. Reykjavík 1892. (Íslendinga sögur. 4.). 8°. pp.
xvi+328.

DANISH.—† En Historie om Eigill Skallagrimssön. Udsat af
Islandsk paa Latin, og af Latinen paa Dansk, og nu forbedret
med nogle Vers og Riim af T. N. Tryckt i dette Aar [1738].
s. l. 8°. pp. 142.

"Truid Nitter, Amanuensis hos Torfæus ved Aar 1690, tror jeg har
oversat de Dele af Torfæus, som er Uddrag af Egilssaga. Han var
senere Præst i Finmarken " (*G. Storm*).

Fortælling om Egil Skallagrimsen. *In* Historiske Fortællinger
om Islændernes Færd ude og hjemme, ved N. M. Petersen.
Kjöbenhavn 1839 I. pp. 320, *map.*—2. Udgave. Kobenhavn
1862, *has also a special t.-p.*: Egils saga eller Fortælling om
Egil Skallagrimsen *etc.* 8°. pp. (4)+287, *map.*

Egils Saga eller Fortællingen om Egil Skallegrimsson. Efter
det islandske Grundskrift ved N. M. Petersen. 3. Udgave
ved Verner Dahlerup og Finnur Jónsson. Versene ved Olaf
Hansen. Kóbenhavn 1901. 8°. pp. (4)+236, *map.*

Egils Saga gjenfortalt af H. H. Lefolii. Versene ved Svend
Grundtvig. Ved Udvalget for Folkeoplysnings Fremme.
Kjöbenhavn 1867. 8°. pp. (2)+168.—2. Oplag. Kjöbenhavn
1875. 8°. pp. (2)+168.

Konge og Bonde.—Egil Skallagrimssön. *In* Nordahl Rolfsen's
Vore Fædres Liv. Oversættelsen ved Gerhard Gran. Bergen
1888. pp. 22–82.—*2. edition.* Kristiania 1898. pp. 26–91, 3
illustr.

Abstract. The illustrations are by A. Bloch.

ENGLISH.—The Story of Egil Skallagrimsson : being an Icelandic Family History of the Ninth and Tenth Centuries,
translated from the Icelandic by Rev. W. C. Green. London
1893. 8°. pp. xviii+222.

Review. Saturday Review. 1894. LXXVII. p. 211.

GERMAN.—Die Geschichte des Skalden Egil Skallagrimsson. Ein germanisches Dichterleben aus dem zehnten Jahrhunderte. Dem Altisländischen nacherzählt von Ferdinand Khull. Wien 1888. 8°. pp. (8)+184.—† 2. edition. Wien 1898. 8°. pp. viii+184.

Reviews : Zeitschr. f. das Realschulwesen. XIII. p. 413, by K. Reissenberg ;—† Allg. Literaturbl. 1901. p. 603, by H. Krtička v. Jaden.

Geschichte des Skalden Egil Skallagrimssohn. In Arthur Bonus's Isländerbuch. München 1907. 8°, pp. 1–77.

Abstract. Extracts also in † Christliche Welt, 1906. No. 20. Cf. † Die Zukunft. 1906. 56. Bd. pp. 334-335.

LATIN.—G. Magnússon's version in the edition of 1809 (see above).

Cf. T. Torfæus's Hist. rer. Norveg. pars II. 1711. fol. pp. 151-194.

SWEDISH.—Egil Skalla-Grimssons Saga från fornistänskan af A. U. Bååth. Stockholm 1883. 8°. pp. viii+253+(2).

Reviews : Ny svensk tidskr. 1884. V. pp. 555-556, by G. Cederschiöld ; —Literaturbl. f. g. u. r. Phil. 1885. coll. 225-226, by E. Mogk.

In all the editions and many of the translations given above, the three principal poems of Egill are to be found : Höfuðlausn, Sonatorrek, and Arinbjarnardrápa. But there are several separate editions and translations of them. Höfuðlausn was first printed in O. Worm's Danica literatura, 1636. 4°. pp. 227-241 (2. ed. 1651. fol. pp. 207-218), the Icelandic text in Runic characters with Latin version and notes. From Latin it was translated into English by Thomas Percy (Five Pieces of Runic Poetry, 1763. pp 43-56 ; reprinted in Mallet's Northern Antiquities, 1809. II. pp 317-324) ; into German together with Sonatorrek by H. W. von Gerstenberg († Briefe über die Merkwürdigkeiten der Litteratur I.-II., 1766. pp. 73-77 ; a new edition by A. von Weilen, Strassb. 1890) ; and into German verse by J. N. C. M. Denis ¹ Ossians und Sineds Lieder, 1784. 4° IV. pp. 70-80) ; there are also German metrical versions of Höfuðlausn and Sonatorrek by G. T. Glückselig (Legis : Die Runen und ihre Denkmäler, 1829. pp 175-189) ; German prose version (with Icel. text) of Höfuðlausn by Ludwig Ettmüller in his edition of Vaulu-spá (Leipzig 1830. pp. xxviii-xxxviii). A revised Icelandic text is in Rask's Sýnishorn, 1819 pp. 141-159 Swedish version : Egil Skallagrimssons Hofuðlausn öfversatt och förklarad. Akademisk afhandling af P. Sörensen. Lund 1868 8°. pp. (4)+61.—Arinbjarnardrápa with Swedish version : Forsök till tolkning och förklaring af Arinbjarnardrápa. Akademisk afhandling af K. S. Björlin. Upsala 1864. 8°. pp. (4)+31.—A very free English version of Sonatorrek is in S. Baring-Gould's Iceland, 1863. pp. 54-56 ; a Swedish one by A. U. Bååth ¦ E S.'s qwad wid sonen Bödwars död) in Läsning för folket, 1878. X. pp. 173-178; a Russian prose version (Vykup golovy) by A. N. Chudinoff in : Drevne-sievernyia sagi i piesni skaldov v perevodakh russkikh pisatelei. Izdanie I. Glazunova St. Petersburg 1903. pp 175-177 —All these poems in Icel. and Engl. in : Corpus poeticum boreale. I pp. 266-280, 534-553, and other verses of Egill, II. pp. 71-73. Höfuðlausn and Sonatorrek in Th. Wisén's Carmina norrœna, 1886. I. pp. 20-25 The improvisations of the saga in K. Gíslason's Udvalg af oldnord. Skjaldekvad, 1892. pp. 4-6, 49-60.

† Bredman, L. Om Egill Skallagrimsson. *In* Förr och nu. Utg. af B. Wadström. Stockholm 1886. I. pp. 111-116, 131-134, 197-204.

Brynjúlfsson, Gísli. Tvær vísur eftir forn höfuðskáld. I. Vísa eftir Egil Skallagrímsson. *In* Fjallkonan. 1885. fol. II. pp. 2-3, 9-13.

Detter, Ferd. Die Lausavísur der Egils saga. Beiträge zur ihrer Erklärung. Halle a. S. 1898 (Sonderabzug aus : Abhandlungen zur germanischen Philologie, Festgabe für Richard Heinzel). 8°. pp. (2)+29.

   Reviews: Anz. f. deut. Altert. 1900. XXVI. pp. 36-38, by Finnur Jónsson ;—Gött. gel. Anz. 1901. CLXIII. 2. pp. 427-428, by A. E. Schönbach.

Dodge, D. K. On a verse in the Old Norse "Höfuðlausn." *In* Modern Language Notes. 1888. III. coll. 15-18.

Falk, Hjalmar. Bemerkungen zu den Lausavísur der Egils saga. *In* P. u. B. Beiträge z. Gesch. d. deut. Spr. u. Lit. 1888. XIII. pp. 359-356.

Finnbogason, Guðm. Egill Skallagrímsson. *In* Skírnir. 1905. LXXIX. pp. 119-134.

   Includes a note by B. M. Ólsen : Um vísu í Sonatorreki, pp. 133-134.

Friðriksson, Halldór Kr. Egils saga 1886 88, bls. 423. *In* Arkiv f. nord. filol. 1896. XII. pp. 372-374.

   On a verse of Sonatorrek.

────── Athugagrein við ritgjörð Jón próf. Jónssonar "Um Eirík blóðöx." *In* Tímarit h. ísl. Bókmentafél. 1897. XVIII. pp. 80-86.

Gjessing, G. A. Egils saga's Forhold til Kongesagaen. *In* Arkiv f. nord. filol. 1885. II. pp. 289-318. *Also separate reprint,* 8°. pp. 30.

G[osse], E. W. The " Egils Saga." *In* The Cornhill Magazine. 1879 XL. pp. 21-39.

Green, W. C. On a Passage of "Sonar Torrek " in the "Egil's Saga." *In* Saga Book of the Viking Club. 1901. II. 3. pp. 386-389.

Grímsson, Magnús. Athugasemdir við Egils sögu Skallagrímssonar. *In* Safn til sögu Íslands. 1861. II. pp. 251-276.

Jessen, C. A. E. Über die Glaubwürdigkeit der Egils-Saga und anderer Isländer-Sagas. *In* Sybel's Historiche Zeitschrift. 1872. XXVIII. pp. 61-100.

Jónsson, Bryn. Rannsókn í Mýra-, Hnappadals- og Snæfellsnessýslum sumarið 1896. *In* Árbók h. ísl. Fornleifafél. 1897. pp. 1-17.

Jónsson, Finnur. Litteratur Historie. I. pp. 481-503 ; II. pp. 415-422.

────── Egil Skallagrimsson og Erik Blodöxe. Höfuðlausn. *In* Oversigt over d. kgl. danske Videnskab. Selsk. Forhandl. 1903. No. 3. pp. 295-312.

   Review: Eimreiðin. 1904. X. pp. 156-157, by Matth. Þórðarson.

Jónsson, Rev. Jón. Um Eirík blóðöx. *In* Tímarit h. ísl. Bókmentafél. 1894. XVI. pp, 176-203.

   Cf. Friðriksson's and Ólsen's articles in vol. XVIII.

Maurer, Konrad. Zwei Rechtsfälle in der Egla. *In* Sitzungsber. d. philos.-philol. u. hist. Cl. der k. b. Akad. der Wissensch. Jahrg. 1895. pp. 65-124. *Also separate reprint.* München 1905.

Reviews : †Tidsskr. f. Retsvidensk. XII. pp. 67–68, by E. Hertzberg ;— Eimreiðin. 1896. II. pp. 158–159, by V. Guðmundsson.

Müller, P. E.   Sagabibliothek. I. pp. 109–129.

Translated into English by E. Burritt in The American Eclectic, 1841, I. pp. 488–492

Ólsen, Björn M.   Kvæði Egils Skallagrímssonar gegn Egils sögu. *In* Tímarit h. ísl. Bókmentafél. 1897. XVIII. pp. 87–99.   *Also separate reprint.* 8°. pp. 15.
Cf. the articles of J. Jónsson in vol. XVI. and of Friðriksson in vol. XVIII.

—— Til versene i Egils saga. *In* Arkiv f. nord. filol. 1903. XIX. pp. 99–133.

—— Landnáma og Egils saga. *In* Aarb. f. nord. Oldk. og Hist. 1904. pp. 167–247.
Review : Skírnir. 1905. LXXIX. pp. 274–278, by Finnur Jónsson ; a reply by Ólsen . "Er Snorri Sturluson höfundur Egils sögu ?" ibid. pp. 363–368 ;—Jahresber. f. germ. Philol. 1904. p. 76, by R. Meissner.

Storm, Gustav.   Kylvingerne i Egilssaga. *In* Akademiske Afhandlinger til Prof. Sophus Bugge. Kristiania 1889. pp. 73–79.

Vigfússon, Guðbr.   Um tímatal í Íslendinga sögum. pp. 311–321.

—— Um nokkrar Íslendingasögur. V. Arinbjarnardrápa. *In* Ný félagsrit. 1861. XXI. pp. 126–127.

Vigfússon, Sig.   Rannsókn í Borgarfirði 1884.—Mosfell   *In* Árbók h. ísl. Fornleifafél. 1884–85. pp. 62–77.

—— Rannsóknir í Borgarfirði 1884.—Egils saga Skallagrímssonar. *Ibid.* 1886. pp. 1-6, 49–50.

Wadstein, Elis.   Till Höfoðlausn. *In* Arkiv f. nord. filol. 1897. XIII. pp. 14–29.

Wisén, Theodor.   Emendationer och exegeser till norröna dikter I–III. Lund 1886–88. 4°. pp. 80.
Höfuðlausn str. 6 and 12, pp. 30–32 ; Sonatorrek str. 18, pp. 73–80.

Egils þáttr Síðu-Hallssonar, *or* Egils þáttur Síðu-Hallssonar ok Tófa Valgautssonar.

C. 1020–30. Written probably in the first decades of the 13th century. In the Ólafs saga helga of the Tómasskinna, a vellum-codex from c. 1400 (Gl. kgl. Sml. 1008. fol.), and in the Flateyjarbók.

Þáttr Egils Hallssonar ok Tófa Valgautssonar.   *In* Fornmannasögur. 1830. V. pp. 321–329,

In Ólafs saga hins helga. Udg. af R. Keyser og C. R. Unger. Christiania 1849. pp. 38–41.

Þáttr af Egli Síðuhallssyni. *In* Sex sögu-þættir, sem Jón Þorkelsson hefir gefið út. Reykjavík 1855. pp. iii–vii, 1–12.—*2. anastatic edition.* Kaupmannahöfn 1895.
Edited from a paper-MS.

In Flateyjarbók. Christiania 1862. II. pp. 142–148.

Egils þáttr Síðu-Hallssonar. *In* Fjörutíu Íslendinga þættir.
Þórleifr Jónsson gaf út. Reykjavík 1904. pp. 15–27.

DANISH.—Fortælling om Egil Hallssön og Tove Valgautssön.
In Oldnordiske Sagaer. 1831. V. pp. 291–299.

LATIN.—Membrum historicum de Egile Halli et Tovio Valgöti
filiis. [*Trl. by* Svb. Egilsson]. *In* Scripta historica Islandorum. 1833. V. pp. 299–306.

Jónsson, Finnur. Litteratur Historie. II. p. 551.
Müller, P. E Sagabibliothek. III. pp 300–303
Eigla. *See* Egils saga Skallagrímssonar

Einars þáttr Skúlasonar.
C. 1120-30. In the Morkinskinna.
Af Einari Skúlasyni. *In* Fornmanna sögur. 1832. VII. pp.
355–357.
In Morkinskinna. Christiania 1867. pp. 226–228.
Einars þáttr Skúlasonar. *In* Fjörutíu Íslendinga þættir. Þórleifr
Jónsson gaf út. Reykjavík 1904. pp. 28–31.
The þáttr is followed by : Kvæði Einars Skúlasonar, pp. 31–63.

DANISH.—Om Einar Skulesön. *In* Oldnordiske Sagaer. 1832.
VII. pp. 298–300.

LATIN.—De Einare Skulii filio. [*Trl. by* Svb. Egilsson]. *In*
Scripta historica Islandorum. 1836. VII. pp. 343–346.

Of Einar Skúlason's principal poem "Geisli" or "Ólafsdrápa" there
are two separate editions : Geisli. Einarr Skúlason orti. Öfversättning
med anmärkningar. Akademisk afhandling af Lars Wennberg. Lund
1874. 8⁰. pp. ii + 73 + (3) —Geisli eða Ólafs drápa ens helga. Efter
"Bergsboken" utg. af G. Cederschiöld. Lund 1874. 4⁰. pp. (4)+xvi
+30.—The poem was first printed with Danish and Latin versions by
Sk. Thorlacius in Schoning and Thorlacius's edition of Heimskringla.
1783. fol. III. pp 461–480; then in Fornmanna sögur. 1830. V. pp.
349–370; in Flateyjarbók. 1860. I. pp. 1–7; in Th Wisén's Carmina
norræna. 1886. I. pp. 53–62; *cf.* Diplomat. Island. I. pp. 205–206.
Danish version in Oldnordiske Sagaer. 1831. V. pp 318–338. Latin
version in Scripta historica Islandorum. 1833. V. pp. 323–349; *cf.*
Antiquités Russes 1850. fol. I pp. 477–480. For all poems of Einar,
with English translation, see Corpus poeticum boreale. 1883. II. pp.
252, 267–272, 277–278, 283–294.

Jónsson, Finnur. Litteratur Historie. II. pp. 62–73, 548.
Thorlacius, Skúli Einar Skulesöns Levnets-Beskrivelse. (*Danish and
Latin*). *In* Heimskringla ed. Schöning et Thorlacius. Havniæ 1783.
fol. III. pp. 481–494.

Einars þáttr Sokkasonar *or* Grænlendinga þáttr (II.).

C. 1120-1130 (establishment of the Garðar see, Greenland). Written in Iceland in the 13th century ; in the Flateyjarbók.

Fortælling om Einar Sokkesön. *In* Grönlands historiske Mindesmærker. Kjöbenhavn 1838. II. pp. 669-724.

Text with Danish version, introduction and notes.

Grænlendingaþattr. *In* Flateyjarbók. Christiania 1868. III. pp. 443-454.

DANISH.—*In* Grönl. hist. Mindesm. 1838. (*see above*).

ENGLISH.—A Memoir of Einar Sokkason. By Thorleif Gudmundsson Repp. *In* Memoires de la Soc. Roy. des Antiq. du Nord. 1840-44. pp. 81-100.

Grænlendinga tháttr (The Tale of the Greenlanders). *In* Origines Islandicæ, by G. Vigfusson and F. Y. Powell. Oxford 1905. II. pp. 748-756.

Jónsson, Finnur. Litteratur Historie II. pp. 648-649.

Maurer, Konrad. Zur geschichte des bergräbnisses "more Teutonico." *In* Zeitschr. f. deut. Philol. 1893. XXV. p 139.

Müller, P. E. Sagabibliothek. I. pp. 288-290.*

Eiríks saga rauða *or* Þorfinns saga karlsefnis ok Snorra Þorbrandssonar.

The first title is older and more appropriate. C. 985-1014. (Northmen in Greenland and Wineland). Written probably in the earlier part of the 13th century (Storm places it in the last third of the century). In the Hauksbók (AM. 544. 4°, beginning of 14th cent.) and AM. 557. 4° (vellum from the 15th cent.).

Saga Þorfinns karlsefnis ok Snorra Þorbrandssonar. *In* Antiquitates Americanæ opera et studio C. C. Rafn. Hafniæ 1837. 4°. pp. 84-187.

Text with Latin and Danish version and notes.

Thorfinn Karlsefnes Saga. *In* Grönlands historiske Mindesmærker. Kjöbenhavn 1838. I. pp. 281-494.

Text with Danish version, introduction and notes by F. Magnússon.

Eiríks saga rauða. *In* An Icelandic Prose Reader, by G. Vigfússon and F. Y. Powell. Oxford 1879. pp. 123-141, 377-385.

Text from A M. 557. 4°. For variants see Origines Islandicæ. 1905. II. pp. 595-597.—Reprinted (Amerikas förste Opdagelse) in . Oldnordiske Læsestykker, udg. af V. Levy. Köbenhavn 1888. 3. Hefte. pp. 3-19, 60-69.

---

*For other works see foot-note on p. 18.

Porfinns saga karlsefnis (Hauksbók pp. 93a–101b).—Eiríks saga rauða (AM. 557. 4°. pp. 27a–35b). *In* The Finding of Wineland the Good, by A. M. Reeves. London 1890. 4°. pp. 104–139, 18 *facsim.-ff.*

Phototype-edition of the MSS. containing the two recensions; Icelandic text printed on the pages facing the facsimile-pages. English version, pp. 19–52. *Reviews:* The Nation (N. Y.). 1891. LII. pp. 54–56, by W. Fiske ,—Arkiv f. nord. filol. 1891. VII. pp. 383–386, by Kr. Kålund ;—Zeitschr. f. deut. Philol. 1892. XXIV. pp. 84–89, by H. Gering ;—Beil. zur Allgem. Zeit. 1891. No. 68, by E. P. Evans ;—Proceed. of the Roy. Geogr. Soc. 1891. N. S. XIII. pp. 127–128, by C. R. Markham ;—Deut. Lit. Zeit. 1897. coll. 258–260, by K. Kretschmer.

Eiríks saga rauða og Flatöbogens Grænlendingaþáttr samt Uddrag fra Ólafssaga Tryggvasonar udg. for Samfund til Udgivelse af gammel nordisk Litteratur ved Gustav Storm. Köbenhavn 1891. 8° pp. (4)+xvi+(2)+79.

Critical edition based on AM. 557. 4°.—*Review:* Literaturbl. f. g. u. r. Philol. 1892. col. 193, by G. Morgenstern.

[Eiríks saga rauða]. *In* Hauksbók udg. [ved Finnur Jónsson og Eiríkur Jónsson] efter de Arnamagnæanske håndskrifter no. 371, 544 og 675. 4°. Köbenhavn 1894 (1892–96). pp. lxxxi–lxxxvi, 425–444.

Porfinns saga karlsefnis. Búið hefir til prentunar Vald. Åsmundarson. Reykjavík 1892. (Íslendingasögur. 35.) 8°. pp. (4)+40.

DANISH.—*In* Antiquit. Americ. 1837 *and* Grönl. hist. Mindesm. 1838 (*see above*).

Torfin Karlsæmnes Saga. *In* Billeder af Livet paa Island, ved Fr. Winkel Horn. Kjöbenhavn 1876. III. pp. 271–297.

Erik den rödes Saga eller Sagaen om Vinland oversat af Gustav Storm. Illustreret af Hjalmar Johnssen og Ch. Krogh og forsynet med historiske Karter. Kristiania 1899. 8°. pp. 36. 4 *illustr.*

ENGLISH.—Eirik the Red's Saga : A translation read before the Literary and Philosophical Society of Liverpool, Jan. 12. 1880, by the Rev. J. Sephton. Liverpool 1880. 8°. pp. 34.

Sep. repr. of the Proceedings of the Lit. and Philos. Soc. of Liverpool 1879–80. No. 34. pp. 183–212.—Translated from the Prose Reader.

In Reeves's The Finding of Wineland the Good. 1890. pp. 19–52 (The Saga of Eric the Red), *see above*.

This version is reprinted with the editor's introduction in :

The Northmen, Columbus and Cabot 985–1503. The Voyages of the Northmen ed. by Julius E. Olson . . . New York 1906. (Original Narratives of Early American History). pp. 14–44.

2

Review: Amer. Histor. Review. 1907. XIII. pp. 654-656, by C. R. Beazley.

In N. L. Beamish's The Discovery of America by the Northmen. 1841. pp. 81-105 is a version of chap 6-15 of this saga, reprinted in : Voyages of the Northmen to America, ed. by E. F. Slafter, publ. by the Prince Society, 1877. pp. 45-54. Beamish's and Reeves's translations are reproduced in R. B. Anderson and J. W. Buel's so-called "Norræna" series : The Norse Discovery of America, 1906, with 2 illustr.

The Story of Thorfinn Carlsemne. *In* Origines Islandicæ, by G. Vigfusson and F. Y. Powell. Oxford 1905. II. pp. 610-625.

LATIN.—*In* Antiqv. Americ. 1837 (*see above*).

RUSSIAN.—Saga ob Eirik krasnom. Per. S. N. Syromiashnykova. *In* Drevne-sievernyia sagi i piesni skaldov v perevodakh russkikh pisatelei. Izdanie I. Glazunoya. S.-Petersburg 1903. (Russkaia klassnaia biblioteka. Red. A. N. Chudinova. II. 25). pp. 141-168, 258-264.

Jónsson, Finnur. Litteratur Historie. II. 646-648.
Müller, P. E. Sagabibliothek. I. pp. 291-294.*

Eiríks þáttr rauða. *See* Grænlendinga þáttr.

Esphælinga saga. *See* Víga-Glúms saga.

Eyrbyggja saga *or* Þórsnesinga saga *or* Álptfirðinga saga.
All the three names used in the saga itself. 884-1031. Written originally about 1200, but in its present form is of somewhat later date Paper-MSS., copies of the lost Vatns-hyrna codex ; several vellum fragments, the oldest from c. 1280 (AM 162 E. fol.).

Eyrbyggja-saga sive Eyranorum historia qvam mandante et impensas faciente P. F. Suhm. versione, lectionum varietate ac indice rerum auxit G. J. Thorkelin. Havniæ 1787. 4°. pp. xii+354 +(2).
The Latin translation was made in 1776-77, and the printing begun in 1784. The preface (signed by Thorkelin) and the index are by Jón Ólafsson (Hypnonensis), explanation of verses by Gunnar Pálsson. *Reviews:* †Lærde Efterretn. 1787. Nr. 48;—Gött. Anz. 1788. pp. 267-268.

Uddrag af Eyrbyggja. *In* Grönlands historiske Mindesmærker. Kjöbenhavn 1838. I. pp. 494-786.
Extracts with Danish version, introduction and notes by Finnur Magnússon.

---

*All other works treating of this and the other sagas relating to the Icelandic colony in Greenland and the discovery of America by the Northmen will be found in a special catalogue to be issued later.

Extracts relating to American voyages, with Latin and Danish versions, and notes by C. C. Rafn *in* Antiquitates Americanæ. 1837. 4°. pp. 195, 215-255.

Eyrbyggia saga herausgg. von Guðbrandr Vigfússon. Leipzig 1864. 8°. pp. liii+144+(2), *map*.
Critical edition. *Review:* Germania. 1865. X. pp. 479-498, by K. Maurer.

Eyrbyggja saga. [*Ed. by* Þorleifr Jónsson.] Akureyri 1882. 8°. pp. vi+151.

Eyrbyggja saga. Búið hefir til prentunar Vald. Ásmundarson. Reykjavík 1895. (Íslendinga sögur. 12.) 8°. pp. viii+203.

Eyrbyggja saga herausgg. von Hugo Gering. Halle a. S. 1897. (Altnordische Saga-Bibliothek. 6.) 8°. pp. xxxi+264.
Annotated edition. *Cf.* a note by the editor in Zeitschr. f. deut. Philol. 1898. XXX. pp. 266-267. *Reviews:* Revue critique. 1898. N. S. XLVI. pp. 14-15, by V. Henry;—Literaturbl. f. g. u. r. Philol. 1898. coll. 325-330, by R. C. Boer;—Literar. Centralbl. 1898. coll. 1653-54;—Deut. Lit. Zeit. 1899. coll. 1220-21, by F. Detter;—The Athenæum. 1898. II. pp. 450-451.

The Thorsness Settlement (Chap. 1-11 of Eyrbyggja saga). *In* Origines Islandicæ, by G. Vigfusson and F. Y. Powell. Oxford 1905. I. pp. 252-266.

For the verses see Corpus poeticum boreale. 1883. II. pp. 57-60, and K. Gíslason's Udvalg af oldnord. Skjaldekvad. 1892. pp. 20, 104-106.

DANISH.—Fortælling om Eyrbyggerne. *In* Historiske Fortællinger om Islændernes Færd hjemme og ude, ved N. M. Petersen. Kjöbenhavn 1844. IV. pp. 133-220. —2. Udgave. [*Ed. by* Guðbr. Vigfússon.] Köbenhavn 1863. III. pp. 1-98 ; *has also a special t.-p.*: Eyrbyggja saga og Laxdælasaga eller Fortællinger om Eyrbyggerne og Laxdælerne *etc.*

Eyrbyggja saga og Laksdöla saga eller Fortællinger om Eyrbyggerne og Laksdölerne. Efter de islandske Grundskrifter ved N. M. Petersen. 3. Udgave ved Verner Dahlerup og Finnur Jónsson. Versene ved Olaf Hansen. Köbenhavn 1901. pp. 1-79.

Styr og Berserkerne. Text af P. A. Munch. Tegning af Flintöe. *In* Norsk Folkekalender for 1848. Christiania. pp. 106-111.

ENGLISH.—Abstract of the Eyrbiggia-Saga. *In* Illustrations of Northern Antiquities from the earlier Teutonic and Scandinavian Romances [*ed. by* R. Jamieson and H. Weber]. Edinburg 1814. 4°. pp. 475-513.

The abstract is dated at end : Abbotsford, October 1813, and signed : W. S. (Walter Scott).—It was later published in vol. v of Scott's prose works with the title : Paul's Letters to his Kinsfolk, and Abstract of the Eyrbiggia saga. By Sir Walter Scott. Edinburgh 1834, pp. 355-413 ; it also was embodied in Mallet's Northern Antiquities, trl. by Percy and ed. by Blackwell, London † 1847, and 1859, pp. 517-540.

The Story of the Ere-Dwellers (Eyrbyggja saga) with the Story of the Heath-Slayings (Heiðarvíga saga) as appendix. Done into English out of the Icelandic by William Morris and Eiríkr Magnússon. London 1892. (The Saga Library. II.) 8°. pp. lii+(2)+410, 2 *maps*.

A facsimile of a page of Morris's MS. (dated 1871) in " The Art Journal. Extra Number: Easter Art Annual. The Art of William Morris." London 1899. 4°. p. 29.—*Reviews :* The Saturday Review. 1891. II. p. 482 ; The Academy. 1891. XL. p 448, by C. Elton.

The Thorsness Settlement.—Eyrbyggia saga.—The Tale of Beorn, the Broadwick-men's champion. *In* Origines Islandicæ, by G. Vigfusson and F. Y. Powell. Oxford 1905. I. pp. 252-266 ; II. pp. 88-135, 625-628.

GERMAN.—Die Geschichte eines Heiligtums.—Die Geschichte von den Zauberinnen Geirrid und Katla und vom Fall des Goden Arnkel.—Ein Kampf auf dem Eise.—Die Geschichte von Björn und Thurid.—Die Geschichte vom Spuk zu Froda. *In* Arthur Bonus's Isländerbuch. München 1907. II. pp. 147-273.

Selections appeared in Deutsche Rundschau. 1906. CXXVIII. pp. 66-78 (Eine altnordische Bauerngeschichte:Die Geschichte von Björn und Thurid), and in † Kunstwart. 1. März 1906 (Der Fall des Goden Arnkel).

Halli und Leikner, oder Tod für die Braut [*trl. by* F. D. Gräter] *in* Bragur, herausgg. v. Böckh u. Gräter. 1791. I pp. 207-218.

LATIN.—Thorkelin's *version in the edition of* 1787 (*see above*).

SWEDISH.—Eyrbyggarnes Saga. Från fornnordiskan af C. J. L. Lönnberg. Stockholm 1873. (Fornnordiska sagor. II.) 8°. pp. (4)+196.

---

† Grönvold, D. Skikkelser i den islandske Ættesaga. III. Snorre Gode. *In* Folkevennen. 1898. N. R. XII. pp. 209-240.

Holmboe. C. A. Commentar til to mærkelige Steder i Eyrbyggja saga. *In* Videnskabs-Selskabets Forhandlinger. Christiania 1863. pp. 221-225.— *Also separate reprint :* Thorolfs Bægifots Begravelse, belyst af C. A. H. *etc.* 8°. pp. 7.

Jónsson, Bryn. Rannsókn í Mýra-, Hnappadals- og Snæfellsnessýslum sumarið 1896. *In* Árbók h. ísl. Fornleifafél. 1897. pp. 1-17.

Jónsson, Finnur. Litteratur Historie. I. pp. 510–512; II. pp. 431–440.

Jónsson, Janus. Athugasemdir við vísurnar í Eyrbyggju og skýringar á þeim. *In* Arkiv f. nord. filol. 1898 XIV. pp. 360–379.

Jónsson, Jón (*of* Hlíð). Örnefni í Snóksdalssókn. *In* Safn til sögu Íslands. 1876. II. pp. 319–324.

Maurer, Konrad. Zwei Rechtsfälle aus der Eyrbyggja. *In* Sitzungsber. d. philos.-philol. u. histor. Classe d. k. b. Akad. d. Wissensch. zu München. 1896. pp. 3–48.

Reviews: †Tidsskr. f. Retsvidensk. XII. pp. 67–68, by E. Hertzberg;— Eimreiðin. 1896. II. pp. 158–159, by V. Guðmundsson.

Müller. P. E. Sagabibliothek. I. pp. 189–198.

Ólsen, Björn M. Ströbemærkninger til norske og islandske skjaldedigte. Eyrb. 40. k.—B. Hítd. 21. k. *In* Arkiv f. nord. filol. 1902. XVIII. pp. 204–210.

—— Landnáma og Eyrbyggja. *In* Aarb. f. nord. Oldk. og Hist. 1905. pp. 81–117.

Thorlacius, Árni. Skýringar yfir örnefni í Landnámu og Eyrbyggju, að svo miklu leyti sem viðkemr Þórnes þingi hinu forna. *In* Safn til sögu Íslands. 1861. II. pp. 277–298.

Vigfússon, Guðbr. Um tímatal í Íslendinga sögum. pp. 328–340, 444–446.

Vigfússon, Sig. Rannsókn í Breiðafjarðardölum og í Þórnesþingi og um hina nyrðri strönd 1881. *In* Árbók h. ísl. Fornleifafél. 1882. pp. 60–105, 2 *pls*.

—— Rannsókn í Rangárþingi . . . svo og í Breiðafirði (síðast rannsakað 1889). *Ibid.* 1888–92. pp. 1–34.

—— Rannsóknir í Breiðafirði 1889. *Ibid.* 1893. pp. 1–23.

Finnboga saga ramma.

A fictitious saga about an historic person of the latter part of the 10th century. Written about 1300. In the Möðruvallabók (AM. 132. fol.; 14th cent.).

Vatnsdæla saga ok saga af Finnboga hinum rama. Vatnsdölernes Historie og Finnboge hiin Stærkes Levnet. Bekostede af Jacob Aal. Udgivne af E. C. Werlauff. Kjöbenhavn 1812. 4°. pp. xvii–xxi, 207–361.

With Danish version. *Review:* Dansk Litterat. Tid. 1813. pp. 325–340, by P. E. Müller.

Chap. 16 and 19 in Antiquités Russes. 1852. fol. pp. 320–327.

Saga Finnboga hins ramma. Útgefandi: Sveinn Skúlason. Akureyri 1860. (Íslendinga sögur. 2. hepti). 8°. pp. (2)+92.

Finnboga saga hins ramma herausgg. von Hugo Gering. Halle a. S. 1879. 8°. pp. (4)+xl+115.

Critical edition with glossary. *Reviews:* Germania. 1879. XXIV. pp. 368-373, by O. Brenner;—Literar. Centralbl. 1879. coll. 779–780, by A. Edzardi;—Revue critique 1879. N. S. VIII. pp. 350–351, by C.;— Zeitschr. f. deut. Philol. 1880. XI. pp. 372–375, by B. Sijmons;—Jenaer Literat. Zeit. 1879. pp. 138–139, by K. Maurer;—Jahresber. d. germ.

Philol. 1879. pp. 81–82 ;—† Magaz. f. die Literat. d. Ausl. 1879. Nr. 27 ;
—"Nogle bemærkninger til det Dr. Gerings udgave af Finnbogasaga
vedföjede glossar af Sigurðr Sigurðarson" in Aarb. f. nord. Oldk. og
Hist. 1881. pp. 57–68.

Finnboga saga. Búið hefir til prentunar Vald. Ásmundarson.
Reykjavík 1897. (Íslendinga sögur. 18.) 8°. pp. vii+104.

DANISH.—Werlauff's *version in the edition of* 1812 (*see above*).
Fortælling om Finboge den Stærke. *In* Historiske Fortællinger
om Islændernes Færd hjemme og ude, ved N. M. Petersen.
Kjöbenhavn 1844. IV. pp. 107–132. —2. Udgave [*ed. by* G.
Vigfússon.] Köbenhavn 1868, *also with the title :* Fortælling-
erne om Vatnsdælerne, Gunlaug Ormetunge, Kormak og
Finboge den Stærke *etc.* pp. 201–225.

RUSSIAN.—Saga o Finnbogie silnom. Izsliedovanie F. Batiusch-
kova. S.-Petersburg¦ 1885. 8°. pp. (2)+117.—2. *edition in :*
Drevne-sievernyia sagi i piesni skaldov v perevodakh russkikh pisatelei. Izdanie I. Glazunova. S.-Petersburg 1903.
(Russkaia klassnaia biblioteka. Red. A. N. Chudinova. II.
25). pp. 62–141, 209–239.

Jónsson, Bryn. Rannsókn sögustaða í vesturhluta Húnavatnssýslu sumarið
1894. IV. Finnboga saga. *In* Árbók h. ísl. Fornleifafél. 1895. pp. 9–10.
Jónsson, Finnur. Litteratur Historie. III. pp. 81–82.
Müller, P. E. Sagabibliothek. I. pp. 281–288.
Vigfússon, Guðbr. Um tímatal í Íslendinga sögum. pp. 378–379.

Fljótsdæla saga. *See* Droplaugarsona saga.

Flóamanna saga *or* Þorgils saga Örrubeinsstjúps.

C. 900–1022. Written in the last quarter of the 13th century, but there
may have been an older recension. Paper-MS., copy of the Vatnshyrna
(AM. 516. 4°); vellum fragment of a different recension AM. 445 B.
4°. (15th cent.)

Uddrag af Flóamanna-saga, indeholdende Thorgils Thordarsöns,
kaldet Orrabeinsfostres, Liv og Levnet. *In* Grönlands historiske Mindesmærker. Kjöbenhavn 1838. II. p. 1–221.

Chap. 8–34 with Danish version, introduction and notes by Finnur
Magnússon.

Flóamannasaga. *In* Fornsögur herausgg. von Guðbrandr Vigfússon und Theodor Möbius. Leipzig 1860. pp. xxii–xxviii,
117–161, 168–185.

The fragments printed as appendices, pp. 168–185, and addenda to the
saga from Landnáma, pp. 195–204.—*Cf.* Sturlunga saga. 1878. II. pp.
501–502.

Flóamanna saga. Þórleifr Jónsson gaf út. Reykjavík 1884. 8°. pp. vii+76.

Flóamanna saga. Búið hefir til prentunar Vald. Ásmundarson. Reykjavík 1898. (Íslendinga sögur. 23.) 8°. pp. (4)+74.

The Story of Thorgisl, Scarleg's Stepson. *In* Origines Islandicæ, by G. Vigfusson and F. Y. Powell. Oxford 1905. II. pp. 629–672.
Text with English translation.

DANISH.—En nordisk Helt fra det tiende Aarhundrede, Thorgils's, kaldet Orrabeens-Stifsöns, Historie, oversat af det gamle Skandinaviske, med en Indledning, af B. Thorlacius. Kiöbenhavn 1809. 8°. pp. 114.
Separate reprint from Det skandinaviske Litteraturselskabs Skrifter. 1808. V. pp. 194-336.—The notes are are by Skúli Thorlacius.

F. Magnússon's *version in* Grönl. hist. Mindesm. 1838. (*see above*).

ENGLISH.—Vigfússon *and* Powell's *version in* Orig. Isl. II. (*see above*).
Extracts from the saga (Thorgils Nursling, a Saga about Greenland) in Iceland, by S. Baring-Gould. London 1863. pp. 368-384.

Jónsson, Bryn. Um Haugavað og Böðvarstóftir. *In* Árbók h. ísl. Fornleifafél. 1900. pp 29-31.
Jónsson, Finnur. Litteratur Historie. II. pp. 756-758.
Müller, P. E. Sagabibliothek. I. pp. 308-314.
Vigfússon, Guðbr. Um tímatal í Íslendinga sögum. pp. 421-422.
Vigfússon, Sig. Rannsókn við Haugavað. *In* Árbók h. ísl. Fornleifafél. 1882. pp. 47-59.
Abstract by M. Lehmann Filhés in Verhandl. d. Berl. anthropolog. Gesellsch. 1894. pp 85-88.*

Fóstbræðra saga *or* Þorgeirs saga Hávarssonar ok Þormóðar Kolbrúnarskálds.
C. 1000-1030. There are various recensions (Hauksbók, Flateyjarbók etc.), but all probably derived from the same original, presumably of the middle of the 13th century.

Fóstbrædra-saga edr Sagan af Þorgeiri Havarssyni og Þormódi Bersasyni Kolbrúnarskalldi. Nú útgengin á prent eptir handritum. Kaupmannahöfn 1822. 8°. pp. (6)+217.
Edited from AM. 141. fol. by Gunnlaugur Oddsson. *Review:* Gött. gel. Anz. 1823. pp. 1751-52.

---

*For other works see foot-note on p. 18.

Uddrag af Fostbrædra-saga, angaaende Thorgeir Havarssöns
Drab og Thormod Kolbruneskalds Ophold i Grönland. *In*
Grönlands historiske Mindesmærker. Kjöbenhavn 1838. II.
pp. 250–419.

Extracts from the Icelandic text of AM. 544. 4°., with introduction,
Danish version and notes by Finnur Magnússon.

Extracts in Antiquités Russes. 1853. fol. II. pp. 343-350.

Fóstbræðra saga, udgivet for det nordiske Literatur-Samfund af
Konrad Gislason. 1. Hefte. Kjöbenhavn 1852. (Nordiske
Oldskrifter. XV.) 8°. pp. (4)+112.

Text of the saga from AM. 132. fol. (pp. 3-63), and AM. 544. 4°. (pp.
63-112). No more published.

In Flateyjarbók. [*Ed. by* G. Vigfússon *and* C. R. Unger.]
Christiania 1862. II. pp. 91–108, 148–168, 199–226, 339–343,
358–366.

The heading of the 1st sect.: Vpphaf Fostbræðra soghu; of the 2d:
Her hefr upp þaatt Þormodar Kolbrunar skalldz; of the 3d: Þaattr
Þormodar er hann er med Knuti konungi i Danmork, the last two
having no special heading.

In Hauksbók. [*Ed. by* F. Jónsson *and* E. Jónsson]. Köbenhavn
1892–96. pp. lxxiv-lxxxi, 370–416.

This recension (AM. 544. 4°.) begins with chap. 11.

Fóstbræðra saga. Búið hefir til prentunar Vald. Ásmundarson.
Reykjavík 1899. (Íslendinga sögur. 26.) 8°. pp. (4)+168.

Text reprinted from the edition of 1852 and from the Hauksbók, with
appendix from the Flateyjarbók.

The Story of Thormod, wrongly but commonly called the Story
of the Foster-brethren. *In* Origines Islandicæ, by G. Vigfusson and F. Y. Powell. Oxford 1905. II. pp. 673–747.

The editors distinguish between two independent sagas of Þormóðr,
one ecclesiastical (The Story of Thormod St. Olave's Champion or
Poet), and the other secular (The Story of Thormod Coalbrow's Poet).
The English version being thus divided, pp. 709-743, while the Icelandic text is without divisions, pp. 679-708.—The Tale of the foster-
brothers Thorgeir and Eywulf ("a little story inserted piecemeal into
the Story of Thormod, but it is, if we may judge, of wholly independent
origin"), in Icelandic and English, pp. 743-747.—*Cf.* Arkiv f. nord.
filol. 1906. XXIII. p. 205.

For the poems of Þormóðr see Corpus poeticum boreale. 1883. II. pp.
172-177.

DANISH.—Fostbrödrenes Saga. *In* Billeder af Livet paa Island,
ved Fr. Winkel Horn. Kjöbenhavn 1874. II. pp. 273-353.

Fostbrödre. *In* N. Rolfsen's Vore Fædres Liv. Oversættelsen
ved Gerhard Gran. Bergen 1888. pp. 245-269.—*2. edition.*
Christiania 1898. pp. 236-265, 3 *illustr.*

Abstract. The illustrations are by A. Bloch.

ENGLISH.—Vigfússon *and* Powell's *version in* Orig. Isl. II. (*see above*).

FRENCH.—La vendette dans le nouveau monde au XI* siècle d'après les textes scandinaves par Eugéne Beauvois. Extrait du Muséon. Louvain 1882. 8°. pp. 28.
The Greenland portion with introduction.

Boer, R. C. Kritische und exegetische bemerkungen zu skaldenstrophen. II. Zur Fóstbræðrasaga. *In* Zeitschr. f. deut. Philol. 1899. XXXI. pp. 149-157.

Gaertner, K. H. Zur Fóstbræðra saga. I. Teil. Die Vísur. *In* P. u. B. Beiträge z. Gesch. d. deut. Spr. u. Lit. 1907. XXXII. pp. 299-446.

Jónsson, Bryn. Rannsókn í Þverárþingi 1903. (Þorgeirshróf). *In* Árbók h. ísl. Fornleifafél. 1904. pp. 7-8.

Jónsson, Finnur. Litteratur Historie. I. pp. 581-587; II. pp. 465-471.

Jónsson, Þorleifur. Örnefni nokkur úr Breiðafjarðardölum. *In* Safn til sógu Íslands. 1876. II. pp. 558-577.

Müller, P. E. Sagabibliothek. I. pp. 153-159.

Vigfússon, Guðbr. Um tímatal í Íslendinga sögum. pp. 462-468.

Geirmundar þáttr heljarskinns.

850-900. Written probably about 1300 partly from other sagas (Land-náma and Hálfs saga), partly from oral tradition. By the compiler of the Sturlunga saga it was placed at the beginning of that collection.

ENGLISH. — The Tale of Gar-mund Hell-skin. *In* Origines Islandicæ, by G. Vigfusson and F. Y. Powell. Oxford 1905. I. pp. 274-276.

For editions and other translations see Sturlunga saga.

Jónsson, Finnur. Litteratur Historie II. pp. 727-728, 729.

Ólsen, Björn M. Um Sturlungu. pp. 205-206.

Gests saga Bárðarsonar.

A fictitious saga, forming a continuation of Bárðar saga Snæfellsáss (*q. v.*), but of different authorship; written early in the 14th century,

Gils (*or* Gísls) þáttr Illugasonar.

1096. Written at the end of the 12th century. Two recensions.

In Fornmanna sögur. 1832. VII. pp. 29-40.

In Jóns saga helga [*ed. by* G. Vigfússon], *in* Biskupa sögur. Kaupmannahöfn 1858. I. pp. 221-227.

The other saga of bishop John has also a short account of the incident. pp. 556-557.

Gísls þáttr Illugasonar. *In* Fjörutíu Íslendinga þættir. Þórleifr Jónsson gaf út. Reykjavík 1904. pp. 64-75.

Followed by "Brot úr erfikvæði eptir Magnús konungs berfætt," by Gils, pp. 75-77.—*Cf.* Corpus poeticum boreale. 1883. II. pp. 240-243.

DANISH.—*In* Oldnordiske Sagaer. 1832. VII. pp. 25–35.
LATIN.—Svb. Egilsson's *version in* Scripta historica Islandorum.
1836. VII. pp. 30–40.
Cf. T. Torfæus's Hist. rer. Norvegic. p. III. 1711. fol. pp 432–436.

Jónsson, Finnur. Litteratur Historie. II. pp. 55–57, 548.
Müller, P. E. Sagabibliothek. III. pp. 386–398 (*containing a literal Danish translation*).

Gísla saga Súrssonar.
C. 950–978. Written about 1200. Two recensions, the longer being interpolated and later. Vellum-MS. of the 15th cent. (AM. 556 A. 4°.), the longer in paper MSS. only.

Sagann af Gijsla Swrs-syne og þeim Sijrdælingum fleirum ödrum. *In* Agiætar Fornmanna Sögur, ad Forlage Biörns Marcus-Sonar. Hólar 1756. pp. 127–180. (*The shorter saga*).

Uddrag af Gisle Sursöns Saga, især indeholdende Helge Vestein-söns, een af Grönlands förste Indbyggeres, Levnet. *In* Grön-lands historiske Mindermærker. Kjöbenhavn 1838. II. pp. 576–608.
Extract with Danish version, introduction and notes.

Tvær sögur af Gísla Súrssyni, udgivne af det nordiske Literatur-Samfund ved Konrad Gislason, med Forklaring over Qvadene af S. Egilsson. Kjöbenhavn 1849. (Nordiske Oldskrifter. VIII.) 8°. pp. (2)+xxii+212.
The shorter saga (AM. 556 A. 4°, pp. 1–74; the longer saga (AM. 149 fol. and AM. 482. 4°), pp. 75–160; diplomatic reproduction of the verses from AM. 556 A. 4°., pp. 161–168, followed by Egilsson's commentary and a glossary.—*Review:* Ný félagsrit. 1858. XVIII. pp. 165–168, by Guðbr. Vigfússon; Gíslason's reply in Norðri. VI. p 137, VIII. pp 66, 121–122;*cf.* Þjóðólfur. XI. p. 119, by G. Vigfússon.

Saga Gísla Súrssonar I. og II. Búið hefir til prentunar Vald. Ásmundarson. Reykjavík 1899. (Íslendinga sögur. 25.) 8°. pp. vii+210+(2).

Gísla saga Súrssonar herausgg. von Finnur Jónsson. Halle a. S. 1903. (Altnordische Saga-Bibliothek. 10.) 8°. pp. xxix+107.
Annotated edition of the shorter saga. *Review:* Jahresber. f. germ. Philol. 1903. pp. 62–63, by R. Meissner.

Gísla saga. *In* Origines Islandicæ, by G. Vigfusson and F. Y. Powell. Oxford 1905. II. pp. 188–237.
The shorter saga. English version of two incidents of the saga (The murder of Westan; The slaying of Thorgrim Thorstansson) pp. 562–566.

Gísli's verses with notes in K. Gíslason's Udvalg af oldnord. Skjaldekvad. 1892. pp. 13-15, 88-92; with Engl. version in Corpus poeticum
boreale. 1883. II. pp. 332-335.

DANISH.—Saga eller Fortælling om Gisle Suursson eller Syrdö-
lerne, oversat fra det ældre norske Sprog af P. A. Munch.
Christiania 1845. [Sagaer eller Fortællinger om Nordmænds
og Islænderes Bedrifter i Oldtiden. I.] 8°. pp viii+62+(2).
Gisle Surssöns Saga. *In* Billeder af Livet paa Island, ved Fr.
Winkel Horn. Kjöbenhavn 1871. (I.) pp. 1-59.
Gisle Surssön. *In* N. Rolfsen's Vore Fædres Liv. Oversættelsen
ved Gerhard Gran. Bergen 1888. pp. 115-137.—*2. edition.*
Kristiania 1898. pp. 133-159, 3 *illustr.* (*by* A. Bloch).
Fortællinger om Vatnsdölerne, Gisle Sursen, Gunlaug Orms-
tunge, Gretter den Stærke. Efter de islandske Grundskrifter
ved N. M. Petersen. 3. Udgave ved Verner Dahlerup og
Finnur Jónsson. Versene ved Olaf Hansen. København 1901.
(Historiske Fortællinger om Islændernes Færd hjemme og
ude). pp. 87-138.
This is the first edition of the translation of Gísla saga.

ENGLISH.—The Story of Gisli the Outlaw. From the Icelandic
by George Webbe Dasent. With illustrations by C. E. St.
John Mildmay. Edinburgh 1866. 4°. pp. xxxv+(2)+123; 7
pls., *2 maps.*
   Reviews: The Spectator. 1866. XXXIX. pp. 183-195 ;—The Examiner
   (London). 1866. p. 96;—† Lond. Quarterly Review. 1871. XXXVI.
   pp. 35-65.

GERMAN.—Gisli der Geächtete. Eine altgermanische Geschichte
von Heldentrotz und Gattentreue. Der altnordischen Quellen
nacherzählt von Ferdinand Khull. Wien 1893. 8°. pp. 63.
   Separate reprint from the July-number of † Der Kyffhäuser. 1893. VII.
   —The copy in Fiske Icelandic Collection has the imprint of Graz 1894
   pasted over the original one.
Geschichte des Skalden Gisli. *In* Arthur Bonus's Isländerbuch.
München 1907. I. pp. 79-150.
Die Geschichte von Gisli dem Geächteten. Aus dem Island-
ischen des 12. Jahrhunderts deutsch von Friedrich Ranke.
München [1907]. (Statuen deutscher Kultur. XIII. Bd.).
8°. pp. 95.
Extracts in A. E. Wollheim da Fonseca's Die National Literatur der Skan-
dinavier. Berlin 1875. I. pp. 287-299.

Jónsson, Finnur.   Litteratur Historie. I. pp. 517-519 ; II. pp. 458-465.
Jónsson, Janus. Á við og dreif. Smáathuganir við fornan kveðskap. II.
    Gísla saga Súrssonar. *In* Arkiv f. nord. filol. 1899. XV. pp. 380-384.
Müller, P. E.   Sagabibliothek. I. pp. 167-175.
Ólsen, Björn M.   Rannsóknir á Vestfjörðum 1884. II. Rannsókn á Valseyri.
    In Árbók h. ísl. Fornleifafél. 1884-85. pp. 7-23.
Vigfússon, Guðbr.   Um tímatal í Íslendinga sögum. pp. 362-364.
Vigfússon, Sig.   Rannsókn um Vestfirði 1882 einkanlega í samanburði við
    Gísla sögu Súrssonar. *In* Árbók h. ísl. Fornleifafél. 1883. pp. 1-70, 3
    pls.
——— Rannsókn á Vestfjörðum 1888. *Ibid.* 1888-92. pp. 124-142.
——— Rannsóknir í Breiðafirði 1889. (Að Auðshugi.—Á Vaðli. Þorska-
    fjarðarþing). *Ibid.* 1893. pp. 2-5, 8-9, 15-18.
Þorkelsson, Jón.   Skýringar á vísum í Gísla sögu Súrssonar. Reykjavík
    1873. 8º. pp. 24. (*Program*).

Gizurar saga (ok Skagfirðinga).

A few chapters of the Sturlunga saga (Íslendinga saga) are by some
critics considered to be from a special saga of Gizur Þorvaldsson (d.
1268) ; the saga is, however, mentioned nowhere and if it ever existed,
is entirely lost excepting these few chapters. *See* Sturlunga saga.

Ólsen, Björn M.   Um Sturlungu. pp. 304-383.

Glúma. *See* Víga-Glúms saga.

Grænlendinga þáttr *or* Eiríks þáttr rauða.

The subject is the same as that of Eiríks saga (the discovery of Greenland and Wineland), but treated differently. It is in the Flateyjarbók,
and is compiled by Jón Þórðarson, the priest, who about 1387 for Jón
Hákonarson wrote the sagas of Olaf Tryggvason and Olaf the Saint in
the Flateyjarbók. Magnús Þórhallsson continued the work and divided
the þáttr into two sections with the headings Eiríks þáttr rauða and
Grænlendinga þáttr, the former title being found in the MSS. used for
the compilation, the latter being applied by Jón Þórðarson.—In two
editions (1838 and 1902) it is wrongly styled Eiríks saga.

Pattr Eyreks Ravda oc Leifs ens Hepna. *In* Saga Olafs Tryggva-
    sonar. Skálholt 1688. 4º. II. pp. 223-227.

In Heimskringla eller Snorre Sturlusons Nordländska Konunga
    Sagor, illustravit Joh. Peringskiöld. Stockholm 1697. fol. I.
    pp. 326-350.
    Text with Swedish and Latin versions.

In Heimskringla edr Noregs Konunga-Sögur af Snorra Sturlu-
    syni. Opera Gerhardi Schöning. Havniæ 1777. fol. I. pp. 304-
    326.
    Text with Danish and Latin versions.

Particula de Eiriko Rufo.—Particula de Grænlandis. *In* Anti-
    quitates Americanæ. Opera C. C. Rafn. Hafniæ 1837. 4º.
    pp. 7-76.
    Text with Danish and Latin versions and notes.

Erik den röde Saga eller Fortælling om Erik den röde og Grön-
lænderne. *In* Grönlands historiske Mindesmærker. Kjöbenhavn 1838. I. pp. 194–281.
Text with Danish translation, introduction aud notes.

Paattr Eireks rauda.—Her hefr Grænlendinga þaatt. *In* Flateyjarbók [*ed. by* G. Vigfússon *and* C. R. Unger]. Christiania
1860. I. pp. 429–432, 539–549.

Eiríks þáttr rauða (Flateyjarbók, Col. 221b–223b).—Grænlendinga þáttr (Flateyjarbók, Col. 281b–288). *In* The Finding
of Wineland the Good, by Arthur M. Reeves. London 1890.
4°. 140–158, 10 *facsim.-ff*.
Phototype-edition of the Flateyjarbók texts; printed Icelandic text
facing the MS.-page.—English version (The Wineland History of the
FlateyBook), with introduction, pp. 53-78. *For reviews see* Eiríka
saga rauða.

Eiríks saga rauða og Flatöbogens Grænlendingaþáttr samt
Uddrag fra Ólafs saga Tryggvasonar udg. for Samf. til udg. af
gl. nord. Litt. ved Gustav Storm. Köbenhavn 1891. pp. xiv–
xvi, 51–74.

Flateyjarbók. The "Flatey Book." "Flatö Bogen." Published by the Royal Danish General Staff Topographical De-
partment. Copenhagen, May 1893. fol. pp. (28).
Facsimile-edition of the two þættir of the Flateyjarbók, with printed
Icelandic text, Danish and English translations. Publ. on the occasion
of the Chicago exhibition 1893. *Review:* The Saga of Eric the Red,
by Hjalmar H. Boyesen, in The Cosmopolitan (Magazine) 1893. XVI.
pp. 467-469.

Eiríks saga rauða ok Grænlendinga þáttr. Búið hefir til prentunar Vald. Ásmundarson. Reykjavík 1902. (Íslendinga
sögur. 34.) 8°. pp. (4)+31.

DANISH.—Schöning's *version in* Heimskringla 1777 (*see above*).
Versions in Antiq. Americ. 1837, *and* Grönl. hist. Mindesm.
1838 (*see above*).

Om Viinlands Opdagelse. *In* Snorre Sturlesons norske Kongers
Sagaer. Oversatte af Jacob Aall. Christania 1847. fol. II. pp.
219–228, *map*.

Fortælling om Erik den röde. *In* Billeder af Livet paa Island,
ved Fr. Winkel Horn. Kjöbenhavn 1876. III. pp. 249–270.

Version in the edition of 1893 (*see above*).

ENGLISH.—Saga of Eric the Red. *In* The Discovery of America
by the Northmen, by N. L. Beamish. London 1841. pp. 45–80.

Reprinted in Voyages of the Northmen to America, ed. by E. E. Slafter, publ. by the Prince Society, Boston 1877. pp. 23-45.

In The Heimskringla transl. from the Icel. of Snorro Sturleson by Samuel Laing. London 1844. III. pp. 344-361.—2. edition, revised by Rasm. B. Anderson. London 1889. II. pp. 229-247.

Reeves's *version in* The Finding of Wineland the Good, 1890. pp. 53-78 ; *reprinted in* The Northmen, Columbus and Cabot 985-1503. The Voyages of the Northmen edited by Julius E. Olson . . . New York 1906. pp. 45-60.

See Eiríks saga rauða.—Beamish's and Reeves's versions also reproduced in the vol. of the "Norræna" series (1906) mentioned under Eiríks saga.

Version in the edition of 1893 (*see above*).

The Story of the Wineland Voyages, commonly called the Story of Eric the Red. *In* Origines Islandicæ, by G. Vigfusson and F. Y. Powell. Oxford 1905. II. pp. 598-609.

GERMAN.—Fahrten der Normänner nach Winland. *In* Heimskringla von Snorre Sturlason. Aus dem Isländischen von Gottlieb Mohnike. Stralsund 1837. pp. 285-304.

LATIN.—Peringsskiöld's *version in the* Heimskringla 1697. Schöning's *version in the* Heimskringla 1777. *Version in* Antiq. Americ. 1847. (*For all these see above.*)

Cf. Historia Vinlandiæ antiqvæ . . . . per Thorm Torfæum. Havniæ 1705.

SWEDISH.—Peringskiöld's *version in the* Heimskringla 1697 (*see above*).

In Konungaboken af Snorre Sturleson. Öfvers. och förkl. af H. O. H. Hildebrand. Örebro 1869. I. pp. 275-290.—*2. edition.* Stockholm 1889. pp. 203-218.

Jónsson, Finnur. Litteratur Historie II. pp. 778-779.

Storm, G. Om Betydningen af "Eyktarstaðr" i Flatöbogens Beretning om Vinlandsreiserne. *In* Arkiv f. nord. filol. 1886. VII. pp. 121-131.

Þorkelsson, Jón. Dagmálastaðr og eyktarstaðr. *In* Ísafold. 1874. fol. I. pp. 2-3.*

Grœnlendinga þáttr (II). *See* Einars þáttr Sokkasonar.

Grautar-Halla þáttr. *See* Sneglu-Halla þáttr.

Grettis saga *or* Grettla.

1000-1031. In its present shape it dates from the end of the 13th century, but it is doubtless based on an older saga now lost. The oldest

*For other works see foot-note p. 18.

MSS. now extant are from the 15th century (AM. 551 A. 4°). The last chapters of the saga (89-95) are a separate þáttr called Spesar þáttr or Þorsteins þáttr drómundar.

Sagan af Grettir Åsmundssyni sterka. *In* Nockrer Marg-Frooder Sögu-Pættir Islendinga, ad Forlage Biörns Marcus-Sonar. Hólar 1756. 4°. pp. 81-163.

Extracts (chap. 89-95, Spesar þáttr) with introduction, Latin version and notes in Antiquités Russes. 1852. fol. II. pp. 290 315.

Grettis saga ved G. Magnússon og G. Thordarson. Oversat af G. Thordarson. Udgivet af det nordiske Literatur-Samfund. Kjöbenhavn 1859. (Nordiske Oldskrifter. XVI., XXV.) 8°. pp. (4)+ 208+(2)+234+(2).

The first part containing the Icelandic text appeared in 1853. *Review:* Ný félagsrit. 1858. XVIII. pp. 162-165, by Guðbr. Vigfússon.

Grettis saga Åsmundarsonar herausgg. von R. C. Boer. Halle a. S. 1900. (Altnordische Saga-Bibliothek. 8.) 8°. pp. lii+ 348.

Annotated edition. *Reviews :* Zeitschr. f deut. Philol. 1904. XXXVI. pp. 560-561, by A. Gebhardt ;—Revue critique. 1901. N. S. LI. pp. 269-270, by L. Pineau ;—Folk-Lore. 1900. XI. pp. 406-414, by F. Y. Powell ; —Anz. f. deut. Altert. 1902. XXVIII. pp. 216-235, by W Ranisch ;— Literar. Centralbl. 1902. coll. 770 771, by O. Brenner.

Grettis saga. Búið hefir til prentunar Vald. Åsmundarson. Reykjavík 1900. (Íslendinga sögur. 28.) 8°. pp. vii+318+(2).

Grettisrímur, a poetical rendering of chap. 14-24 of the saga, made about year 1400, is printed in : Rímnasafn. Samling af de ældste islandske rimer Udg. for Samf. til udg. af gl. nord. litt. ved Finnur Jónsson. Köbenhavn 1905. pp. 43-104.

DANISH.—Fortælling om Gretter den Stærke. *In* Historiske Fortællinger om Islændernes Færd hjemme og ude, ved N. M. Petersen. Kjöbenhavn 1844. IV. pp. 221-258.

This paraphrase was not included in the 2d edition of Petersen's translations.

Fortællinger om Vatnsdölerne, Gisle Sursen, Gunlaug Ormstunge, Gretter den Stærke. Ved N. M. Petersen. 3. Udgave ved Verner Dahlerup og Finnur Jónsson. Köbenhavn 1901. pp. 171-201.

Gunnl. Þórðarson's *version in the edition of* 1859 (*see above*).

Grettes Saga. *In* Fortællinger og Sagaer fortalte af H. H. Lefolii. 2. Udgave. Kjöbenhavn 1874. II. pp. 1-118.— † *1. edition.* Kjöbenhavn 1861.

Grettes Saga. *In* Billeder af Livet paa Island, ved Fr. Winkel Horn. Kjöbenhavn 1874. II. pp. 1–212.

ENGLISH.—Grettis saga. The Story of Grettir the Strong. Translated from the Icelandic by Eiríkr Magnússon and William Morris. 2. edition. London 1869. 8°. pp. xxiv+304, *map.*—† *1. edition.* London 1869. 8°. pp. xxiv+306, *map.*— *3. edition.* London 1901. 8°. pp. xxiv+306.—† *A new edition, limited to 315 copies, as one volume of an eight volume series of the works of W. Morris, printed with the golden type of the Kelmscott Press in black and red on hand-made paper.* London (Chiswick Press) 1901. 4°. *with map.*

> Of the 1st ed. 25 copies were printed on Whatman hand-made paper (have been sold at auction for from £3.10 to £9.10). *Review :* †Lond. Quarterly Review. 1871. XXXVI. pp. 35-65.—*Cf.* C. A. Stephen's Off to the Geysers, Philadelphia 1873, which contains abstract of this version.

Grettir the Strong. [By E. H. Jones]. *In* Tales of the Teutonic Lands, by G. W. Cox and E. H. Jones. London 1872. pp. 247–324.

> This paraphrase was later embodied in the 2d edition of the same authors' Popular Romances of the Middle Ages. † London 1880, and the American edition, New York 1880. pp. 400–457.

Grettir the Outlaw. A Story of Iceland. By S. Baring-Gould. With 10 page illustrations by M. Zeno Diemer, and a coloured map. London 1890. 8°. pp. 384.

> "I have told the story in my own words and in my own way" (*preface*). *Review:* Tímarit h. ísl. Bókmentafél. 1893. XIV. pp. 264-266, by V. Guðmundsson.—Baring Gould has in his "Iceland, its Scenes and Sagas" (London 1863) given many extracts from this saga.

GERMAN.—E. Dagobert Schoenfeld : Gretter der Starke. Einer alten Isländischen Urkunde nacherzählt. Berlin 1896. 8°. pp. (8)+272, *map.* (*Bastard-title :* Aus Islands Vorzeit).

Extracts from Grettis saga in A. E. Wollheim da Fonseca's Die National-Literatur der Skandinavier. Berlin 1875. I. pp. 327-338.

SWEDISH.—Sagan om Grette den Starke, tolkad från fornisländ-skan af A. U.Bååth. Lund 1901. 8°. pp. xi+281.

Sagan om Grette den fredlöse *in* Hedda Anderson's Nordiske sagor. Stockholm 1896. II. pp. 103-136, a paraphrase, with two illustrations by Jenny Nyström-Stoopendaal.

Boer, R. C. Zur Grettissaga. *In* Zeitschr. f. deut. Philol. 1898. XXX. pp. 1-71.

Boer, R. C. Die handschriftliche überlieferung der Grettissaga. *Ibid.* 1899.
XXXI. pp. 40–60.

—— Kritische und exegetische bemerkungen zu skaldenstrophen. I. Zur
Grettissaga. *Ibid.* 1899. XXXI. pp. 141–148.

Daae, Ludv. Til Gretters Saga. *In* (Norsk) Historisk Tidsskrift. 1871. I.
pp. 498–500.

Gering, Hugo. Der Beówulf und die isländische Grettis saga. *In* Anglia.
1879. III. pp. 74–87.

Gunnlaugsson, Björn. Um fund Þórisdals. *In* Skírnir. 1835. IX. pp. 104–
107.

—— Um Þórisdal. *In* Sunnanpósturinn. 1836. II. pp. 111–124.

Jónsson, Bryn. Grettisbæli í Sökkólfsdal. *In* Árbók h. ísl. Fornleifafél.
1894. pp. 30–31.

—— Rannsókn sögustaða í vesturhluta Húnavatnssýslu sumarið 1894.
VII. Grettis saga. *Ibid.* 1895. pp. 14–17.

Jónsson, Finnur. Litteratur Historie. I. pp. 521–524 ; II. pp. 748–752 ; III.
pp. 82–83.

Jónsson, Janus Um vísurnar í Grettissögu, útg. 1853. *In* Arkiv f. nord.
filol. 1901. XVII pp. 248–273.

Jónsson, Þorleifur. Örnefni nokkur í Breiðafjarðardölum. *In* Safn til
sögu Íslands. 1876. II. pp. 558–577.

Müller. P. E. Sagabibliothek. I. pp. 249–263.

Smith, Chas. Sprague. Beówulf Gretti. *In* The New Englander. 1881.
No. CLVIII. (Vol. IV. no. 19). pp. 49–67.

Storm, Gustav. Sagn om Gretter fra Sætersdalen. *In* (Norsk) Historisk
Tidsskrift. 1880. II. R. II. Bd. pp. 377–385.

Vigfússon, Guðbr. Um tímatal í Íslendinga sögum. pp. 468–484.

—— Um nokkrar Íslendinga sögur. IV. Grettisfærsla. *In* Ný félagsrit.
1861. XXI. pp. 125–126,

Vigfússon, Sig. Rannsóknir á Vestrlandi 1891. *In* Árbók h. ísl. Fornleifafél. 1893. pp. 61–93.

Þorkelsson, Jón. Aldur vísnanna í Grettis sögu og fáeinar leiðrjettingar
við hana. *In* Norðanfari. 1868. VII. fol. pp. 45–46.

—— Skýringar á vísum í Grettis sögu. Reykjavík 1871. 8°. pp. 36.
(*Program*).
A few additional notes are found in Þorkelsson's Skýringar á vísum í
Guðmundar sögu. 1872. pp. 38–40.

Guðmundar saga dýra *or* Önundar-brennu saga.

1184–1200. Written probably before the middle of the 13th century as
an independent saga, but is now only found embodied in the Sturlunga
saga (*q. v.*).

Jónsson, Finnur. Litteratur Historie. II. pp. 561–564.

Ólsen, Björn M. Um Sturlungu. pp. 232–243.

3

Guðmundar saga biskups góða I–III.

I. Prestssaga Guðmundar.

Story of the life of Guðmundur Arason from his birth in 1161 until he was consecrated as bishop of Hólar 1202. Written probably in the first or second decade of the 13th century, but if the authorship of Lambkárr Þorgilsson (d. 1249) be accepted, it may be from the fifth decade. It is now found embodied in the Sturlunga saga (*q. v.*), and also combined with the Biskupssaga Guðmundar (*q. v.*), in a vellum codex from about 1300 (Codex Resenianus, AM. 399. 4°.; *cf.* Kålund's Palæografisk Atlas. 1905 No. 40.)

Jónsson, Finnur. Litteratur Historie. II. pp. 572-575.

Ólsen, Björn M. Um Sturlungu. pp. 224-232.

II. Biskupssaga Guðmundar.

Story of the life of bishop Guðmundr the Good from his consecration as bishop in 1202 until his death in 1237, a continuation of the Prestssaga, but by another pen. It seems to have been composed in the latter part of the 13th century, and largely based upon Sturla Þórðarson's Íslendinga saga and other sagas, but it is doubtful whether there ever existed an earlier saga of this period of the bishop's life. It is found in two recensions, a longer in AM. 399. 4° (Cod. Resen ', and a shorter in AM. 657 C. 4° (a vellum codex from the 14th cent.), the latter being usually called "Miðsagan."

Saga Guðmundar Arasonar Hóla-biskups hin elzta. *In* Biskupa sögur. Kaupmannahöfn 1858. I. pp. liii–lxv, 405–558.

The Prestssaga and the Biskupssaga together (from AM. 399, 4°. and AM. 394,4° edited by Guðbr. Vigfússon ; appended is : Brot úr miðsögu Guðmundar, pp. 559-618.

Extracts from the Prestssaga with introduction, notes and Danish version in Grönlands historiske Mindesmærker. 1838. II. pp. 749-762.

The Election of Bishop Godmund, a few chapters of the Biskupssaga translated into English, in Origines Islandicæ. 1905. I. pp. 601-613.

Jónsson, Finnur (*bishop*). Historia Ecclesiastica Islandicæ. Havniæ 1772. 4°. I. pp. 335-361.

Jónsson, Finnur. Litteratur Historie. II. pp. 735, 769-771.

Ker, W. P. The Life of Bishop Gudmund Arason. *In* Saga-Book of the Viking Club. 1907. V. 1. pp. 86-103.

Ólsen, Björn M. Um Sturlungu. pp. 272-304.

Þorkelsson, Jón. Skýringar á vísum í Guðmundar sögu Arasonar og Hrafns sögu Sveinbjarnarsonar. Reykjavík 1872 pp. 3-25. (*Program*).

III. Guðmundar saga Arngríms ábóta.

About the middle of the 14th century abbot Arngrímr of Þingeyrar (d. 1361) wrote this life of bishop Guðmundr. It was doubtless originally written in Latin and afterwards translated into Icelandic. It is, of course, based upon the earlier sagas, but is diffuse and full of miracle stories.

Saga Guðmundar Arasonar, Hólabiskups, eptir Arngrím ábóta. *In* Biskupa sögur. Kaupmannahöfn 1862. II. pp. 1–187 (*cf.* I. pp. liii–lxv.).

Edited from Cod. Holm. No. 5. fol. and various other MSS. (AM. 396. 4°, 398. 4°, 219–220 fol.) by Guðbr. Vigfússon.—Appended to it are : 1. Guðmundar drápa Hólabiskups, sem bróðir Arngrímr orti 1345, pp. 187–201 ; 2 Guðmundar drápa Hólabiskups, sem bróðir Árni Jónsson orti, ábóti á Múnkaþverá 1371–79, pp. 202–220 ,—Arngrímr's poem was later issued separately with glossary and Swedish prose version under the title : Kvæði Guðmundar byskups efter skinnboken no 5 fol. á Kongl. Bibliotheket i Stockholm. Akademisk afhandling af Arvid Isberg. Lund 1877. 8°. pp (2)+97.

Nokkur blöð úr Hauksbók og brot úr Guðmundar sögu gefin út af Jóni Þorkelssyni. Reykjavík 1865. 8°. pp. xxiv+55.

A fragment of the saga found on a vellum leaf in the Archeological Museum, Reykjavík, pp. 43–47 (*Cf.* Biskupa sögur II. pp. 67-71).

Jónsson, Finnur. Litteratur Historie III. pp. 68–71

Maurer, Konrad. Der Elisabeth von Schönau Visionen nach einer islándischen Quelle. Aus den Sitzungsberichten der philos.-philol. u. histor. Classe der k. bayer. Akad. d. Wiss. 1883. Heft III. pp, 401–423.

Ólsen, Björn M. Um Sturlungu. pp. 297–301.

Guðmundar saga ríka. *See* Ljósvetninga saga.

Gull-Ásu-Þórðar þáttr.

C. 1100–1120. Written in the earlier part of the 13th century. In the Morkinskinna.

In Fornmanna sögur. 1832. VII. pp. 111–118.   \

Þáttr af Gull-Ásu-Þórði. *In* Sex sögu-þættir, sem Jón Þorkelsson hefir gefið út. Reykjavík 1855. pp. xviii–xix, 72–78.— 2. (*anastatic*) útgáfa. Kaupmannahöfn 1895.

Edited from a paper-MS.

Scipti Eysteins konvngs oc Jngimars vm Asoþorþ. *In* Morkinskinna. Christiania 1867. pp. 170–174.

Gull-Ásu-Þórðar þáttr. *In* Fjörutíu Íslendinga þættir. Þórleifr Jónsson gaf út. Reykjavík 1904. pp. 78–84.

DANISH.—*In* Oldnordiske Sagaer. 1832. VII. pp. 95–100.

LATIN.—Svb. Egilsson's *version in* Scripta historica Islandorum. 1836. VII. pp. 115–121.

Jónsson, Finnur. Litteratur Historie. II. pp. 53-54, 551.

Müller, P. E. Sagabibliothek. I. pp. 346–347.

Gull-Þóris saga *or* Þorskfirðinga saga.

900–930. Written in the earlier part of the 13th century, and is now found only in one vellum MS. (AM. 561, 4°, from c. 1400) with some lacunæ.

Die Gull-Þóris saga oder Þorskfirðinga saga. Herausgegeben von Konrad Maurer. Leipzig 1858. 8°. pp. viii+87.

Review: †Leipz. Repertorium (hgg. v. Gersdorf). 1858. XVI. pp. 62, 162-164.—After this edition was printed Guðbr. Vigfússon succeeded in deciphering the last page of the MS. and published it in Nÿ félagsrit. 1861. XXI. pp. 118-121, and afterwards in his and Powell's Icelandic Prose Reader. 1879. pp. 121-122, 375-376.

Gull-Þóris saga. Þorleifr Jónsson gaf út. Reykjavík 1878. 8°. pp. iv+52.

Here the lacunæ are filled from paper-MSS. *Review:* Skuld. 1879. III. coll. 220-221, by Jón Ólafsson.

Þorskfirðinga saga. Búið hefir til prentunar Vald. Ásmundarson. Reykjavík 1897. (Íslendinga sögur. 17.) 8°. pp. (4)+67.

Gull-Þóris saga eller Þorskfirðinga saga udg. for Samfund til udgivelse af gammel nordisk litteratur ved Kr. Kålund. Köbenhavn 1898. 8°. pp. (4)+xxii+(2)+72.

Reviews: Zeitschr. f. deut. Philol. 1899. XXXI. pp. 505-509, by K. Maurer;—Deut. Lit. Zeit. 1899. col. 1630, by W. Golther;—Literar. Centralbl. 1900. col. 206, by E. Mogk.

Borgfirðingur, Sighv. Grímsson. Skÿringar yfir nokkur örnefni í Gull-Þóris sögu að því leyti sem viðkemr Þorskafjarðar þingi hinu forna. *In* Safn til sögu Íslands. 1876. II. pp. 578-592.

Jónsson, Bryn. Rannsókn í Barðastrandarsÿslu sumarið 1898. *In* Árbók h. ísl. Fornleifafél. 1899. pp. 6-13.

Jónsson, Finnur. Litteratur Historie. II. pp. 453-458.

Jónsson, Þorleifur. Endnu lidt om lakunerne i Gullþóris saga. *In* Arkiv f. nord. filol. 1886. III. p. 286.

Kålund, Kr. Om lakunerne i Gull-Þóris saga. *Ibid.* 1882. I. pp. 179-191.

Müller, P. E. Sagabibliothek. I. pp. 101-103.

Vigfússon, Guðbr. Um tímatal í Íslendinga sögum. pp. 355-358.

Gunnars saga Keldugnúpsfífls.

Fictitious saga, the scene is laid in the 11th century. Was supposed to be a 14th century composition, but is doubtless later. Paper-MSS. from the 17th century, being copies of earlier MSS.

Krókarefssaga, Gunnars saga Keldugnúpsfífls og Ölkofra þáttr. Kaupmannahöfn 1866. pp. 39-63.

Edited (from AM. 156 fol.) by Þorvaldur Björnsson. *Review:* Germania. 1867. XII. pp. 486-489, by K. Maurer.

Gunnars saga (*or* þáttr) Þiðrandabana.

C. 1000. Written in the 13th century. It has been generally supposed that this saga is identical with Njarðvíkinga saga, which is mentioned in the Landnáma and Laxdæla saga, but this is uncertain. Paper MSS.

Þáttr af Gunnari Þiðranda-bana. *In* Laxdæla saga. Hafniæ 1826. 4°. pp. 364-385.

Text (AM. 552 E. 4°) with Latin version by Þ. G. Repp.

Laxdæla saga og Gunnars þáttr Þiðrandabana. [*Ed. by* Jón Þorkelsson.] Akureyri 1867. pp. 245-259.

Gunnars saga Þiðrandabana. *In* Austfirðinga sögur udg. ved Jakob Jakobsen. Köbenhavn 1903. pp. lxv-lxxvi, 192-211. Critical edition (AM. 156 fol.).

Gunnars þáttr Þiðranda-bana. *In* Fjörutíu Íslendinga þættir. Þórleifr Jónsson gaf út. Reykjavík 1904. pp. 85-100.

DANISH.—Njardvikinga saga eller Fortælling om Gunnar Thidrandebane. *In* Historiske Fortællinger om Islændernes Færd hjemme og ude, ved N. M. Petersen. 2. Udg. Köbenhavn 1863. III. pp. 313-322.

ENGLISH.—The Tale of Gunnere Thidrand's bane. *In* Origines Islandicæ, by G. Vigfusson and F. Y. Powell. Oxford 1905. II. pp. 567-575.

LATIN.—Repp's *version in the edition of* 1826 (*see above*).

Gunnarsson, Sig. Örnefni frá Jökulsá í Axarfirði austan að Skeiðará. 9. Gunnars þáttr Þiðrandabana. *In* Safn til sögu Íslands. 1876. II. pp. 476-478.

Jónsson, Finnur. Litteratur Historie. II. p. 551.

Müller, P. E. Sagabibliothek. I. pp. 144-145

Gunnlaugs saga ormstungu *or* Gunnlaugs saga ormstungu ok Skáld-Hrafns.

983-1008. Written in the last decades of the 12th century. It is erroneously ascribed to Ari the Learned. MSS. : Cod. Holm. No. 18. 4º, vellum from c. 1350, and AM. 557. 4º, vellum from the 15th century, imperfect.

Sagan af Gunnlaugi ormstungu ok skalld-Rafni, sive Gunnlaugi vermilingvis et Rafnis poetæ vita. Ex manuscriptis Legati Magnæani cum interpretatione latina, notis, chronologia, tabulis genealogicis, et indicibus, tam rerum qvam verborum. Hafniæ 1775. (Sumptibus Legati Magnæani). 4º. pp. (8)+ xxxii+318+(80), 2 *pls.*, 4 *engrs. in text.*

Edited by Jón Eiríksson. Text from AM. 557. 4º. The preface is by B. W. Luxdorph, the indices by Hannes Finnsson, and the explanations of verses by Gunnar Pálsson. The "Annotationes uberiores" consist of : 1. De expositione infantum apud veteres Septentrionales ejusque causis (by Jón Eiríksson), pp. 194-219; 2. Pauli Vidalini de lingvæ septentrionalis appellatione : dönsk tunga i. e. lingva danica commentatio, ex islandico latiné versa, et supplementis aucta, pp. 220-297; 3. De vocibus víkingr et víking (by Jón Eiríksson), pp. 298-306. The plates represent interiors of Icelandic houses in the 10th century ; the third pl. (containing MSS.-facsims. according to Möbius) is lacking in Fiske Collection copy. For controversial writings about the chronology of the saga occasioned by this edition see below under Bp. Finnur Jónsson and Jón Eiríksson. *Reviews :* † Gatterer's Histor. Journal. XVI. pp. 192-204 ;—Kjøbenh Nye Kritisk Journal. 1775. coll. 305-310, by Jacob Baden ;—† Götting. Anzeig. 1778. pp. 223 ff.—The publication of this first scholarly edition of an Icelandic saga was celebrated in a poem by Gunnar Pálsson, which was issued separately : Nýprentadri Saugu af Gunnlaugi Ormstungu fagnad under gaumlu kvædis vidlagi. *S. l. et a.* [Copenhagen 1775 ?] 4°. pp. (4).

Sagan af Hrafni ok Gunnlaugi ormstungu. *In* Íslendinga sögur. Kjöbenhavn 1847. II. pp. xx-xxxii, 187-276.

> Critical edition by Jón Sigurðsson.   Text chiefly following Cod. Holm.

Gunnlaugs saga ormstungu ok Skáld-Hrafns. *In* Analecta norræna herausgg. von Th. Möbius. Leipzig 1859. pp. 135-166.

—2. Ausgabe. Leipzig 1877. pp. 103-135.

Gunnlaugs saga ormstungu. Med forklarende Anmærkninger og Ordsamling ved O. Rygh. Christiania 1862. (Det norske Oldskriftsselskabs Samlinger. III.) 8°. pp. iv+120.

Gunnlaugs saga ormstungu. *In* Oldnordisk Læsebog af L. F. A. Wimmer. Köbenhavn 1870. pp. 73-104, 133-139.

> With Icelandic-Danish glossary ; in all subsequent editions of this reader : 1877 ; 1882 ; 1889 ; 1896; and 1903 (pp. 74-107, 137-154).

Gunnlaugs saga ormstungu. Jón Þorkelsson gaf út. Reykjavík 1880. 8°. pp. viii+64.

> *Reviews :* Literar. Centralbl. 1880. col. 563 ;—Ísafold. 1880. VII. pp. 35-36, by H. Kr. Friðriksson ; reply by J. Þ., ibid. pp. 37-39 ; rejoinder by H. Kr. F., ibid. pp. 61-62, 66-68 ; by J. Þ., ibid. pp. 78-79, 83-84, 85-86.

Saga þeira Hrafns ok Gunnlaugs ormstungu. *In* Einleitung in das Studium des Altnordischen von J. C. Poestion. Hagen i W. 1887. II. pp. 39-73.

> With Icelandic-German glossary.

Gunnlaugssaga Ormstungu. Mit einleitung und glossar herausgg. von E. Mogk. Halle a. S. 1886. (Altnordische texte. I.) 8°. pp. xx+57.

> Text from AM. 557. 4°. *Reviews :* Zeitschr. f. deut. Philol. 1887. XIX. pp. 494-501, by H. Gering (*cf.* Mogk's article below) ;—Literar. Centralbl. 1886. coll. 732-733 —† Wissenschaftl. Beil. der Leipziger Zeit. 1886. p. 69 ;—Modern Lang. Notes. 1887. II. pp. 198-199, by W. H. Carpenter.

Gunnlaugs saga ormstungu. Búið hefir til prentunar Vald. Ásmundarson. Reykjavík 1893. (Íslendinga sögur. 9.) 8°. pp. viii+64.

> The stanzas of the saga in Corpus poeticum boreale. 1883. II. pp. 109-113, and in K. Gíslason's Udvalg af oldnord. Skjaldekvad. 1892. pp. 27-28, 124-142.

DANISH.—†Fortællingen om Gunlaug Ormetunge og Rave [!]
Skald oversat af det gamle nordiske Sprog [ved W. H. F.
Abrahamson]. *In* Det Almindelige danske Bibliothek. Kjö-
benhavn 1778. IV. pp. 276–319 ; 1779. I. pp. 25–45.

Gunlaugs og Rafns Saga. *In* Saga. Nytaarsgave for 1812 ved
N. F. S. Grundtvig. Kiöbenhavn. pp. 1–50.

Fortælling om Gunlaug Ormstunge og Skjald-Rafn. *In* Historiske Fortællinger om Islændernes Færd hjemme og ude,
ved N. M. Petersen. Kjöbenhavn 1840. II. pp. 3–46.—2.
Udg. [*ed. by* G. Vigfússon]. Köbenhavn 1868. IV. pp. 103–
146, *also with special t.-p.:* Fortællingerne om Vatnsdælerne,
Gunlaug Ormetunge, Kormak og Finboge den Stærke *etc.*

Fortællinger om Vatnsdölerne, Gisle Sursen, Gunlaug Ormstunge, Gretter den Stærke. Efter de islandske Grundskrifter
ved N. M. Petersen. 3. Udgave ved Verner Dahlerup og F.
Jónsson. Versene ved Olaf Hansen. Köbenhavn 1901. pp.
139–170.

Reprinted in : Jón Svensson, Islandsblomster. Köbenhavn 1906. pp. 65–
105.

Gunlög Ormstunge og Helga den Favre. *In* Sagaer, fortalte af
Brynjolf Snorrason og Kristian Arentzen. Kjöbenhavn 1849.
I. pp. 131–177.

Sagaen om Gunnlaug Ormstunge og Skalde-Ravn. Oversat fra
Gammelnorsk af O. Rygh. Udg. af Selskabet for Folkeoplysnings Fremme. Tillægshefte til Folkevennen VIII. Kristiania 1859. 8°. pp. 39.

Review : † Illustr. Nyhedsbl. 1859. No. 39.—Rygh's translation is reprinted *in* H. Lassen's Læsebog i Modersmaalet for Skolernes höjere
Klasser. 2. Udgave. Christiania 1875. pp. 1–20.—† *1. edition.* Christiania 1861 ;—*and*

in Nordahl Rolfsen's Vore Fædres Liv. Bergen 1888. pp. 82–
103.—*2. edition.* Christiania 1898. pp. 92–116, 2 *illustr.* (*by*
A. Bloch).

Gunlögs Saga. *In* Fortællinger og Sagaer, fortalte for Börn af
H. H. Lefolii. 2. Udg. Kjöbenhavn 1874. II. pp. 119–163.—
† *1.edition.* Kjöbenhavn 1861.

Sagaen om Gunlög Ormstunge og Helga den Fagre. Forkortet
og fremstillet paa Dansk ved Johan Skjoldborg. *In* Wisbech's
Almanak for 1900. Odense. pp. (16), 5 *illustr.*

ENGLISH.—The Saga of Gunnlaug the Worm-tongue and Rafn
the Skald. (Transl. by Eiríkr Magnússon and William
Morris). *In* The Fortnightly Review. 1869. XI. (N. S. V.)
pp. 27-56.—*Reprinted in :* Three Northern Love Stories and
other Tales. Transl. from the Icelandic by E. M. and W. M.
London 1875. pp. 1-93.—New edition. London 1901. pp. 1-68.
—† *Another edition, limited to 315 copies, is found in the eight
volume series of the works of William Morris, printed with
golden type of the Kelmscott Press in black and red on hand-
made paper.* London (Chiswick Press) 1901. 4°.

A separate edition of this translation was printed for Morris, with title
as follows :

† The Story of Gunnlaug the Worm-Tongue and Raven the
Skald even as Ari Thorgilsson the learned, the priest, hath
told it. . . Printed at the Chiswick Press for William Morris,
1891. 4°.

In Caxton black letter type. Only 75 copies printed on paper and 3 on
vellum. A vellum copy was sold to Tregaskis at auction March 25,
1903 for £42, in which connection the "Book prices current 1903"
(no 3042) notes : "Of this story, which first appeared in the Fortnightly Review for Jan. 1869, and which was here reprinted at the
Chiswick Press for W. M only 75 copies were printed on Whatman paper
and 3 copies only on vellum. The spaces left blank for initial letters
were never rubricated and the book was therefore not published. In
the case of the vellum copies, it was Morris's intention to illuminate
the spaces, which he, however, did in one only. There is, therefore,
but one other copy in a similar state to the above."

Gunnlaug and the fair Helga. [By E. H. Jones.] *In* Tales of
the Teutonic Lands, by G. W. Cox and E. H. Jones. London
1872. pp. 325-345.

This was later embodied in the 2d edition of the same authors' Popular
Romances of the Middle Ages †London 1880, and the American edition,
New York 1880, pp. 345-473.

FAROESE.—† Sögan um Gunnleyg Ormstungu, utlögd úr Ís-
lendskum av J. Jakobsen. *In* Ársbók Fröja bókafjelags 1901.
I. pp. 28-58.—† *Also a separate reprint.*

FRENCH.—La saga de Gunnlaug Langue de Serpent. Traduite
de l'ancien islandais avec une introduction par Félix Wagner.
Gand 1899. 8°. pp. 100.

Reviews : Arkiv f. nord. filol. 1901. XVII. pp. 383-384, by R. C. Boer ;
—Deut. Lit. Zeit. 1900. coll. 354-355, by E. Mogk ;—Literaturbl. f. g.
u. r. Philol. 1900. col. 278, by W. Golther ;—Literar. Centralbl. 1900.
col. 940, by O. Brenner (?).

GERMAN.—Die Geschichte von Gunnlaug Schlangenzunge. Aus dem isländischen Urtexte übertragen von Eugen Kölbing. Heilbronn 1878. 16°. pp. xiii+(2)+72.

A few remarks and amendments by the translator (Zur Gunnlaugs saga ormstungu) in Wissenschaftl. Monatsblatter. (Königsberg) 1878. VI. pp. 110–111. *Reviews*. Nord. Tidskr. f Filol. 1878 III. pp. 301–303, by J. Hoffory,—Jenaer Lit. Zeit. 1878 pp. 227–228, by A. Edzardi;—Arch. f. d. Studium d. neu Spr. u. Lit. 1878 LIX. pp. 459–460, by Hans Löschhorn;—† Edlinger's Literaturbl. 1878. II. 436;—† Europa Chronik. 1878. 9.

Ein alt-isländisches Dichterleben. *In* Aus Hellas, Rom und Thule. Cultur- und Literaturbilder von J. C. Poestion. Leipzig 1882. pp. 105–128. (*A paraphrase*).

Die Saga von Gunnlaug Schlangenzunge. Aus dem Altisländischen übersetzt von Alexander Tille. Leipzig [1890]. (Reclam's Universal-Bibliothek. 2756.) 16°. pp. 69.

Review: Timarit h. isl. Bókmentafél. 1893. XIV. p. 268, by V. Guð-mundsson.

Die Saga von Gunnlaug Schlangenzunge. *In* Nordische Heldensagen. Aus dem Altisländischen übersetzt und bearbeitet von Carl Küchler. Bremen 1892. pp. 1–75.

Reviews: Deut. Lit. Zeit. 1893. coll. 1134–36, by E. Kölbing,—Literaturbl. f. g. u. r. Philol. 1894. coll. 388–389, by B. Kahle;—†Blätt. f. liter. Unterhalt. 1892. no. 48, by E. Mogk.

LATIN.—J. Eiríksson's *version in the edition of* 1775 (*see above*).

NORWEGIAN.—Soga um Gunnlaug Ormstunga. Umskrivi fraa Gamallnorsk av Matias Skard. 2. Utgaava. Christiania 1902. 8°. pp. 48.—† *1. edition*. Christiania 1870. 8°. pp. 48.

SWEDISH.—Gunlögs Saga från Island. På Swenska utgifwen och bearbetad af S[olon Hammargre]n. Örebro 1856. 8°. pp. 42.

Sagan om Gunnlög Ormtunga och Skald-Ram, på svenska tolkad af P. Aug. Gödecke. Stockholm 1872. (Läsning för folket. Tilläggshäfte, No. 3). 8°. pp. 47.—Ny, omarbetad upplaga. Stockholm 1881. 8°. pp. 47.

Review· †Göteborg Handelstidning, Dec. 30, 1872, by Viktor Rydberg, reprinted under the heading "Fornnordiskt" in his Skrifter. Stockholm 1899. XIV. pp. 524–532.

Sagan om Gunnlög Ormtunga och Skald-Ram. *In* Hedda Anderson's Nordiska sagor. Stockholm 1896. II. pp. 74–102, 2 *illustr*. (*by* J. Nyström-Stoopendaal). (*A paraphrase*.)

Sagan om Gunnlaug Ormstunga. *In* Isländsk och fornsvensk litteratur i urval, af Richard Steffen. Stockholm 1905. pp. 65–97.

Boer, R. C.   Kritische und exegetische bemerkungen zur skaldenstrophen.
III. Zur Gunnlaugs saga ormstungu. *In* Zeitschr. f. deut. Philol. 1899.
XXXI. pp. 157-159.

Eiríksson, Jón.   Ad Finnum Johannæum Epistola de chronologia Gunnlaugs-sagæ ad Hist. Eccles. Island. Tom. IV. p. 358-368 et Vitam
Gunnlaugi Ormstungæ not 82. 101 et 111. Accesserunt Gunnari Pauli
F. curæ posteriores in Gunnlaugi Vitam et maximæ in qvædam carmina antiqva in eadem obvia. Hafniæ 1778. 4°. pp. 31.

———— Observationes et emendationes ulteriores in Gunnlaugi Vermilingvis
et Hrafni Poetæ vitam ex eruditorum quorundam in Islandia amicorum
ad se epistolis collectæ, et maximam partem ex Island. Latine versæ
nunc vero editæ per J. E.   Havniæ 1786. 4°. pp. 8.
Extracts from letters of Gunnar Pálsson, Guðlaugur Sveinsson and
Magnús Ketilsson.

Jónsson, Finnur (*bishop*).   Historia Ecclesiastica Islandiæ. Havniæ 1778.
4°. IV. pp. 358-368.

———— † Responsio apologetica ad Johannis Erici epistolam de chronologia
Gunnlaugs-sagæ occasionem subministrante Hist. Eccles. Island. Tom.
IV. pag. 358-368. Havniæ 1780. 4°.

Jónsson, Finnur.   Litteratur Historie. I. pp. 569-573; II. pp. 290-292,
422-425.

Mogk, E.   Zur Gunnlaugssaga. *In* P. u. B. Beiträge z. Gesch. d. deut. Spr.
u. Lit. 1891 XVI. pp. 537-539.

Müller. P. E.   Sagabibliothek. I. pp. 62-70.
Translated into English by E. Burritt in The American Eclectic. 1841.
I. pp. 105-107.

Vigfússon, Guðbr.   Um tímatal í Íslendinga sögum. pp. 437-441.

Þorkelsson, Jón.   Skýringar á vísum í nokkurum íslenzkum sögum.
Reykjavík 1868. pp. 15-26. (*Program*).

Halldórs þáttr Snorrasonar.

C 1050. There are two different þættir of Halldór, one in the Flateyjarbók (Halldór and Einar þambarskelfir), the other in the Morkinskinna (Halldór and King Haraldr); they are probably both written
in the 13th century, the Morkinskinna þáttr being possibly a little
older than the other.

Þattr Halldors Snorrasunar. [*I.*]   *In* Saga Olafs Tryggvasonar.
Skálholt 1689. 4°. pp. 315-321.

Þáttr Halldórs Snorrasonar. [*I.*]   *In* Fornmanna sögur. 1827.
III. pp. 152-174. [*II.*] *Ibid.* 1831. VI. pp. 240-251.

Einarr hjalpaði Halldori.—Saga Einars.—(Þattr Halldors Snorrasonar). *In* Flateyjarbók. Christiania 1860-68. I. pp. 506-
511; III. pp. 428-431.

In Morkinskinna. Christiania 1867. pp. 46-51.

Halldórs þáttr Snorrasonar. [*I.-II.*]   *In* Fjörutíu Íslendinga
þættir. Þórleifr Jónsson gaf út. Reykjavík 1904. pp. 101-125.

DANISH.—En Fortælling om Haldor Snorroson. [*II.*] *In* Dansk Minerva for Juni 1818. pp. 543–558, *and* [*I.*] for October 1818. pp. 322–333.
Translated by Þorleifur G. Repp.

Fortælling om Haldor Snorresön. [*I.*] *In* Oldnordiske Sagaer. 1827. III. pp. 136–154. [*II.*] *Ibid.* 1832. VI. pp. 196–205.

Halldór Snorrason. [*II.*] *In* Udvalgte Sagastykker fordanskede ved Grímur Thomsen. Kjöbenhavn 1846. pp. 3–5.

Haldor Snorressön. [*II.*] *In* Sagaer, fortalte af Brynjolf Snorrason og Kristian Arentzen. Kjöbenhavn 1850. IV. pp. 199–213.
A paraphrase of the second þáttr in Fortællinger og Sagaer, ved H. H. Lefolii. 3. Udg. Kjöbenhavn 1869. I. pp. 136–139. † *1. ed.* 1859. † *2. ed.* 1862.

LATIN.—Particula de Haldore Snorrii filio. [*I.*] *In* Scripta historica Islandorum. 1829. III. pp. 155–174. [*II.*] *Ibid.* 1835. VI. pp. 223–232.
Translated by Svb. Egilsson.
Cf. Torfæus's Histor. rer. Norvegic. p. III. 1711. fol. pp. 325–329. (De Haldore Snorrii filio narratio).

Jónsson, Finnur. Litteratur Historie. II. p. 548.

Müller, P. E. Sagabibliothek. III. pp. 330–337.

Hallfreðar saga vandræðaskálds.

C. 960–1007. Date of composition about 1200. Two recensions, the older in the Möðruvallabók (AM. 132 fol.), the younger, which has been called Hallfreðar þáttr vandræðaskálds, embodied in Ólafs saga Tryggvasonar of the Flateyjarbók (Gl. kgl. Sml. 1005 fol.)

[*II.*] *In* Saga Olafs Tryggvasonar. Skálholt 1689. 4°. II. pp. 78–87, 98, 109–115, 126–132, 247–250, 304–307 ; Appendix, pp. 19–22.
The first and the last (appendix) sections have the heading Þattr Hallfreds (Hallfredar) Vandræda Skalds, which is taken from the Flateyjarbók.

[*II.*] *In* Fornmanna sögur. 1826–1827. II. pp. 1–17, 39–43, 50–62, 79–88, 211–213, 246–251 ; III. pp. 20–29.

[*II.*] *In* Flateyjarbók [*Ed. by* G. Vigfússon *and* C. R. Unger.] Christiania 1860. I. pp. 299–308, 316–317, 326–332, 340–345, 448–451, 497–500, 533–536.

Hallfreðar saga [*I.*]. *In* Fire og fyrretyve Pröver af oldnordisk Sprog og Literatur, udg. af Konr. Gíslason. Kjöbenhavn 1860. pp. 6–41.

Hallfreðar saga [*I.*].   *In* Fornsögur herausgg. von Guðbrandr
Vigfússon und Theodor Möbius. Leipzig 1860. pp. ix–xiv,
81–116.

Appended are: Aus Heimskringla, Ólafs saga Tryggvasonar, kap. 90,
113, pp. 115–116; Kvæði Hallfreðar (Drápa um Hákon jarl; Ólafs
drápa, Drápa um Eirík jarl; Erfidrápa Ólafs Tryggvasonar) pp. 204–
210, 215–225.—For a few text emendations see Origines Islandicæ. 1905.
II. pp. 277.

Hallfreðar saga [*I.*].   Búið hefir til prentunar Vald. Ásmundarson. Reykjavík 1901. (Íslendinga sögur. 31.) 8°. pp. (4)+
83.

Appended are the poems by Hallfreðr, pp. 50–62.

The Ólafs drápa of Hallfreðr has been published twice separately: Ólafs
drápa Tryggvasonar er Hallfredr orti Vandrædaskáld, útgefin af
Sveinbirni Egilssyni. Videyar Klaustri 1832 8°. pp. 22. (Program).—
Ólafs drápa Tryggvasonar. Fragment ur "Bergsboken." Akademisk
afhandling af Hjalmar Gullberg. Lund 1875. 8°. pp. (4)+49.—His
poems and improvisations are also in. Corpus poeticum boreale. 1883.
II. pp. 87–97; Tb. Wisén's Carmina norræna. 1886 I. pp. 33–40, 135–
137; K. Gíslason's Udvalg af oldnord. Skjaldekvad. 1892. pp. 21–23,
107–113.

DANISH.—[*II. trl. by* C. C. Rafn.] *In* Oldnordiske Sagaer. 1827.
II. pp. 1–16, 35–38, 45–56, 71–79, 188–190, 218–223; III. pp.
17–25.

Hallfreds Saga [*I.*].   *In* Billeder af Livet paa Island, ved Fr.
Winkel Horn. Kjöbenhavn 1876. III. pp. 187–222.

Hallfred Vandraadeskald.   *In* Nordahl Rolfsen's Vore Fædres
Liv. Oversættelsen ved Gerhard Gran. Bergen 1888. pp.
103–115.—*2. edition.* Christiania 1898. pp. 117–132, 2 *illustr.*

Abstract. The illustrations are by A. Bloch.

ENGLISH.[*II.*]   *In* The Saga of King Olaf Tryggwason. Translated by J. Sephton. London 1895. pp. 210–221, 235–238,
243–251, 261–267, 351–352, 374–377, 441–447.

Origines Islandicæ. 1905. II. pp. 312–314, has a version of the first
three chapters of the saga.—A two-page drawing "Thor's Hammer or
Christ's Cross" by Allan Stewart in Illustrated London News. Dec.
22. 1906, illustrating the sword-verse episode.

LATIN.—[*II. trl. by* Svb. Egilsson.] *In* Scripta historica Islandorum. 1828–1829. II. pp. 1–17, 35–39, 46–59, 73–82, 198–200,
230–235; III. pp. 23–33.

Cf. T. Torfæus's Histor. rer. Norvegic. p. II. 1711. fol. pp. 466–483. (Vita
Hallfredi Vandrædaskaldi, sev periculosi poetæ).

SWEDISH.—Hallfreds Saga [*I.*]. Öfversättning från Isländskan
jemte Anmärkningar. Akademisk afhandling af S. H. B,
Svensson. Lund 1864. 8°. pp. viii+82.

† Giesebrecht, Ludwig. Halfred Vandrädaskald. Stettin 1830. 4°. pp. 30.
(*Program*).

Hjelmquist, Th. Var Hallfreðr vandræðaskáld arian? *In* Arkiv f. nord.
filol. 1907. XXIII. pp. 155-179.

Jónsson, Bryn. Rannsókn sögustaða í vesturhluta Húnavatnssýslu. III.
Hallfreðar saga. *In* Árbók h. ísl. Fornleifafél. 1895. pp. 7-9.

Jónsson, Finnur. Litteratur Historie. I. pp. 556-566; II. pp. 474-477.

—— Versene i Hallfredssaga. *In* Arkiv f. nord. filol. 1902. XVIII. pp.
305-330.

Müller, P. E. Sagabibliothek. III. pp. 269-287.

Vigfússon, Guðbr. Um tímatal í Íslendinga sögum. pp. 382-384.

Hallfreðar þáttr vandræðaskálds. *See* Hallfreðar saga vandræðaskálds.

Hænsa-Þóris saga.

C. 963-970. Date of composition uncertain, by some put in the earlier
period of sagawriting (about 1200), by others in the middle or latter
part of the 13th century which is, perhaps, more probable. Vellum
fragment from the 15th century (AM. 162 G, fol.), but the saga is complete only in paper-MSS.

Hænsa-Þóris saga. *In* Íslendinga sögur. Kjöbenhavn 1847. II.
pp. xiv-xx, 119-186.

Critical edition (AM. 501. 4°) by Jón Sigurðsson.

Hænsa-Þóris saga. Þorleifr Jónsson gaf út. Reykjavík 1892.
(Íslendinga sögur. 5.) 8°. pp. vii+41.

Zwei Isländer-Geschichten, die Hænsna-Þóres und die Bandamanna saga mit Einleitung und Glossar herausgg. von Andreas
Heusler. Berlin 1897. 8°. pp. (4)+xlii+164.

Introduction, pp. i-xxviii, text, pp. 1-26.—*For reviews see* Bandamanna saga.

The Story of Thore the Henpeddler. *In* Origines Islandicæ,
by G. Vigfusson and F. Y. Powell. Oxford 1905. II. pp. 2-
42.

Icelandic text with English translation.

DANISH.—Hönse-Thorers Saga ˙eller Fortællingen om Hönse-
Thorer, oversat fra det ældre norske Sprog af P. A. Munch.
Christiania 1845. (Sagaer eller Fortællinger om Nordmænds
og Islænderes Bedrifter i Oldtiden. II.) 8°. pp. (2)+v+36.

Hönsetores Saga. *In* Billeder af Livet paa Island, ved Fr.
Winkel Horn. Kjöbenhavn 1871. (I.) pp. 61-90.

ENGLISH.—The Story of Hen Thorer. *In* The Saga Library,
by W. Morris and E. Magnússon. London 1891. I. pp. xxviii-
xlvii, 123-163, *map*.

For reviews see Bandamanna saga.—A special edition in black letter
type on heavy paper, restricted to 350 numbered copies, is :

The Saga of Hen Thorer. Done into English out of the Icelandic by William Morris and Eiríkr Magnússon. With
decorations by A. E. Goetting. Cincinnati, Ohio. (Byway
Press). [1903.] 8°. pp. (2)+87.
Vigfússon *and* Powell's *version in* Orig. Isl. II. (*see above*).

GERMAN.—Die Geschichte vom Hühnerthorir. Eine altisländische Saga übersetzt von Andreas Heusler. Berlin 1900. 8°.
pp. (4)+91.

Reviews. Revue critique. 1900. I. pp. 452-453, by L. Pineau;—Deut.
Lit. Zeit. 1900. coll. 1701-02, by B. Kahle;—Literaturbl. f. g. u. r.
Philol. 1901. coll. 6-8, by A. Gebhardt,—Eimreiðin. 1900. VI. p. 155,
by V. Guðmundsson;—Literar. Centralbl. 1901. col. 370, by O.
Brenner.

Die Saga vom Hühner-Thor. Eine altisländische Bauernnovelle
des Xten Jahrhunderts. Aus dem Altisländischen übersetzt
von Alwin Wode. Diessen 1902. 8°. pp. 77+(2).

Jónsson, Finnur. Litteratur Historie. II. pp. 233-237, 744-746.
Jónsson, Jón (*of* Hlíð). Örnefni í Snóksdalssókn. *In* Safn til sögu
Íslands. 1876. II. pp. 319-324.
Maurer, K. Ueber die Hænsa-Þóris saga. Aus den Abhandlungen der k.
bayer. Akademie der Wiss. I. Cl. XII. Bd. II Abtheil. München 1871.
4°. pp. 60.
Müller, P. E. Sagabibliothek. I. pp. 78-85.
Ólsen, Björn M. Landnáma og Hænsa-Þóris saga. *In* Aarb. f. nord.
Oldk. og Hist. 1905. pp. 63-80.
Vigfússon, Guðbr. Um tímatal í Íslendinga sögum. pp. 321-323.
Vigfússon, Sig. Rannsóknir í Borgarfirði 1884. (Örnólfsdair. Blund-
ketilsbrenna). *In* Árbók h. ísl. Fornleifafél. 1884 85. pp. 133-138.

Harðar saga, *or* Harðar saga Grímkelssonar ok Geirs, *or* Harðar
saga ok Hólmverja, *or* Hólmverja saga.

C. 940-986. In its present shape the saga cannot be older than the
latter part of the 13th century, but there must have been another saga
from the earlier period of sagawriting, which is now lost except a small
portion of a recension of it, now among the fragments of the Vatnshyrna-
codex (c. 1400) in AM. 564 A, 4°.

Sagann af Haurde og hans Fylgiurum, þeim Hoolmverium. *In*
Agiætar Fornmanna Sögur, ad Forlage Biörns Marcussonar.
Hólar 1756. pp. 69-126.
Harðar saga Grímkelssonar ok Geirs. *In* Íslendinga sögur.
Kjöbenhavn 1847. II. pp. iii-xiv, 1-118, 476-480.

Critical edition (AM. 556 A. 4°) by Jón Sigurðsson. The fragments of
the Vatnshyrna, pp. 476-480 (reprinted in G. Vigfússon and F. Y.
Powell's Icel. Prose Reader. 1879. pp. 94-99.)—Chap. 17 with notes in
Antiquités Russes. 1852. II. fol. pp. 317-320.

Harðar saga ok Hólmverja. Þórleifr Jónsson gaf út. Reykjavík 1891. (Íslendinga sögur. 3.) 8⁰. pp. vii+104.

Holmverja saga or Hardar saga. *In* Origines Islandicæ, by G. Vigfusson and F. Y. Powell. Oxford 1905. II. pp. 43–87.

Text with English translation of the chapters which the editors consider to be historical.

DANISH.—Hörd Grimkjeldssöns saga eller de fredlöse paa holmen. En historisk skildring fra det 10de århundredes anden halvdel. Oversat fra oldnorsk af Fr. Brandt. Kristiania 1849. (Skildringer af de gamle Nordboeres færd.) 8⁰. pp. 96.

Review. † Morgenbladet, 1849. No. 175, by P. A. Munch.

Hörd Grimkelssön og Geir. *In* Sagaer, fortalte af Brynjolf Snorrason og Kristian Arentzen. Kjöbenhavn 1849. II. pp. 109–194.

Hörd Grimkelssöns Saga. *In* Billeder af Livet paa Island, ved Fr. Winkel Horn. Kjöbenhavn 1876. III. pp. 1–62.

Hord Grimkelssön. *In* Nordahl Rolfsen's Vore Fædres Liv. Oversættelsen ved Gerhard Gran. Bergen 1888. pp. 183–196.

—*2. edition*. Christiania 1888. pp. 160–176, 2 *illustr*.

A paraphrase The illustrations are by A. Bloch.

ENGLISH.—Vigfússon *and* Powell's *version in* Orig. Isl. II. (*see above*).

_____

Jónsson, Bryn Rannsókn sögustaða í Grafningi í maí 1898. 1. Grímkelsstaðir. *In* Árbók h. ísl. Fornleifafél. 1899. pp. 1–3.

——— Um Haugsnesshauginn.—Um Stykkisvöll. *Ibid*. 1904. pp. 19–20.

——— Rannsókn í Árnesþingi 1904. (Grímsstaðir í Þingvallasveit). *Ibid*. 1905. pp. 44–46.

Jónsson, Finnur. Litteratur Historie. II. pp. 429–431; III. p. 81.

Jónsson, Janus. Um vísurnar í Harðar sögu Grímkelssonar. *In* Tímarit h. ísl. Bókmentafél 1892. XIII. pp. 259–275.

Lehmann-Filhés, M. Grabhügelraub im isländischen Alterthum. *In* Globus. 1902. LXXXI. 4°. pp. 64–66

Müller. P. E. Sagabibliothek. I. pp. 274–280.

Vigfússon, Guðbr. Um tímatal í Íslendinga sögum. pp. 309–311.

Vigfússon, Sig Rannsókn á blóthúsinu að Þyrli og fleira í Hvalfirði og um Kjalarnes *In* Árbók h. ísl. Fornleifafél. 1880–81. pp 65–78

——— Rannsóknir í Borgarfirði.—Hoftóttin á Lundi í Syðra Reykjadal. *Ibid* 1884–85. pp. 97–103.

Þorkelsson, Jón. Skýringar á vísum í nokkurum íslenzkum sögum. Reykjavík 1868. pp. 7–14. (*Program*).

Haukdæla þáttr.

Five chapters in the Íslendinga saga (Oxford ed. 1878. I. pp. 203–208, chap. 12–16) concerning the descendants of Ketilbjörn gamli, the famous Haukdælir; an interpolation serving as an introduction to the saga of Gizur Þorvaldsson (q v.) *See* Sturlunga saga.

Ólsen, Björn M.   Um Sturlungu.   pp. 304-383.

Hávarðar saga Ísfirðings *or* Ísfirðinga saga.

C. 970-1003.   Written towards the end of the 13th century; now only found in paper MSS. (AM. 160, fol.)

Sagann af Haavarde Isfirdingi.   *In* Nockrer Marg-Frooder Sögu-Pætter Islendinga, ad Forlage Biörns Marcussonar. Hólar 1756. 4°. pp. 38-58.

Hávarðar saga Ísfirðings besörget og oversat af G. Thordarson, med et Tillæg om Sagaen og Forklaring af Viserne, ved G. Brynjúlfsson.   Udg. af det Nordiske Literatur-Samfund. Kjöbenhavn 1860. (Nordiske Oldskrifter. XXVIII.) 8°. pp. iv+191.

Text, pp. 1-55, and Danish version, pp. 69-111.

Saga Hávarðar Ísfirðings.   Texta-útgáfa.   Ísafjörður 1889. 8°. pp. 41.

Hávarðar saga Ísfirðings.   Búið hefir til prentunar Vald. Ásmundarson.   Reykjavík 1896. (Íslendinga sögur. 15.) 8°. pp. vi+(2)+84.

Review: Eimreiðin. 1897. III. p. 56, by V. Guðmundsson.

Havardz Saga.   *In* Origines Islandicæ, by G. Vigfusson and F. Y. Powell.   Oxford 1905. II. pp. 238-274.

Text with English version.—*Cf.* Arkiv f. nord. filol. 1906. XIII. pp. 204-205.

DANISH.—Gunnl. Þórðarson's *version in the ed. of* 1860 (*see above*).

Haavard Isfjordings Saga.   *In* Billeder af Livet paa Island, ved Fr. Winkel Horn. Kjöbenhavn 1871. (I.) pp. 257-304.

En Fader.   *In* Nord. Rolfsen's Vore Fædres Liv. Oversættelsen ved Gerhard Gran.   Bergen 1888.   pp. 1-22.—*2. edition.* Christiania 1898.   pp. 1-25, 2 *illustr.*

The illustrations are by A. Bloch.

ENGLISH.—The Story of Howard the Halt.   *In* The Saga Library, by W. Morris and E. Magnússon. London 1891. pp. xii-xxiii, 1-69, *map.*

For *reviews see* Bandamanna saga.

Vigfússon *and* Powell's *version in* Orig. Isl. II. (*see above*).

GERMAN.—Die Hovard Isfjordings-Sage.   Aus dem altisländischen Urtexte übersetzt von Willibald Leo. Heilbronn 1878. 16°. pp. xv+142.

There is a † title edition of 1883, styled "neue Ausgabe."

Brynjúlfsson, Gísli *jr.* Bemærkninger om Haavard Isfirdings Saga med Forklaring over Viserne m. m. Kjöbenhavn 1860. 8°. pp. 83 (*Sep. repr. from the ed. of* 1860, pp. 112-191).

Jónsson, Finnur. Litteratur Historie. I. p. 519; II. pp. 752-754.

Müller, P. E. Sagabibliothek. I. pp. 267-269.

Vigfússon, Guðbr. Um tímatal í Íslendinga sögum. pp. 365-367.

Heiðarvíga saga, *or* Víga-Barða saga, *or* Víga-Styrs saga ok Heiðarvíga.

C. 1005-1014. One of the oldest sagas, written probably in the latter part of the 12th century, but now imperfect. The only known MS. of it, a vellum from c. 1300, was brought from Iceland to Sweden about 1680 and it was then defective. In 1725 rni Magnússon borrowed it and had a copy made of it, but both the original and the copy were destroyed by fire in Copenhagen 1728. Jón Ólafsson who had made the copy, wrote, in the year following, from memory the saga, and this is all that is known of that portion (the Víga-Styrs saga). It was found afterwards, that the whole MS. had not been sent to Copenhagen, so the latter part of the saga (the larger part of Heiðarvíga saga proper) is still preserved in the Royal Library, Stockholm (No 18. 4°. *cf.* Kålund's Palæografisk Atlas. 1905. No 39), but even this portion has a lacuna.

Heiðarvígasögu brot.—Ágrip af Vígastýrssögu ok fyrra parts Heiðarvígasögu, ritat af Jóni Ólafssyni frá Grunnavík. *In* Íslendinga sögur. Kaupmannhöfn 1829. I. pp. 261-350.

Edited by Þorgeir Guðmundsson and Þorsteinn Helgason The vol. has also a special t.-p., *see* Íslendingabók.

Saga af Víga-Styr ok Heiðarvígum. *In* Íslendinga sögur. Kjöbenhavn 1847. II. pp. xxxii-xlvi, 277-394, 480-483.

Edited by Jón Sigurðsson ; the text of the vellum fragment printed from a copy made by Ólafur Pálsson.

Extracts with introduction and notes in Antiquités Russes 1852. fol II. pp. 263-268.

Víga-Styrs saga ok Heiðarvíga. Búið hefir til prentunar Vald. Ásmundarson. Reykjavík 1899. (Íslendinga sögur. 27.) 8°. pp. vi+(2)+117.

Heiðarvíga saga udg. for Samfund til udgivelsen af gammel nordisk litteratur ved Kr. Kålund. Köbenhavn 1904. 8°. pp. (2)+xxxiv+135.

With explanations of the stanzas by Finnur Jónsson. *Reviews:* Skírnir. 1905. LXXIX. pp. 186-190, by B. M. Ólsen ;— Literar. Centralbl. 1905. coll. 1067-68, by Aug. Gebhardt ;—Jahresber. f. germ. Philol. 1904. pp. 76-77, by R. Meissner.

ENGLISH.—The Story of the Ere-dwellers (Eyrbyggja saga) with the Story of the Heath-Slayings (Heiðarvíga saga) as appendix. Done into English out of the Icelandic by William

4

Morris and Eiríkr Magnússon. London 1892. (The Saga Library. II.) pp. xxxiv–xlvii, 191–259, *map*.
For reviews see Eyrbyggja saga.

Jónsson, Bryn.   Rannsókn sögustaða í vesturhluta Húnavatnssýslu sumarið 1894. VIII. Heiðarvíga saga. *In* Árbók h. ísl. Fornleifafél. 1895. pp. 17–19.

Jónsson, Finnur.   Bidrag til en rigtigere forståelse af Tindr Hallkelssons vers. *In* Aarb. f. nord. Oldk. og Hist. 1886. pp. 309–368.
Concerning the two stanzas of the Heiðarvíga saga see pp. 361–368.
——— Litteratur Historie. II. pp. 485–490.

Ólsen, Bjorn M.   Borgarvirki. *In* Árbók h. ísl. Fornleifafél. 1880–81. pp. 99–113, *wdct.*
An abstract in German (Das Borgarvirki auf Island) by M. Lehmann-Filhés, in Verhandl. der Berliner anthropol. Gesellsch. 1894. pp. 40–43.—*Cf.* Daniel Bruun: Arkæologiske Undersögelser paa Island foretagne i Sommeren 1898. (Árbók h. ísl. Fornleifafél. 1899. Fylgirit). pp. 39–47, illustr.
——— "Mest" eða "melt." *In* Tímarit h. ísl. Bókmentafél. 1881. I. pp. 271–272.

Vigfússon, Guðbr.   Um tímatal í Íslendinga sögum. pp. 459–462.

Vigfússon, Sig.   Rannsókn í Borgarfirði 1884.—Heiðarvíga-saga, Gullteigr. *In* Árbók h. ísl. Fornleifafél. 1884–85. pp. 128–133.

Þorkelsson, Jón.   Skýringar á vísum í nokkurum íslenzkum sögum. Reykjavík 1868. pp. 27–35. (*Program*).
——— Vísa í Víga-Styrssögu, 26. kap. [Ísl. sög. 1847. II] 354. bls. *In* Norðanfari. 1872. fol. XI. pp. 103–104.

Heiðarvígs saga.   *See* Sturlu saga.

Helga saga ok Gríms Droplaugarsona, *or*

Helganna saga.   *See* Droplaugarsona saga.

Hólmverja saga.   *See* Harðar saga.

Hrafnkels saga Freysgoða.
C. 920–952. Written about 1200; it is found in paper-MSS. only, most of which are from the 17th century, a vellum fragment from c. 1400, A.M. 162 I. fol.

Sagan af Hrafnkeli Freysgoða. Udg. af P. G. Thorsen og Konráð Gíslason   Köbenhavn 1839. 8°. pp. (6)+34+54.
Cf. Fjolnir. 1843. VII. pp. 66-67, by K. Gíslason.—*Reviews* · Tidsskr. f. Lit. og Kritik (udg. af F. C Petersen). 1840. II. pp. 167-198, b N. M. Petersen ;—† Fædrelandet. 1840. No. 135.

Sagan af Hrafnkeli Freysgoða, 2. Udgave, besörget ved K. Gíslason, og oversat af N. L. Westergaard, udg. af det nordiske Literatur-Samfund. Kjöbenhavn 1847. (Nordiske Oldskrifter. I.) 8°. pp. (4)+32+34.
Icelandic text with Danish version —A brief extract from the saga in Antiquités Russes. 1852. fol. II. pp. 260-263.

Sagan af Hrafnkeli Freysgoda med forklarende Anmærkninger
udg. til Skolebrug af Karl L. Sommerfeldt. Kristiania 1879.
8°. pp. 55.

Sagan af Hrafnkeli Freysgoda. *In* Einleitung in das Studium
des Altnordischen von J. C. Poestion. Hagen i. W. 1887. II.
pp. 13–39.
With Icelandic-German glossary.

Hrafnkels saga Freysgoða. Búið hefir til prentunar Vald. Ásmundarson. Reykjavík 1893. (Íslendinga sögur. 8.) 8°. pp.
v +(2)+43.

Hrafnkels saga Freysgoða. *In* Austfirðinga sögur udg. af
Jakob Jakobsen. Köbenhavn 1902. pp. xxxviii–liii, 93–137.
Critical edition (AM. 156 fol.)

The Story of Hrafnkel (Ravencetil) the Priest of Frey. *In*
Origines Islandicæ, by G. Vigfusson and F. Y. Powell.
Oxford 1905. II. pp. 486–527.
Text with English translation.

DANISH.—† Hrafnkel Freysgodes Saga. Efter det Islandske.
In Dansk Minerva, Aug. 1818. pp. 97–140.

† Fortælling om Ravnkild Halfredsön, oversat af L. C. Müller.
In Dannebroge (udg. af J. C. Lindberg). 1841. Nos. 26–27.

Westergaard's *version in the edition of* 1847 (*see above*).

Hrafnkel Freysgodes Saga. Gjenfortalt af H. H. Lefolii. *In*
Danske Folkeskrifter. XLIV. Blandinger. Ny Samling. Ha-
derslev 1863. pp. 1–40.

Ravnkel Fröjsgodes Saga. *In* Billeder af Livet paa Island, ved
Fr. Winkel Horn. Kjöbenhavn 1871. (I.) pp. 91–121.

Fortællingen om Ravnkel Freysgode oversat af O. A. Överland.
2. Oplag. Kristiania 1896. (Historiske Fortællinger. 6.) 8°.
pp. 40.—† *1. edition*. Kristiania 1895. 8°. pp. 40.

Sagaen om Ravnkel Fröisgode oversat af Alexander Bugge.
Kristiania 1901. (Udvalgte Sagaer oversatte af A. B) 8°. pp.
viii+39.

ENGLISH.—The Story of Hrafnkell, Frey's Priest. *In* Summer
Travelling in Iceland, by John Coles. London 1882. pp. 230–
249.

Vigfússon *and* Powell's *version in* Orig. Isl. II. (*see above*).

GERMAN.—Die Saga von Hrafnkell Freysgoði. Eine isländische
Geschichte aus dem 10. Jahrh. n. Chr. Aus dem altisländi-

schen Urtexte zum erstenmale in's Deutsche übersetzt und mit ausführlichen Erläuterungen nebst einer kurzen Einführung in die isländische Sagaliteratur versehen von Heinrich Lenk. Wien 1883. 8°. pp. xiii+132.

Reviews: Anz. f. deut. Altert. 1884. X. pp. 357-362, by E. Mogk ;— Literar. Centralbl. 1883. coll. 1275-76,—†Deut. Lit. Zeit. 1883. No. 28, by K. Lehmann.

SWEDISH.—Sagan af Hrafnkel Freysgode. Öfversättning med inledning och anmärkningar af Nore Ambrosius. Halmstad 1882. 4°. pp. xxvi.

---

† Grönvold, D. Ravnkell Freysgode. *In* Folkevennen. Christiania 1887. pp. 395-418.

Gunnarsson, Sig. Örnefni frá Jökulsá í Axarfirði austan að Skeiðará. 2. Sagan af Hrafnkeli Freysgoða. *In* Safn til sögu Íslands. 1876. II. pp. 453-458.

Jónsson, Finnur. Litteratur Historie. II. 521-525.

Müller, P. E. Sagabibliothek. I. pp. 103-108.

Opet, Otto. Zuverlässigkeit der rechtsgeschichtlichen Angaben der Hrafnkelssaga. *In* Mittheilungen des Instituts für oesterreichische Geschichtsforschung. III. Ergänzungsband. 1890-1894. pp. 586-618.— *Also separate reprint.* Innsbruck 1894. 8°. pp. 33.

Vigfússon, Guðbr. Um tímatal í Íslendinga sögum. pp. 407-408.

Vigfússon, Sig. Rannsókn í Austfirðingafjórðungi 1890. *In* Árbók h. ísl. Fornleifafél. 1893. pp. 28-60.

Hrafns saga Sveinbjarnarsonar, *or* Hrafns saga ok Þorvalds.

1190-1213. Written not long after Hrafn's death (1213), apparently by an eye-witness (Valde, the priest?). In paper-MSS., copies of a vellum destroyed in 1728; a fragment of another vellum MS. of the 15th century, AM. 557 4°. The last ten chapters, slightly abridged, are embodied in the Sturlunga saga.

[*Chap. 11-20.*] *In* Sturlunga saga. Kaupmannahöfn 1818. I. 2. 4°. pp. 20-36.

Udtog af Rafn Sveinbjörnsöns Saga. *In* Grönlands historiske Mindesmærker. Kjöbenhavn 1838. II. pp. 725-749.
Extracts with introduction, notes and Danish version by Finnur Magnússon.

Rafns saga Sveinbjarnarsonar. *In* Biskupa sögur. Kaupmannahöfn 1858. I. pp. lxviii-lxxii, 639-676.
Edited (from AM. 155 fol.) by Guðbr. Vigfússon.

Hrafns saga. *In* Sturlunga saga, ed. by Gudbr. Vigfusson. Oxford 1878. II. pp. 275-311.—Hrafns saga ok Þorvaldz [chap. 11-20]. *Ibid.* I. pp. 175-187. (*Cf.* pp. cxv-cxvi).

[*Chap. 11-20*]. *In* Sturlunga saga, udgiven [ved Kr. Kålund].
Köbenhavn 1906. I. pp. 297-317.

DANISH.—[*Chap. 11-20*]. *In* Sturlunga saga i dansk oversættelse ved Kr. Kålund, versene ved Olaf Hansen. Köbenhavn 1904. I. pp. 268-284.

Jónsson, Finnur. Litteratur Historie. II. pp. 558-561.
Müller, P. E. Sagabibliothek. I. pp. 236-243.
Ólsen, Björn M Um Sturlungu. pp 244-253.
Þorkelsson, Jón. Skýringar á vísum í Guðmundar sögu Arasonar og
Hrafns sögu Sveinbjarnarsonar. Reykjavík 1872. pp. 26-37. (*Program*).

Hrafns þáttr Hrútfirðings *or* Hrafns þáttr Guðrúnarsonar af
Hrútafirði.

C. 1045. Written about 1200. In the Hrokkinskinna (Gl. kgl. Saml.
1010, fol.; 15th cent.).

In Fornmanna sögur. 1831. VI. pp. 102-119.

Hrafns þáttr Hrútfirðings. *In* Fjörutíu Íslendinga þættir.
Þórleifr Jónsson gaf út. Reykjavík 1904. pp. 126-143.

DANISH.—Rafn Rutfyrding og Einar den Nommedalske. En
Fortælling efter det Islandske [ved P. G. Repp.] *In* Dansk
Minerva. Juli 1818. pp. 46-66.

In Oldnordiske Sagaer. 1832. VI. pp. 83-98.

LATIN.—Svb. Egilsson's *version in* Scripta historica Islandorum.
1835. VI. pp. 98-112.

Jónsson, Finnur. Litteratur Historie. I. p. 627; II. pp. 549.
Müller, P. E. Sagabibliothek. III. pp. 322-325.

Hreiðars þáttr heimska Þorgrímssonar.

C. 1045. In the Morkinskinna, but probably written about 1200.

In Fornmanna sögur. 1831. VI. pp. 200-218.

Fra Hreiþare heimska. *In* Morkinskinna, udg. af C. R. Unger.
Christiania 1867. pp. 35-44.

Hreiðars þáttr heimska. *In* Fjörutíu Íslendinga þættir. Þórleifr Jónsson gaf út. Reykjavík 1904. pp. 144-162.

DANISH.—Fortælling om Hreidar Tosse. Oversat af det Islandske
ved P. E. Müller. *In* Det Skandinaviske Litteratur Selskabs
Skrifter. 1816-1817. pp. 208-233.

Hreidar den Dumme, en Fortælling af det Islandske [ved P.
G. Repp.] *In* Dansk Minerva. Juni 1818. pp. 524-543.

In Oldnordiske Sagaer. 1832. VI. pp. 163-178.

Hreidar Tosse. *In* Sagaer, fortalte af Brynjolf Snorrason og Kristian Arentzen. Kjöbenhavn 1850. III. pp. 113-133.

LATIN.—Svb. Egilsson's *version in* Scripta historica Islandorum. 1835. VI. pp. 189-204.

Jónsson, Finnur. Litteratur Historie. I. p. 641 ; II. pp. 550.
Müller, P. F. Sagabibliothek. III. pp. 325-329.

Hrómundar þáttr halta.

10th century. In the Flateyjarbók, the date of composition being probably early in the 13th century. The same story is briefly narrated in the Landnámabók (*see ed. of* 1900, pp. 53-57, 177-180).

Pattr Hromundar Halta. *In* Saga Olafs Tryggvasonar. Skálholt 1689. II. 4°, pp. 201-206.

Þáttr Hrómundar halta. *In* Fornmanna sögur. 1827. III. pp. 142-151.

Paattr Hromundar hallta. *In* Flateyjarbók. Christiania 1860. I. pp. 409-414.

Hrómundar þáttr halta. *In* Fjörutíu Íslendinga þættir. Þórleifr Jónsson gaf út. Reykjavík 1904. pp. 163-172.

DANISH.—Fortælling om Romund Halte [*trl. by* C. C. Rafn]. *In* Oldnordiske Sagaer. 1837. III. pp. 127-135.

LATIN.—Particula de Hromundo Claudo [*trl.. by* Svb. Egilsson]. *In* Scripta historica Islandorum. 1829. III. pp. 144-154.

Gering, Hugo. Eine lausavísa des Hrómundr halti. *In* Zeitschr. f. deut. Philol. 1890. XXII. pp. 383-384.
Jónsson, Finnur. Litteratur Historie. I. pp. 525-526.
Müller, P. E. Sagabibliothek. III. pp. 462-464.

Hungrvaka.

History of the first five bishops of Skálholt, 1056-1176, written by an ecclesiastic connected with the Skálholt see, the author's principal authority being Gizur Hallsson (d 1206); it was written probably about 1200, and is now found only in paper copies of a lost vellum.

Hungurvaka, sive Historia primorum quinque Skalholtensium in Islandia Episcoporum, Páls biskups saga, sive Historia Pauli Episcopi et Pattr af Thorvalldi vidförla, sive Narratio de Thorvalldo Peregrinatore, ex manuscriptis Legati Magnæani, cum interpretatione Latina, annotationibus, chronologia, tabulis genealogicis, et indicibus tam rerum quam verborum.

Hafniæ 1778. (Ex Legato Magnæano). 8°. pp. (28)+441+ (7), 4 *tbls.*

Text (AM. 207 fol.) edited and translated by Jón Ólafsson of Grunna-vík, pp. 1-141. The preface is by G. Schöning, the chronological index and notes by Hannes Finnsson, the index of names and subjects by G. J. Thorkelin, the glossary by Jón Ólafsson. *Review:* Nye kritisk Journal for 1779. coll. 209-212, by Jacob Baden.

Húngrvaka. *In* Biskupa sögur. Kaupmannahöfn 1858. I. pp. xxv-xxviii, 57-86.

Edited (from AM. 379. 4°) by Guðbr. Vigfússon.

Saga Páls Skálaholts biscups oc Hungrvaka. Útgefandi : Stefán Sveinsson. Winnipeg 1889. 8°. pp. 1-30.

Kristni saga . . . Hungrvaka herausgg. von B. Kahle. Halle a. S. 1905. pp. xxiii-xxxiii, 87-126.

Annotated edition *Cf.* Kristni saga.

Hungrvaca. *In* Origines Islandicæ, by G. Vigfusson and F. Y. Powell. Oxford 1905. I. pp. 420-458.

Icelandic text with English translation

ENGLISH.—Húngrvaka (The Hunger-waker). *In* The Stories of the Bishops of Iceland, translated by the Author of "The Chorister Brothers" [Mrs. Disney Leith]. London 1895. pp. 33-71.

Vigfússon *and* Powell's *version in* Orig. Isl. I. (*see above*).

LATIN.—Jón Ólafsson's *version in the ed. of* 1778 (*see above*).

Jónsson, Finnur. Litteratur Historie. II. pp. 565-567.
Kahle, B. Die handschriften der Hungrvaka. *In* Arkiv f. nord. filol. 1904. XX. pp. 228-254.
Müller, P. E. Sagabibliothek. I. pp. 186-188.

Ísfirðinga saga. *See* Hávarðar saga Ísfirðings.

Íslands bygging.

A brief account of the discovery of Iceland and the principal settlers, embodied in the Ólafs saga Tryggvasonar of the Flateyjarbók and other codices.

In Saga Olafs Tryggvasonar. Skálholt 1689. 4°. II. pp. 10-20.

In Fornmanna sögur. 1825. I. pp. 233-255.

In Flateyjarbók. Christiania 1860. I. pp. 247-248, 263-268.

DANISH.—C. C. Rafn's *version in* Oldnordiske Sagaer. 1826. I. pp. 210-230.

ENGLISH.—*In* The Saga of King Olaf Tryggwason transl. by J. Sephton. London 1905. pp. 157-174.

LATIN.—Svb. Egilsson's *version in* Scripta historica Islandorum. 1828. I. pp. 259–281.

Ísleifs þáttr biskups.

> C. 1025-1056. In the Flateyjarbók. (Ísleifr Gizurarson, b. 1006, d.
> 1080, bishop 1056-1080).

Kristni saga . . . nec non Þattr af Isleifi biskupi, sive Narratio
de Isleifo Episcopo . . . Hafniæ 1773. pp. 130–141.

> Text with Latin version by Hannes Finnsson. *See* Kristni saga.

Páttr af Ísleifi biskupi. [*Ed. by* G. Vigfússon.] *In* Biskupa
sögur. Kaupmannahöfn 1858. I. pp. xxv, 51–56.

Jsleifr feck Döllu er siþan var biskup. *In* Flateyjarbók. Christiania 1862. II. pp. 140–142.

Kristnisaga . . . Þáttr Ísleifs biskups Gizurarsonar . . . herausgg.
von B. Kahle. Halle a. S. 1905. pp. xxii, 83–86.

DANISH.—Om Islejf Bisp. *In* Billeder af Livet paa Island, ved
Fr. Winkel Horn. Kjöbenhavn 1876. III. pp. 246–248.

ENGLISH.—The Stories of Thorwald the Far-farer and of
Bishop Isleif. Translated from the Icelandic by the Author
of "The Chorister Brothers" [Mrs. Disney Leith.] London
1894. pp. 25–32. —*Also in the same translator's* Stories of the
Bishops of Iceland. London 1895. pp. 25–32.

Tales of Bishop Is-laf. *In* Origines Islandicæ, by G. Vigfusson
and F. Y. Powell. Oxford 1905. I. pp. 595–596.

LATIN.—H. Finnsson's *version in the ed. of* 1773 (*see above*).

Íslendingabók.

> A brief history of Iceland from 870-1120, by Ari Þorgilsson hinn fróði
> (b. 1067, d. 1148); written probably shortly after 1134 and being an
> abridgment of (or supplement to) a larger Íslendingabók which is now
> lost. The title given to it by the author is Libellus Islandorum. It
> is found in two paper copies (AM. 113 A-B fol) made in the 17th
> century by Jón Erlendsson from a vellum which is now lost and which
> probably was the author's original MS.

Schedæ Ara prestz froda Vm Island. Prentadar i Skalhollte af
Hendrick Kruse. Anno 1688. 4°. pp. (2)+14+(8).

> Edited by Bishop Þórður Þorláksson, who has appended to it a list of the
> bishops of Hólar and Skálholt down to the date of publication. Coat-
> of arms of Iceland on final page.

Aræ Multiscii Schedæ de Islandia. Accedit dissertatio De Aræ
Multiscii Vita et Scriptis. Oxoniæ, e Theatro Seldeniano
[*sic*]. An. Dom. MDCCXVI. 8°. in 4s, pp. (2)+88, [169]–
192.

> *Contents :* t.-f.; Icelandic text with Latin version, interpretation and
> notes, pp. 1-88; De Aræ Multiscii vita et scriptis dissertatio, pp [169]-

192 (half-title on p. [169], reverse blank). The present copy is
an imperfect issue, as the "commentarius," pp. 89-152 is lacking; but
all copies of this edition, so far as is known, have a lacuna from p. 153
to p. 168 incl. The only copy we know of with a t.-p. different from
that given above, is in the British Museum, the title being as follows :
"Aræ Multiscii Schedæ de Islandia. Accedit Commentarius, Et Dissertatio de Aræ Multiscii Vita et Scriptis. Oxoniæ, E Theatro Seldo-
niano. An. Dom. MDCCXVI," the contents being the same as de-
scribed except that the Commentarius is there and fills pp. [89]-152
(half-title : In Aræ Multiscii Schedas de Islandia Commentarius, p.
[89]). Möbius (Cat. p. 116) gives this title and gives the contents as if
there were no lacuna, but that is, of course, his mistake. This edition
was printed about 1695 from the notes of Árni Magnússon and without his
permission, the editor being Christen Worm, later bishop of Zeeland
(d 1737). Concerning this edition see Luxdorphiana ved R. Nyerup,
Kiöbenhavn 1791. pp. 333-345 (Om Biskop Worms Udgave af Are
Frode, by B. W. Luxdorph).

Arii Thorgilsis Filii, cognomentô Froda, id est Multiscii vel
Polyhistoris, in Islandia qvondam Presbyteri, Primi in Sep-
tentrione Historici, Schedae, seu Libellus de Is-landia, Islend-
inga-Bok dictus ; E veteri Islandica, vel, si mavis, Danica
antiquâ, Septentrionalibus olim communi Lingvâ, in Latinam
versus ac præter necessarios Indices, qvorum unus est Lexici
instar, brevibus notis et Chronologiâ, præmissâ, qvoqve Auc-
toris vita illustratus ab Andrea Bussæo. Havniæ, Ex Calco-
graphéo B. Joachimi Schmidtgen, Ao. 1733. 4°. pp. (28)+118
+(92)+27+(1)+26.

Contents : t.-f. , dedicatory letter to Count de Plelo, pp. (3)-(8) ; Ad
lectorem, pp. (9)-(12) ; Vita Arii, pp. (13)-(28) ; Schedæ Arii (text
with Latin version and notes), pp. 1-78 ; Jonæ Gam Schediasma de
ratione anni solaris, secundum rudem observationem veterum pagano-
rum in Islandia, ex solis motu restituti, referente Ara Froda cap.
IV. Schedarum (preceded by a letter from Gam to Bussæus', pp. 79-
118 ; Index personarum et rerum, pp (1)-(16) ; Lexicon vocum anti-
quarum, pp. (17)- 92) ; Periplus Otheri et Wulfstani (Anglo-Saxon
text with Latin version, notes and index), pp. 1-27, (1) ; Sicilimenta
præfestinatæ messi reliqvæ adjicienda, pp. 1-26.

Frodæ, filii Arii Thorgilsis Liber Historicus de Islandia una cum
clarissimi viri Andreæ Bussæi versione latina, ex islandico
idiomate congesta, et indicibus, glossario, notis, chronologia
et vita illustratus : Accessit Periplus Otheri ut et Wulfstani
Angli, narrationes de navigationibus eorum in ultimam pla-
gam Septentrionis et Mare Balthicum, jussu Alfredi Magni
Anglorum regis factis, Anglo-Saxonice et Latine. Hafniæ,
apud Christ. Gottl. Mengel et Socium, 1744. 4°. pp. (24)+
118, *etc.*

Except for the new t.-p. and the dedicatory letter being reset so as to
fill only two pages, this edition is identical with that of 1733

Íslendinga bók. *In* Íslendinga sögur. [*Ed. by* Þorg. Guðmundsson *and* Þorst. Helgason]. Kaupmannahöfn 1829. I.
pp. 5-7, 1-20. *This vol. has also a special title :* Íslendingabók Ara prests ens fróða Þorgilssonar, Íslands Landnámabók,
Heiðarvígasögu brot ok ágrip Vígastýrs- ok Heiðarvíga-sögu.
Eptir gömlum handritum útgefnar at tilhlutun hins konúnglega norræna Fornfræða félags. Kaupmannahöfn 1829. 8°.
pp. 12 + 412.
> Extracts with notes in Antiqvitates Americanæ. 1837. 4°. pp. 204-208 ;
> in Grónlands historiske Mindesmærker. 1838. I. pp. 168-173 ; and
> in Antiqvités Russes. 1852. fol. II. pp. 228-231.

Íslendingabók. *In* Íslendinga sögur. Kjöbenhavn 1843. I. pp.
v-xv, 1-20, 362-383.
> Edited by Jón Sigurðsson. Appended is : Prestanòfn (Gl. kgl. Saml.
> 1812. fol) p. 384 (with 2 facsims.), ascribed to Ari (*cf* Diplomatarium
> Islandicum. I. pp 180-194).

Íslendingabók. *In* Analecta norræna, herausgg. von Th.
Möbius. Leipzig 1859. 8°. pp. 98-111.

Úr Íslendingabók [chap. I-IV.]. *In* Fire og fyrretyve Pröver
af oldnordisk Sprog og Literatur, udg. af Konr. Gíslason.
Kjöbenhavn 1860. pp. 505-509.

Are's Isländerbuch im isländischen Text mit deutscher Über-
setzung, Namen- und Wörter-Verzeichniss und einer Karte. . .
herausgg. von Theodor Möbius. Leipzig 1869. 8°. pp. xxii+
(2)+88, *map*.
> *Reviews :* The Academy. 1870. I. pp. 160-161, by Guðbr. Vigfússon ;—
> Zeitschr. f. deut. Philol. 1870. II pp. 220-221, by J. Zacher.
> *A portion of chap. iv. in* Äldsta delen af cod. 1812. 4to Gml kgl. samling,
> i diplomatarisk aftryck utg. af L. Larsson. Köbenhavn 1883. pp. 7-8.

Íslendingabók. *In* Einleitung in das Studium des Altnordischen. Von J. C. Poestion. Hagen i. W. 1887. II. pp. 1-12.
> Without the genealogical supplements ; with glossary.

Íslendingabóc, es Are prestr Þorgilsson görþe. Gefin út af hinu
íslenzka Bókmentafélagi. Finnur Jónsson bjó til prentunar.
Kaupmannahöfn 1887. 8°. pp. xxvii+44.

Íslendingabók, er skrifað hefir Ari Þorgilsson, og Landnámabók. Búið hefir til prentunar Vald. Ásmundarson. Reykjavík
1891. (Íslendinga sögur. 1.-2.) pp. 1-22.

Ares Isländerbuch herausgg. von Wolfgang Gother. Halle a. S.
1892. (Altnordische Saga-Bibliothek. I.) 8°. pp. xxviii+46.
> Annotated edition. *Reviews :* Anz. f. deut. Altert. 1894. XX. pp. 38-
> 43, by Fr. Kauffmann ;—Deut. Lit. Zeit. 1893. coll. 1518-19, by E.

Kölbing ;—Literaturbl. f. g. u. r. Philol. 1892. pp. 335-336, by B. Kahle ; —Literar. Centralbl. 1892. col. 995 ;—Zeitschr. f. deut. Philol. 1897. XXIX. pp. 228-235, by O. L. Jiriczek ;—† Bullet. bibliogr. et pédag. du Musée belge. I. 3., by F. Wagner

Libellus Islandorum. *In* Origines Islandicæ, by G. Vigfusson and F. Y. Powell. Oxford 1905. I. pp. 279-306.

Icelandic text with English version. *Reviews :* Arkiv f. nord. filol. 1906. XXIII pp. 202-204, by Finnur Jónsson ;—Saga Book of the Viking Club, 1906. IV. 2. pp. 464-467, by E Magnússon.—The same editors printed in their "Icelandic Prose Reader" (Oxford 1879) pp. 1-19, several extracts from various works, which they thought were taken from Ari's writings, similar extracts are found in Orig. Isl. following the Libellus.

ENGLISH.—Vigfússon *and* Powell's *version in* Orig. Isl. I. (*see above*).

FRENCH.—Le livre des Islandais du prêtre Ari le Savant traduit de l'ancien islandais, précédé d'une étude sur la vie et les œuvres d'Ari et accompagné d'un commentaire par Félix Wagner. Bruxelles 1898. (Bibliothèque de la faculté de philosophie et lettres de l'Université de Liége, fasc. IV.) 8°. pp. 105+(3), *map.*

Reviews : Journal des Savants. 1899. p. 388, by R. Dareste ;—† Revue de l'instruction publique en Belgique. XLII. pp. 119-125, by A Bley ; —† Musée belge. III. p. 304 ff., by J. P. Waltzing.

GERMAN.—Das Isländerbuch des Priesters Are, des Weisen. *In* F. C. Dahlmann's Forschungen auf dem Gebiete der Geschichte. Altona 1822. I. pp. 457-488.

Möbius's *version in the edition of* 1869 (*see above*).

Chap. vii. (Die Einführung des Christenthums auf Island) trl. by Karl Reuschel, *in* Dresdner Anzeiger, Montags Beilage. I. 30. p. 7.

LATIN.—Bussæus's *version in the ed. of* 1733 (*see above*).

Bley, A. Zur entstehung der jüngeren Íslendingabók. *In* Zeitschr. f. deut. Philol. 1900. XXXII. pp. 336-349.

Craigie, W. A. A Father of History. *In* The Scottish Review. 1900. XXXVI. no. 71. pp. 126-142.

Dahlström, Joh. Fred. Den norske og islandske tidsregning i det 10de århundrede. I anledning af Islands tusendårsfest. Kjöbenhavn 1874. 8°. pp. 26.

Finsen, Vilhjálmur. Om den oprindelige Ordning af nogle af den island-ske Fristats Institutioner. Kjöbenhavn 1888. 4°. pp. 31-98.

Gjessing, A. Undersögelse af Kongesagaens Fremvæxt. I.-II. Christiania 1873-1876. 8°. pp. (4)+115 ; (4)+70.

Vol. I.: Bemerkninger om Ares Forfattervirksomhed, pp. 1-7 ; *vol. II.:* Ares og Sæmunds Tidsregning.

Henning, R. and Hoffory, J.   Zur textkritik der Íslendingabók.   In Zeitschr. f. deut. Altert. 1882. XXVI. pp. 178–192.

Heusler, A.   Are's Íslendingabók und Libellus Islandorum.   In Arkiv f. nord. filol. 1907. XXIII. pp. 319–337.

Jónsson, Finnur.   Litteratur Historie. II. pp. 354–381.

Jónsson, Rev. Jón.   Nokkrar athuganir við Íslendingasögur. I.   Upphafsár Íslands bygðar ekki 874 heldur (870 eða) 871.   In Tímarit h. ísl. Bókmentafél. 1897. XVIII. pp. 190–195

Klempin, Carl Robert.   De Arii frodis chronologia.   In his De criteriis ad scripta historica Islandorum examinanda. Pars prior.   Berolini 1845. pp. 21–54.   (Inaug.-diss.)

Maurer, Konrad.   Über Ari Thorgilsson und sein Isländerbuch.   In Germania. 1870. XV. pp. 291–321.

——— Über Ari fróði und seine Schriften.   Ibid. 1891. XXXVI. pp. 61–96. Review: Tímarit h. ísl. Bókmentafél. 1893. XIV.234–235, by V. Guðmundsson.

Müller, P. E.   Sagabibliothek. I. pp. 34–37.

Ólsen, Björn M.   Om forholdet mellem de to bearbeidelser af Ares Íslændingebog.   In Aarb. f nord. Oldk. og Hist. 1885. pp. 341–371 —Also separate reprint. Kjöbenhavn 1886. 8°. pp. 31.

——— Ari Þorgilsson hinn fróði.   In Tímarit h. ísl. Bókmentafél. 1889. X. pp. 214–240.—Also separate reprint. Reykjavík 1889. 8°.

——— Om Are frode.   In Aarb. f. nord. Oldk. og Hist. 1894. pp. 207–352.— Also separate reprint. Kjöbenhavn 1894.

Schück, H.   Smärre bidrag till nordisk litteraturhistoria I. Den svenska krönikan i Hervararsagan.   In Arkiv f. nord. filol. 1896. XII pp. 217–222.
   Discusses Ari's authorship of this chronicle.   Cf. Rev. Jón Jónsson : Um Svíakonungatal í Hervararsögu, ibid. 1901. XVIII. pp. 172–179.

Sigurðsson, Jón.   Lögsögumannatal og lógmanna á Íslandi.   In Safn til sögu Íslands 1860. II. pp. 1–23.

Vigfússon, Guðbr.   Prolegomena in Sturlunga saga. 1878. I. pp. xxvi–xxxvi.

Werlauff, E. Chr.   Arius multiscius, primus Islandorum historicus. Havniæ 1808. 8°. pp (6)+106.
   Reviews : Kjöbenhavn. lærde Efterretninger for 1808. pp. 681–687, by W. H. F. Abrahamson ;—† Universitets- og Skole-Annaler. 1808. II pp. 69–91, by L. Engelstoft ;—† Zeit f. Litt. u. Kunst in d. kgl. dän. Staaten. 1809. Nr. 14 ,—† Morgenbl. f. gebild. Stände. 1810. Beilag Nr. 3.

Þorkelsson, Jón.   Orðið "gea" í Íslendingabók Ara Þorgilssonar.   In Nýja Öldin. 1898. II. fol. p. 37.

Íslendinga saga.

A history of the Icelandic commonwealth from 1183 to 1242, by Sturla Þórðarson (b. 1214, d. 1284); it forms now the principal part of the Sturlunga saga (q. v.)

Jónsson, Finnur.   Litteratur Historie. II. pp. 730–740.

Ólsen, Björn M.   Um Sturlungu. pp. 385–437.

Íslendings þáttr sögufróða.

C. 1050. Has been wrongly called Þorsteins þáttr sögufróða, the name of the hero being unknown. In the Morkinskinna, but dates problably from c. 1200.

In Fornmanna sögur. 1831. VI. pp. 353–356.

Fra scemton Jslendings. *In* Morkinskinna, udg. af C. R. Unger. Christiania 1867. pp. 72–73.

The Icelander telling Stories at Court. *In* An Icelandic Prose Reader, by G. Vigfusson and F. Y. Powell. Oxford 1879. pp. 141–142.

Íslendings þáttr sögufróða. *In* Fjörutíu Íslendinga þættir. Þórleifr Jónsson gaf út. Reykjavík 1904. pp. 173–175.

DANISH.—*In* Oldnordiske Sagaer. 1832. VI. pp. 290–291.

Sagafortælleren. *In* Udvalgte Sagastykker fordanskede af Grímur Thomsen. Kjöbenhavn 1846. pp. 1–3.

Sagafortælleren. *In* Sagaer, fortalte af Brynjolf Snorrason og Kristian Arentzen. Kjöbenhavn 1850. IV. pp. 215–219.

Sagamanden. *In* Fortællinger og Sagaer fortalte for Börn af H. H. Lefolii. 3. Udg. Kjöbenhavn 1869. I. pp. 133–136.— † *1 ed.* 1859 ; † *2 ed.* 1862.

GERMAN.—*In* Die Geschichte von Gísli dem Geächteten, deutsch von Frd. Ranke. München 1907. pp. 5–7.

LATIN.—Svb. Egilsson's *version in* Scripta historica Islandorum. 1835. VI. pp. 328–330.

SWEDISH.—Sagoberättaren. *In* Isländsk och fornsvensk litteratur i urval af Richard Steffen. Stockholm 1905. pp. 132–134.

Jónsson, Finnur. Litteratur Historie. II pp. 197–198, 553.
Müller, P. E. Sagabibliothek. I. pp. 347–348.

Ivars þáttr Ingimundarsonar.

C. 1120. In the Morkinskinna ; it is also in the Jöfraskinna-codex (now lost, copy in AM. 38. fol.) of the Heimskringla, and is therefore in almost all editions and translations of that work (Finnur Jónsson's edition, 1893-1901, being based on the Kringla, has it as an appendix, III. pp. 500-501), and in the Codex Frisianus (Fríssbók, AM. 45 fol., ed. by C. R. Unger, Christiania 1871. pp. 289-290).

In Fornmanna sögur. 1832. VII. pp. 102–106.

Fra Eysteini konvngi oc Ivari. *In* Morkinskinna, udg. af C. R. Unger. Christiania 1867. pp. 167–168.

Ivar the Love-sick Poet and King Eystein. *In* An Icelandic Prose Reader, by G. Vigfusson and F. Y. Powell. Oxford 1879. pp. 144–146.

Iver Ingimundsson hos kong Östén. *In* Oldnordiske Læsestykker, udg. af V. Levy. Köbenhavn 1888. III. pp. 57–59, 86–87.

Ívars þáttr Ingimundarsonar. *In* Fjörutíu Íslendinga þættir. Þórleifr Jónsson gaf út. Reykjavík 1904. pp. 176–180.

Followed by Ívar's poem, Sigurðar-bálkr slembidjákns, pp. 180–185. *Cf.* Corpus poeticum boreale. 1883. II. pp. 261–266.

DANISH.—*In* Oldnordiske Sagaer. 1832. VII. pp. 87–90.

LATIN.—Svb. Egilsson's *version in* Scripta historica Islandorum. 1836. VII. pp. 107–110.

Jónsson, Finnur. Litteratur Historie. II. pp. 59–60, 553.

Jökuls þáttr Bárðarsonar.

C. 1028. A chapter in the Ólafs saga helga in the Heimskringla, and found in all editions and translations of that work (see especially Finnur Jónsson's edition, Kjöbenhavn 1893–1901, II. pp. 422–424); it is also in the larger Ólafs saga by Snorri Sturluson (Christiania 1853, pp. 190–191), and in the Flateyjarbók (Christiania 1862. II. p. 317). See also : Fornmanna sögur. 1839. V. pp. 28–30 ; Oldnordiske Sagaer. 1831. V. pp. 26–27 ; Scripta historica Islandorum. 1833. V. pp. 35–37.

Jökuls þáttr Bárðarsonar. *In* Fjörutíu Íslendinga þættir. Þórleifr Jónsson gaf út. Reykjavík 1904. pp. 186–187.

Jökuls þáttr Búasonar.

A fictitious tale composed in the 14th century and forming a continuation of the Kjalnesinga saga (*q. v.*).

Paattur of Jökle Syne Bwa Andrijdar-Sonar. *In* Nockrer Marg-Frooder Sögu-Pætter Islendinga, ad Forlage Biörns Marcussonar. Hólar 1756. pp. 182–187.

Þáttr af Jökli Búasyni. *In* Íslendinga sögur. Kjöbenhavn 1847. II. pp. lv–lvi, 461–476.

Critical edition (AM. 504. 4°) by Jón Sigurðsson.

Jökuls þáttr Búasonar. *In* Kjalnesinga saga. Reykjavík 1902. pp. 47–61.

Jónsson, Finnur. Litteratur Historie. III. pp. 84.
Müller, P. E. Sagabibliothek. I. pp. 356–357.
Cf. Grönlands historiske Mindesmærker. III p. 521.

Jóns saga helga.

Life of Jón Ögmundsson the Saint, the first bishop of Hólar (1106-1121), by Gunnlaugr Leifsson, monk of Þingeyrar-cloister (d. 1218 or 1219).

It was written in Latin not long after 1200, and afterwards translated into Icelandic; the Latin original is lost, but three recensions of the translation are extant, the latest of which is from the 14th century, diffuse and unimportant, while the two others are of the 13th century, but which of them is the older is a disputed question, it is beyond doubt, that the saga called by Guðbr. Vigfússon "hin elzta" is a translation of Gunnlaugr's work, but not his source as Vigfússon thought.

Jóns saga helga hin elzta. *In* Biskupa sögur. Kaupmannahöfn 1858. I. pp. xxxiv–xxxviii, 149–202.

Jóns saga helga eptir Gunnlaug múnk. *Ibid.* pp. xxxviii–xlii, 213–260.

Edited from 14th century vellums (the first from AM 234. fol., the second from Cod. Holm. 5. fol.) by Guðbr. Vigfússon In foot-notes and in an appendix, pp. 203–212, are found additions from the latest recension (AM. 392. 4°).

S. John of Holar's Life (Ioans saga). *In* Origines Islandicæ, by G. Vigfusson and F. Y. Powell. Oxford 1905. I. pp. 531–567.

Fragments from Gunlaug's Life of S. John of Holar. *Ibid.* pp. 591–594.

Texts with English versions

ENGLISH.—Vigfússon *and* Powell's *version in* Orig. Isl. I. (*see above*).

Jónsson, Finnur (*bishop*). Historia Ecclesiastica Islandiæ. Havniæ 1772. I. 4°. pp. 320–327.

Jónsson, Finnur. Litteratur Historie. II. pp. 404–407.

Müller, P. E. Sagabibliothek. I. pp. 321–326.

Jóns þáttr biskups Halldórssonar.

Jón Halldórsson was bishop of Skálholt 1332–1339. A tale of very little historical value, written shortly after the bishop's death. MSS.: AM. 764. 4°. (14th cent.) and AM. 624. 4°. (15th cent.).

Söguþáttr af Jóni biskupi Halldórssyni. *In* Biskupa sögur. [*Ed. by* Guðbr. Vigfússon]. Kaupmannahöfn 1867. II. pp. 221–230.

Jóns þáttr biskups Halldórssonar. *In* Íslendzk æventýri, herausgg. von Hugo Gering. Halle a. S. 1882. I. pp. 84–94.

GERMAN.—Jón Halldórsson. *In* Gering's Ísl. æventýri. Halle a. S. 1883. II. pp. 70–77.

Jónsson, Finnur Litteratur Historie. III. p. 71.

Kjalnesinga saga *or* Búa saga Andríðarsonar.

An unhistoric saga, written in the earlier part of the 14th century. MS.: AM. 471. 4°. (15th cent.). A continuation of this, but by another pen, is Jökuls þáttr Búasonar (*q v.*)

Kialnesinga Saga, edur Af Bwa Andrijds-Syne   *In* Agiætar
Fornmanna-Sögur, ad Forlage Biörns Marcussonar. Hólar
1756. pp. 1–34.
Kjalnesinga saga.   *In* Íslendinga sögur. Kjöbenhavn 1847.
II. pp. xlvi–lvi, 395–460.
Critical edition by Jón Sigurðsson.
Kjalnesinga saga.   Búið hefir til prentunar Vald. Ásmundarson.
Reykjavík 1902. (Íslendinga sögur. 36.) 8°. pp. (4)+64.

Jónsson, Bryn.   Rannsókn í Gullbringu- og Árnessýslu sumarið 1902.   *In*
Árbók h. ísl. Fornleifafél. 1903. pp. 31-33.
Jónsson, Finnur.   Litteratur Historie. III. pp. 83–84.
Kahle, B.   Zum kampf des vaters und sohnes.   *In* P u. B. Beitiäge zur
Gesch. d. deut. Spr u. Lit. 1901. XXVI. pp. 319-320.
Müller. P. E.   Sagabibliothek. I. pp. 354-356.
Smith, Robert Angus.   On some Ruins at Ellida Vatn and Kjalarnes in
Iceland.   From the Proceedings of the Society of Antiquaries of Scot-
land, Vol. X. 1872-73. Edinburgh 1874. 8°. pp. 29, 1 *pl.*
Contains letters from K. Maurer and Sig. Guðmundsson, and an extract
from the diary of Jónas Hallgrímsson.   The same subject is treated in
Smith's To Iceland in a Yacht.   Edinburgh 1873. pp. 79–113, which in-
cludes a version of the first four chapters of the saga.
Vigfússon, Sig.   Rannsókn á blóthúsinu að Þyrli og fleira í Hvalfirði og
um Kjalarnes.   *In* Árbók h. ísl. Fornleifafél. 1880-81. pp. 65–78, 1 *pl.*
——— Rannsókn í Kjalarnesþingi 1889.   *Ibid.* 1893. pp. 24-27.

Kjartans þáttr Ólafssonar.

C. 970-1003.   Extracts from the Laxdæla saga embodied in the Ólafs
saga Tryggvasonar of the Flateyjarbók.

Þattr Kiartans Olafssunar.   *In* Saga Olafs Tryggvasonar. Skálholt 1689. 4°. II. pp. 87–95, 96–98, 125, 252–255.

In Fornmanna sögur. 1826. II. pp. 19–34, 36–39, 78–79, 253–
258.

Paattr Kiartans Olafssonar.   *In* Flateyjarbók. [*Ed. by* Vigfússon *and* Unger]. Christiania 1860. I. pp. 308–316, 319, 325,
339, 340, 453–455.

DANISH.—C. C. Rafn's *version in* Oldnordiske Sagaer. 1827. II.
pp. 18–31, 33–35, 69–70, 224–229.

ENGLISH.—*In* The Saga of King Olaf Tryggwason, transl. by
J. Sephton. London 1895. pp. 222–232, 233–235, 260–261, 379–
382.

LATIN.—Svb. Egilsson's *version in* Scripta historica Islandorum.
1828. II. pp. 18–32, 33–35, 72–73, 238–243.

Cf. T. Torfæus's Hist. rer. Norvegic. pars II Havniæ 1711. fol. pp.
483-491 (Vita Kiartani Olafi filii).

Kormáks saga.

C. 937-985. Composed in the latter half of the 13th century as a framing for the verses, which number about eighty, chiefly by Kormákr. In the vellum codex Möðruvallabók (AM. 132 fol., 14th cent.)

Kormaks saga sive Kormaki OEgmundi filii vita. Ex manuscriptis Legati Magnæani cum interpretatione latina, dispersis Kormaki carminibus ad calcem adjectis et indicibus personarum, locorum et vocum rariorum. Havniæ 1832. (Sumptibus Legati Magnæani). 8°. pp. (4)+xvi+340+(2).

Edited and translated by Þorgeir Guðmundsson. Annotationes chorographicæ, by Gunnar Pálsson, p 252 Fragmenta carminum Kormaki in opere vetusto, Skálda dicto, nobis servata, edited with preface, version and notes by Finnur Magnússon, pp. 252-287.

Extract with notes in Antiquités Russes. 1852. fol. II. pp. 272-278.

Kormaks saga herausgg. von Theodor Möbius. Halle a. S. 1886. 8°. pp. (4)+206+(2).

Critical edition, with diplomatic reproduction of the verses (from AM. 132 fol. and AM. 162 F. fol.) *Reviews* Literar. Centralbl. 1886. col. 1695, by E. Mogk,—Deut Lit. Zeit. 1887 coll. 344-345, by E. Kölbing; —Litteraturbl. f. g. u. r Philol. 1887. coll 429-430, by O. Brenner;— † Centralorgan f. die Interessen d. Realschulw. 1887. pp. 126 ff., by H. Lenk;—Germania. 1888. XXXIII. p 116, by Karl Bartsch;—Anz. f. deut. Altert. 1888. XIV. pp. 43-55, by R. Heinzel;—Zeitschr. f. deut. Philol. 1889. XXI. pp. 367-372, by B. Sijmons.

Kormáks saga. Búið hefir til prentunar Vald. Ásmundarson. Reykjavík 1893. (Íslendinga sögur. 6.) 8°. pp. x+(2)+112.

The verses of the saga and the poems by Kormákr are found in : Corpus poeticum boreale. 1883 I. p. 362, II. pp. 32-33, 63-71 ; Th. Wisén's Carmina norræna 1886. I. p. 26; K. Gíslason's Udvalg af oldnord. Skjaldekvad. 1892. pp. 10-13, 74-88.

DANISH.—Fortælling om Kormak. *In* Historiske Fortællinger om Islændernes Færd hjemme og ude, ved N. M. Petersen. Kjöbenhavn 1840. II. pp. 267-321.—2. Udgave [*ed. by* Guðbr. Vigfússon]. Köbenhavn 1868. IV. pp. 147-200 ; *also with special t.-p.:* Fortællingerne om Vatnsdælerne, Gunlaug Ormetunge, Kormak, Finboge den Stærke *etc.*

ENGLISH.—The Life and Death of Cormac the Skald, being the Icelandic Kormáks-saga rendered into English by W. G. Collingwood and Jón Stefánsson. Ulverston 1902. (Viking Club Translation Series. No. 1). 8°. pp. (6)+145, *illustr.*, *map.*

The illustrations (by Collingwood), with the exception of the frontispiece, represent localities mentioned in the saga.

5

Cormac saga. The Story of Cormak and Berse. *In* Origines Islandicæ, by G. Vigfusson and F. Y. Powell. Oxford 1905. II. pp. 315–343.

An abstract of the saga in Mallet-Percy-Blackwell's Northern Antiquities. London 1859. pp. 321–339.

SWEDISH.—Kärlek i hedna dagar. Skalden Kormaks saga från fornisländskan tolkad af A. U. Bååth. Göteborg 1895. 8°. pp. 83.

Brynjúlfsson, Gísli *jr.* Tvær vísur eftir forn höfuðskáld. II. Vísa eftir Kormak. *In* Fjallkonan. 1885. fol. II. pp. 34–35.

Bugge, Sophus. Om Versene i Kormaks Saga. *In* Aarb f. nord. Oldk. og Hist. 1889. pp. 1–88.—*Also separate reprint.* Kjöbenhavn 1889. pp. 88.

Finnbogason, Guðm. Kormakur og Steingerður. *In* Skírnir, 1907. LXXXI. pp. 71–81.

Jónsson, Bryn. Rannsóknir sögustaða í vesturhluta Húnavatnsýslu 1894. VI. Kormakssaga. *In* Árbók h. ísl. Fornleifafél. 1895. pp. 12–13.

Jónsson, Finnur Litteratur Historie. I pp. 537–542, II. pp. 746–748.

Jónsson, Janus. Á víð og dreif. Smáathugasemdir við fornan kveðskap. III. Kormáks-saga. *In* Arkiv f nord. filol. 1899. XV. pp. 384–390.

Jónsson, Þorleifur. Örnefni nokkur í Breiðafjarðardölum. *In* Safn til sögu Íslands. 1876. II pp. 558 577.

Müller. P. E Sagabibliothek. I. pp. 140–144

Ólsen, Björn M. Om versene i Kormaks saga. *In* Aarb. f. nord. Oldk. og Hist. 1888. pp 1–86.—*Also separate reprint.* Kjöbenhavn 1888. 8°. pp. 86.

Sommarin, E. Anteckningar vid lasning af Kormaks Saga. *In* Från Filologiska föreningen i Lund. 1897. pp. 97–104.

Vigfússon, Guðbr. Um tímatal í Íslendinga sögum. pp. 371–375.

Kristni saga.

A brief history of the Icelandic church from the advent of the first missionaries in 981 to 1118 (chiefly concerning the introduction of Christianity in 1000). It was probably written about 1200, partly from oral tradition, partly from written sources; the text is now somewhat interpolated. Found only in the MSS of the Hauksbók (AM. 371, 544 and 675. 4°). It is also partly embodied in the Njáls saga (*q. v.*).—*Cf.* Kristni þáttr.

Christendoms saga Hliodande um þad hvornenn Christen Tru kom fyrst a Island, at forlage þess haloflega Herra, Olafs Tryggvasonar Noregs Kongs ... Prentud i Skalhollti af Hendrick Kruse, Anno M. DC. LXXXVIII. 4°. pp. (4)+26 +(2).

Edited by Bp Þórður Þorláksson, and dedicated to Mich. Vibe and Matth. Moth. On reverse of t.-p. a wood-cut representing King Olaf. On the final-leaf "Stutt Innehald og Registur."

Kristni-saga sive Historia Religionis Christianæ in Islandiam introductæ ; nec non Þáttr af Isleifi biskupi, sive Narratio de Isleifo Episcopo ; ex manuscriptis Legati Magnæani cum interpretatione Latina, notis, chronologia, tabulis genealogicis, et indicibus, tam rerum, quam verborum. Hafniæ 1773. (Sumtibus Legati Magnæani). 8°. pp. (40)+194+(104).

Contents: dedicatory letter, pp. (5)-(12) ; preface, by B. W. Luxdorph, pp. (13)-(40) ; Krıstnısaga (text, version and notes), pp. 1-129 ; Þáttr af Isleifi, pp. 130-141 ; Annotationes uberiores : 1. De berserkis et furore berserkico (by Jón Eiríksson), pp 142-163 ; 2. De centenario argenti (by Björn Halldórsson), pp. 164-174 ; Chronologia, pp. 175-184 ; Genealogiæ, pp. 185-194 ; indices of names, subjects and words, pp. (1)-(103) ; on final page corrigenda. The edition is the work of Hannes Finnson, the translation is by B. W. Luxdorph. *Reviews:* Krıtıske Journal for 1773, coll 465-474 ;—† Götting. Anz. 1774. pp 65-68 (where the version is wrongly ascribed to Ol. Olavius).—To commemorate the publication of this edition Gunnar Pálsson composed a Latin poem, which was printed separately with the title : "In hundrad silfurs cum Kristni-Saga Hafn. 1773 editum, per G. P." 8°. pp. (4).

Extracts from the saga in : Grönlands historiske Mindesmærker 1838. II. pp. 232-234 (*cf.* I. pp. 37-47), and Antiquités Russes. 1852. fol. II. pp. 236-237.

Kristni saga. [*Ed. by* Jón Sigurðsson]. *In* Biskupa sögur. Kaupmannahöfn 1858. I. pp. xi-xxiii, 1-32.

Kristni saga. *In* Hauksbók udg. efter de Arnamagnæanske håndskrifter no. 371, 544 og 675, 4°. samt forskellige papir-håndskrifter [*by* Finnur Jónsson *and* Eiríkur Jónsson]. Köbenhavn 1892-96. pp. lxiv-lxxv, 126-149.

Kristnisaga, Þáttr Þorvalds ens víðförla, Þáttr Ísleifs bıskups Gizurarsonar, Hungrvaka. Herausgg. von B. Kahle. Halle a. S. 1905. (Altnordische Sagabibliothek. 11.) 8°. pp. (4)+ xxxiii+(2)+143.

Kristni saga, pp. v-xv, 1-57. Annotated edition. *Reviews:* Anz f. deut. Altert. 1907. XXXI. pp. 107-113, by G. Neckel ;—Literar. Centralbl. 1907. coll. 513-514, by A. Gebhardt ;—Deut Lit. Zeit. 1907. coll. 1248-49, by W. Ranisch ;—Literaturbl. f. g. u. r. Philol. 1908. coll. 10-11, by W. Golther ;—Revue critique. 1907. N. S. LXIII. pp. 289-290, by L. Pineau.

Christne Saga. *In* Origines Islandicæ, by G. Vigfusson and F. Y. Powell. Oxford 1905. I. pp. 370-406.

Icelandic text with English version.

DANISH.—Kristendomssaga. *In* Billeder af Livet paa Island, ved Fr. Winkel Horn. Kjöbenhavn 1876. III. pp. 223-245.

ENGLISH.—Vigfússon *and* Powell's *version in* Orig. Isl. I. (*see above*).

LATIN.—Luxdorph's *version in the edition of* 1773 (*see above*).

SWEDISH.—Nio kapitel af Kristni saga tolkade og upplysta samt med en kort historisk inledning försedda. Akademisk afhandling af Robert Wilhelm Gillberg. Uppsala 1866. 8°. pp. (4)+40.

Brenner, Oskar. Über die Kristni saga. Kritische Beiträge zur altnordischen Literaturgeschichte. München 1878. 8°. pp. xiv+(2)+158.
Cf. a corrective note by the author in Literaturbl. f. g. u. r. Philol. 1887. col. 51. *Reviews*. Literar. Centralbl. 1879. coll. 381-382, by A. Edzardi ;—Jenaer Literat. Zeit. 1879. pp. 124-127, by K. Maurer (*cf.* Zeitschr. f. deut. Philol. 1879. X. pp. 352-353) ;—Literaturbl. f. g. u. r. Philol. 1880. coll. 97-100, by K. v. Amira.

Jónsson, Bryn. „" Bær Þórodds goða." *In* Árbók h. ísl. Fornleifafél. 1895. pp. 24-29.

—— Rannsókn í Árnesþingi 1904. (Þorvaldur hinn veili). *Ibid.* 1905. pp. 43-44.

Jónsson, Finnur (*bishop*). Historia ecclesiastica Islandiæ. Tom. I. Havniæ 1772. 4°. pp. (8)+598.

Jónsson, Finnur. Litteratur Historie. II. pp. 575-584.

Jörgensen, A. D. Den nordiske Kirkes Grundlæggelse og förste Udvikling. Kjöbenhavn 1874-76. pp. 355-379.

Magnússon, Eiríkur. The Conversion of Iceland to Christianity A. D. 1000. *In* Saga-Book of the Viking Club. London 1901. II. 3. pp 348-376.

Maurer, Konrad. Die Bekehrung des Norwegischen Stammes zum Christenthume, in ihrem geschichtlichen Verlaufe quellenmässig geschildert. I.-II. München 1855-1856. 8°. pp. xii+660, viii+732.
Cf. Maurer's "Über Ari fróði und seine Schriften " in Germania. 1891. pp. 61-96.

Monrad, Sóren. De vita Thangbrandi qvæ exstant, collegit, recensuit et defendit S. M., respondente Joh. Wexelsen   Havniæ 1773. 12°. pp. 24. (*Inaug.-Diss.*)
Review: Kritiske Journal for 1773. coll. 425-427.

Müller, P. E. Sagabibliothek. I. pp. 317-318.

Ólsen, Björn M. Um kristnitökuna árið 1000 og tildrög hennar. Gefið út í minningu 900 ára afmælis kristninnar á Íslandi. Reykjavík 1900. 8°. pp. (6)+108.
Reviews: Eimreiðin. 1901. VII. pp. 1-16, by Finnur Jónsson ; a reply by the author in Andvari. 1901. XXVI. pp. 136-159 ;—Andvari. 1901. XXVI. pp. 213-219, by Matth. Jochumsson ;—Verði ljós! 1900. V. pp. 122-126, 137-141, by Eiríkur Magnússon ;—Sameiningin. 1900. XV. pp. 147-151, by Jón Bjarnason ;—Þjóðólfur. 1900. LII. p. 117, by Hannes Þorsteinsson ;—Literar. Centralbl. 1901. col. 653, by O. Brenner.

—— Om Are frode. *In* Aarb. f. nord. Oldk. og. Hist. 1893. pp. 203-352.

Vigfússon, Guðbr. Um tímatal í Íslendinga sögum. pp. 429-434.

Werneke, Bernh. Die Einführung des Christenthums auf Island. Eine historische Skizze nach altnordischen Quellen. Coesfeld 1856. (28ter Jahresber. d. kgl. Gymnasium). 4°. pp. 22.

Kristni þáttr.

997-1000. In the Ólafs saga Tryggvasonar of the Flateyjarbók. *Cf.* Kristni saga.

In Saga Olafs Tryggvasonar. Skálholt 1689. 4°. II. pp. 214-223, 238-245.

In Fornmanna sögur. 1826. II. pp. 197-211, 232-244.

In Flateyjarbók. Christiania 1860. I. pp. 421-429, 441-447.

DANISH.—C. C. Rafn's *version in* Oldnordiske Sagaer. 1827. II. pp. 175-188, 206-216.

ENGLISH.—*In* The Saga of King Olaf Tryggwason, translated by J. Sephton. London 1895. pp. 342-351, 365-372.

LATIN.—Svb. Egilsson's *version in* Scripta historica Islandorum. 1828. II. pp. 182-198, 217-227.

Króka-Refs saga.

A fictitious saga written in the 14th century, the events placed in the 11th century. In vellum-MS. AM. 471. 4°. (15th cent.)

Lijf-Saga Hinns Kynduga Krooka-Refs, hvör ed Inneheldur alla Hanns Frægd og Mannlega Geórninga : Hagleik, Vitsku, og Hroodrar Smijde. Samannsett af Froodum Fræde-Mönnum. *In* Agiætar Fornmanna-Sögur, ad Forlage Biörns Marcussonar. Hólar 1756. pp. 35-68.

Krókarefssaga, Gunnars saga Keldugnúpsfífls og Ölkofra þáttr. Kaupmannahöfn 1866. 8°. pp. vi+(2)+75.

Krókarefssaga, pp. iii-iv, 1-37. Edited by Þorvaldur Björnsson. *Reviews:* Germania. 1867. XII. pp. 479-490, by K. Maurer ;—Þjóðólfur. 1867. XIX. pp. 147-148, by Jón Þorkelsson.

Króka-Refs saga og Króka-Refs rímur efter hándskrifterne udgivne af Pálmi Pálsson. (Samfund til udg. af gl. nord. litteratur). Köbenhavn 1883. 8°. pp. (2)+xxxviii+(2)+120+(2).

Critical edition. The rímur were probably composed in the earlier part of the 15th century. *Reviews:* †Deut. Lit. Zeit 1884. No. 30, by J. Hoffory ;—Literaturbl. f. g. u. r Philol. 1884 coll. 379-382, by O. Brenner ;—†Nord. Revy. 1883. col. 311, by E. H. Lind.

Saga Krókarefs. Ísafjörður 1890. 8°. pp. 39.

Króka-Refs saga. Útgefandi : Sigurbjörn Jónsson. Selkirk, Man. 1900. 8°. pp. (2)+23+(2).

Jónsson, Finnur. Litteratur Historie. III. pp. 47-48, 86-87.

Magnússon, Finnur. Blandede Optegnelser. *In* Grönlands historiske Mindesmærker. 1845. III. pp. 526-528.

Müller, P. E.   Sagabibliothek. I. pp. 357-359.
See also K. Maurer's article "Der Franz Joseph-Fjord in Grönland"
in Beil. zur Allg. Zeit. 20. Oct. 1870. pp. 4786-87.—*Cf.* W. Fiske's
Chess in Iceland. Florence 1905. pp. 14-16.

Kumlbúa þáttr, *or* Þorsteins draumr Þorvarðssonar.

A legendary tale from the 13th century.

Kumlbúa þáttr. *In* Bárðar saga Snæfellsáss . . . Draumvitranir
. . . ved Guðbrandr Vigfússon. Kjöbenhavn 1860. pp. 129–
130, 169–170.

_____

Jónsson, Finnur. Litteratur Historie. II. p. 765.

Landnámabók *or* Landnáma.

An historical account of the Norwegian settlement of Iceland 874-930.
It is now found in three recensions, viz. the Sturlubók (AM. 107 fol.),
the Hauksbók (AM. 105 fol.; a 14th cent. vellum fragm AM. 371. 4°.
cf. Kålund's Palæografisk Atlas. 1905. Nr. 37), and the Melabók (AM.
445 B. 4°, 15th cent.). The Sturlubók owes its origin to Sturla Þórðarson, and dates from c. 1250-1280. The Hauksbók-text is a compilation, made about 1320 by Haukr Erlendsson, of the Sturlubók and
a recension (now lost) by Styrmir Kárason hinn fróði (d. 1245).   The
Melabók is a fragment of a recension by a member of the Melar
family (Borgarfjörðr) of the first half of the 14th cent.   The so-
called younger Melabók is a 17th century compilation from these three,
which are based upon an older text, the original Landnáma-text, probably written before or about 1200, from various sources, oral traditions
and writings of Kolskeggr Ásbjarnarson (for East Iceland), Ari
Þorgilsson (*cf.* Íslendingabók), Brandr prior (the genealogies of the
Breiðfirðings), possibly also of Sæmundr Sigfússon and others.

Sagan Landnama Vm fyrstu bygging Islands af Nordmönnum
. . . Skalhollte, Pryckt af Hendr. Kruse, A. MDCLXXXVIII.
4°. pp. (10)+182+(20).

Contents. t.-p., on rev. the coat-of-arms of Iceland; dedicatory letter
to King Christian V. from Bp. Þórður Þorláksson, pp. (3)-(5); preface
by the same, pp. (6)-(7); wdct. representing Ingólfr Arnarson, p. (8;
Landnamabok, prologus, pp. (9)-(10), text, pp. 1-174; Appendix
[Viðauki Skarðsárbókar. Mantissa], pp. 175-182; Prefallt registvr (of
persons, places, and subjects), pp. (1)-(17); poems to Bp. Þórður (in
Icel. by Einar Eyjólfsson, in Latin by Þórður Þ. Vidalín and Þorlákur
Grímsson), pp. (18)-(20).—Edited (from five MSS.) by Einar Eyjólfsson.

Islands Landnamabok. Hoc est : Liber Originum Islandiae.
Versione latina, lectionibus variantibus, et rerum, personarum,
locorum, nec non vocum rarissimarum, indicibus illustratus.
Ex manuscriptis Legati Magnæani.   Havniae 1774. 4°. pp.
(20)+510, 1 *facsim.*

Edited and translated by Hannes Finnsson, text based upon the Skálholt edition and AM. 104 fol. Index of poetical and rare words by
Jón Ólafsson (Hypnonensis). *Reviews:* Nye kritisk Journal for 1775.
coll. 97-99, by Jacob Baden ;—† Götting. Anz. 1777. Zug.-Bd. pp. 123 ff.

Íslands Landnámabók. *In* Íslendinga sögur. Kaupmannahöfn
1829. pp. 7–10, 21–260.

> Text based on AM. 104 fol. Edited by Þorgeir Guðmundsson and
> Þorsteinn Helgason. Has also a special t.-p. *see* Íslendingabók.

Extracts from Landnáma in Antiquitates Americanæ. 1837. 4°. pp. 187–190
(P. II. Ch. 14); in Grönlands historiske Mindesmærker. 1838 I. pp.
71–79 (P I. Ch. 8, 14, 29, 30), 150–169 (P. II. Ch. 22), 172–195 (P. II.
Ch. 14), *cf.* II. pp. 784–787; in Antiquités Russes. 1852. fol. II. pp.
231–236 (P. I. Ch. 1; P. II. Ch.9; P. III. Ch. 1, 9).

Landnámabók. *In* Íslendinga sögur. Kjöbenhavn 1843. I. pp.
xiv–lxiv, 21–322, 2 *facsims.*

> Critical edition by Jón Sigurðsson, based on AM. 107 fol. Appended
> are: 1. Viðrauki Skarðsárbókar (AM. 104 fol.), pp. 323-333; 2.
> Viðrauki Melabókar ennar yngri (AM. 106 fol.), pp. 334-340; 3.
> Nýfundið brot Melabókar ennar eldri (AM. 445 B. 4°), pp. 341-353; 4.
> Ættartölubrot : a. Ættartölubrot framan við Melabók ena eldri, pp.
> 353-356; b. Biskupa-ættir (AM. 162 M. fol.), pp. 357-362.

Íslendingabók . . . og Landnámabók. Búið hefir til prentunar
Vald. Ásmundarson. Reykjavík 1891. (Íslendinga sögur.
1.–2.) pp. vii + 6.

> Landnáma-text with appendices, explanation of verses, and index of
> settlers, pp. 23-256.

Landnámabók. *In* Hauksbók udg. efter de Arnamagnæanske
håndskrifter no. 371, 544 og 675, 4°. samt forskellige papir-
håndskrifter [*by* Finnur Jónsson *and* Eiríkur Jónsson]. Köbenhavn 1892 (–96). pp. lxiii–lxv, 3–125.

Landnámabók. I.–III. Hauksbók. Sturlubók. Melabók m. m.
Udg. af det kongelige nordiske Oldskrift-Selskab. Köbenhavn
1900. 8°. pp. (4) + lx + 403.

> Edited by Finnur Jónsson. *Contents:* Indledning, pp. i-lx; Hauksbók
> (cf. above), pp. 1-125; Sturlubók, pp. 127-231; Melabók, pp. 233-
> 242; Den såkaldte "yngre Melabók"s (AM. 106 fol.) vigtigste afvigel-
> ser, pp. 243-260; Tillæg : a. Uddrag af Ólafs saga Tryggvasonar, (AM. 61
> fol.), pp. 261-273; b. Henvisninger til genealogiske uddrag i saga-
> værker, pp. 274-276; c. Kritiske bemærkninger til enkelte steder i
> teksterne, pp. 276-280; d. Kapitelforholdene i denne udg. og den fra
> 1843, pp. 281-283; Registre (of places and persons), pp. 284-403.
> *Reviews:* Literar. Centralbl. 1900. coll. 1946-47, by O. Brenner;—
> Deut. Lit. Zeit. 1900. coll. 2346-48, by A. Heusler;—Eimreiðin. 1900.
> VII. p. 76, by M. Þórðarson;—Literaturbl. f. g. u. r Philol. 1901. coll.
> 66-67, by W. Golther;—Revue critique 1901. N. S. LI. pp. 85-88, by
> E. Beauvois;—Arkiv f. nord. filol. 1902. XVIII. pp. 193-194, by L.
> Larsson;—Anz. f. deut. Altert. 1902. XXVIII. pp. 283-285, by W.
> Ranisch.

Landnama-Book or the Book of Settlements. *In* Origines Islandicæ, by G. Vigfusson and F. Y. Powell. Oxford 1905. I.
pp. 2–236, 266–274.

> Text (Hauksbók) with English version. Mantissa (text and transla-

tion), pp. 266-274. *Review:* Saga Book of the Viking Club. 1906. IV.
2. pp. 415-463, by E. Magnússon.—The edition given in the bibliography for 1888 in Germania XXXVII. p. 485 (no. 1859) is not a
separate edition, but merely advance sheets of the Origines Islandicæ.

ENGLISH.—The Book of the Settlement of Iceland. Translated
from the original Icelandic of Ari the Learned, by Rev. T.
Ellwood. Kendal 1898. 8°. pp. (8)+xxxi+243+(3)+4, *map.*
Follows chiefly the text of the edition of 1843.
Vigfússon *and* Powell's *version in* Orig. Isl. I. (*see above*).

LATIN.—H. Finnsson's *version in the edition of* 1770 (*see above*).

Brím, Eggert Ó.   Víg Gríms á Kálfsskinni eða Þorvalds í Haga. (Landnáma 3. 13; Glúma k. 27). *In* Tímarit h.ísl. Bókmentafél. 1882. III.
pp. 100-112.

Bugge, Alex.   De norske nybygder paa Færöerne og Island í deres forhold
til Vesterlandene og særlig til den keltiske kultur. *In his* Vester-
landenes indflydelse paa Nordboernes og særlig Nordmændenes ydre
kultur, levesæt og samfundsforhold i Vikingetiden.   Christiania 1905.
pp. 353-396.

†Craigie, W A.   The Gaels in Iceland.   *In* Proceedings of the Society of
Antiquaries of Scotland (May 10) 1898.
Reviews. Eimreiðin. 1899. V. p. 118, by V. Guðmundsson,—Revue
celtique. 1899. XX. pp. 101-102, by L. Duvau, reply by Craigie, p. 356.

Gunnarsson, Sig.   Örnefni frá Jökulsá í Axarfirði austan að Skeiðará. I.
Landnámabók. *In* Safn til sögu Íslands. 1876. II. pp. 429-453.

Jónsson. Arngrímur.   Specimen Islandiæ historicum, et magna ex parte
chorographicum, anno Iesu Christi 874. primum habitare cœptœ : quo
simul sententia contraria D. Ioh. Isaci Pontani, Regis Daniæ Historia-
graphi, in placidam considerationem venit.   Amstelodami 1643. 4°. pp.
(12)+174.
A copy with the imprint †Amstelodami 1646, probably a title-edition, was
acquired in May 1906 by the Royal Library, Copenhagen.

Jónsson, Bryn.   Um landnám Sighvats rauða. *In* Árbók h. ísl. Fornleifafél. 1886. pp. 52-61.

——— Nokkur bæjanöfn í Landnámu í ofanverðri Hvítársíðu og Hálsasveit.
Ibid. 1893. pp. 74-80. *Cf. ibid.* 1900. p. 27.

——— Rannsóknir í ofanverðu Árnespingi 1893.—í Skaptafellspingi 1893.
—í Rangárpingi 1893. *Ibid.* 1894. pp. 1-25.

——— Rannsókn sögustaða í vesturhluta Húnavatnssýslu sumarið 1894. I.
Landnáma. *Ibid.* 1895. pp. 1-3.

——— Fornleifar á Fellsströnd. *Ibid.* 1896. pp. 19-21.

——— Rannsókn sögustaða í Grafningi í maímán. 1898. 2. Steinrauðar-
staðir. *Ibid.* pp. 3-5. *Cf. ibid.* 1900. p. 34.

——— Rannsóknir í Snæfellsnessýslu sumarið 1899. *Ibid.* 1900. pp. 9-27.

Jónsson, Bryn. Kirkjutóft á Esjubergi. *Ibid.* 1902. pp. 33-35.
—— Rannsókn í Gullbringu- og Árnessýslu sumarið 1902. *Ibid.* 1903.
pp. 31-33.
—— Rannsókn í Þverárþingi sumarið 1903. *Ibid.* 1904. pp. 8-16.
—— Rannsókn í Árnesþingi sumarið 1904. *Ibid.* 1905. pp. 1-41. *Cf.*
ibid. 1907. pp. 29-38.
—— Rannsókn í Norðurlandi sumarið 1905. *Ibid.* 1906. pp. 8, 15-16,
23-25.
—— Rannsókn í Vestmannaeyjum sumarið 1906. *Ibid.* 1907. pp. 5-10.
—— Rannsókn á Þórsmörk sumarið 1906. *Ibid.* 1907. pp. 16-22.
—— Ölfus=Álfós? *In* Tímarit h. ísl. Bókmentafél. 1895. XVI. pp 164-
172.
Followed by a note (Athugagrein) by B. M. Ólsen, pp. 173-175. *Cf.*
Melsteð's Íslendinga saga. I. p. 215.
Jónsson, Finnur. Litteratur Historie. II. pp. 584-594.
Jónsson, Jón (*of* Hlíð). Örnefni í Snóksdalssókn. *In* Safn til sögu
Íslands. 1876. II. pp. 319-324.
Jónsson, *Rev.* Jón. Rannsóknir í fornsögu Norðurlanda. *In* Tímarit h.
ísl. Bókmentafél. 1890. XI pp. 53-71.
Treats of settlers of Swedish origin.
—— Nokkrar athugagreinir við Íslendinga sögur. III. Um ættmenn
Klypps hersis á Íslandi. *Ibid.* 1898. XIX. pp. 92-109.
Jónsson, Þorleifur. Örnefni nokkur í Breiðafjarðardólum. *In* Safn til
sögu Íslands. 1876. II. pp. 558-577.
Kålund, P. E. Kristian. Bidrag til en historisk-topografisk beskrivelse af
Island. I.-II. Udg. af Kommissionen for det Arnamagnæanske Legat.
Kjöbenhavn 1877-1882. 8°. pp. (12)+638; (12)+527; 18 *maps.*
Treats, of course, of the Icelandic sagas in general. *Reviews.* Ger-
mania. 1879. XXIV. pp. 88-102, by K. Maurer;—Literaturbl. f. g u. r.
Philol. 1880. coll. 14-17, by K. Maurer;—† Nord. tidskr. utg. af
Letterst. fören. 1881, by R. Arpi; sep. repr. 8°. pp. 11.
Magnússon, Eiríkur. On the sailing directions of Landnámabók deter-
mining the course from the Hern-Isles in Norway to Hvarf (Wharf) in
Greenland. (London 1881). 8°. pp. 4. *Sep. repr. of the* Transactions
of the Cambridge Philological Society. I. pp. 316-318.
Melsteð, Bogi Th. Íslendinga saga. Kaupmannahöfn 1903. I. pp. 53-316.
Müller, P. E. Sagabibliothek. II. pp. 225-229.
Munch, P. A. Det norske Folks Historie. Christiania 1852. I. 1. pp. 517-
569.
Nordlander, Joh. Om ortnamnens bildning enligt Landnáma-boken. *In*
Svensk Fornminnesföreningens Tidskrift. 1898. X. pp. 141-157.
Ólsen, Björn M. Rannsóknir á Vestfjorðum. I. Rannsókn á Ingjaldssandi.
In Árbók h. ísl. Fornleifafél. 1884-85. pp. 1-7.
—— Landnáma og Egilssaga. *In* Aarb. f. nord. Oldk. og. Hist. 1904.
pp. 167-247.
For reviews see Egils saga.
—— Landnáma og Hænsa-Þóris saga. *Ibid.* 1905. pp. 63-80.
—— Landnáma og Eyrbyggja. *Ibid.* 1905. pp. 81-117.

Schumann, Oscar. Islands Siedelungsgebiete während der landnámatíð. *In* Mitteil. des Vereins für Erdkunde zu Leipzig. 1899. pp. 85-141, *map*.
Also issued separately as † Inaug.-Diss. of the Leipz Univ. (Leipzig 1900). *Review :* Petermann's Mittheil., Lit.-Ber , 1900. coll. 132-133, by Þorv. Thoroddsen.

Stokes, Whitley. On the Gaelic names in the Landnamabok and Runic inscriptions. *In* Revue celtique. 1876. III. pp. 186-191.

Thorlacius, Árni. Skýringar yfir örnefni í Landnámu og Eyrbyggju, að svo miklu leyti, sem við kemr Þórnes þingi hinu forna. *In* Safn til sögu Íslands. 1861. II. pp. 277-298.

Vigfússon, Guðbr. Um tímatal í Íslendinga sögum. pp. 196-298.

Þorkelsson, Jón. Skýringar á vísum í nokkurum íslenzkum sögum. Reykjavík 1868. pp. 36-48. (*Program*).

Laurentius saga Hólabiskups *or* Lafranz saga biskups.

Life of Laurentius Kálfsson (b. 1267, d. 1330), bishop of Hólar 1323-1330, written by Einar Hafliðason (1307-1393). Imperfect. MSS. : AM. 180 B. fol. (15th cent.), AM 406 A. 4° (16th cent.)

Laurentius saga Hóla biskups. [*Ed. by* Guðbr. Vigfússon]. *In* Biskupa sögur. Kaupmannahöfn 1858. I. pp. lxxxi-xc, 787-914.

Extracts in Munch and Unger's Oldnorsk Læsebog. Christiania 1847. pp. 42-48.

ENGLISH.—The Life of Laurence Bishop of Hólar in Iceland (Laurentius saga) by Einar Haflidason, translated from the Icelandic by Oliver Elton. London 1890. 8°. pp. viii+152, *map*.

Jónsson, Finnur (*bishop*). Historia Ecclesiastica Islandiæ. Havniæ 1774. 4°. II. pp. 169-192.

Jónsson, Finnur. Litteratur Historie. III. pp. 67-68.

Müller, P. E. Sagabibliothek. I. pp. 330-334.

Laxdæla saga *or* Laxdæla.

C. 892-1026. Written in the first part of the 13th century. To it has been added as a continuation the Bolla þáttr Bollasonar (chap. 79-88), which is of later date and of questionable historical value. MSS. : Möðruvallabók (AM. 132 fol., from c. 1350) ; a copy of the Vatnshyrna, Icel. Lit. Soc. (now National Library, Reykjavík) 225, 4°.; two vellum fragments from the 13th century, AM. 162 D-E. fol. (*cf.* Kålund's Palæografisk Atlas. 1905. Nr. 29). *Cf.* Kjartans þáttr Ólafssonar.

A Fragment of Irish History, or a Voyage to Ireland undertaken from Iceland in the tenth century. *In* G. J. Thorkelin's Fragments of English and Irish History in the ninth and tenth century. London 1788. 4°. pp. 1-59.

Extracts with English version. *Reviews :* Götting. Anz. 1790. pp. 633-637 ;—Gentleman's Mag. 1788. LVIII. p. 1001 ;—† Lærde Efterretn. 1789. Nr. 29.

Laxdæla-saga sive Historia de rebus gestis Laxdölensium.   Ex manuscriptis Legati Magnæani cum interpretatione latina, tribus dissertationibus ad calcem adjectis et indicibus tam rerum qvam nominum propriorum.   Hafniæ 1826.   (Sumtibus Legati Magnæani).   4°. pp. (6)+xviii+442.

Contents: Præfatio (by Börge Thorlacius), pp. i–xviii; Laxdæla saga, pp. 1–363; Þáttr af Gunnari Þiðrandabana, pp 364–385; Disqvisitio de imaginibus in æde Olavi Pavonis Hiardarholtensi seculo Xmo extructa, scenas aut actiones mythologicas repræsentantibus, auctore Finno Magnusen, pp 386–394; De vi formulæ "at ganga undir jardarmen," auctore P. E. Müller, pp. 395–400; Nonnulla de notione vocis "Jarteikn," auctore E. Chr. Werlauff, pp 401–406; indices (of persons, places, subjects, and rare words), pp. 407–442   Text (AM. 132 fol.) edited by Gunnlaugur Oddsson and Wium; the Latin version by Þorleifur G Repp; indices by Þorgeir Guðmundsson. *Reviews:* Dansk Literat. Tid. 1829. pp. 328–330, 348–352;—Götting. gel. Anz. 1830. pp. 620–624, by Jacob Grimm;—†Berl. Jahrb. f. wissensch. Critik. 1829. II. pp. 801–808, by G. Mohnike. Extracts with notes in Antiquités Russes. 1852. fol. II. pp. 278–289.

Laxdæla saga og Gunnars þáttr Þiðrandabana.   Kostað hefir : Björn Jónsson.   Akureyri 1867. 8°. pp. xiv+282+(2).

Edited by Jón Þorkelsson.—The printing of an †edition of the Laxdæla by Sveinn Skúlason was begun at the Akureyri press in 1861, but only 4 sheets were printed (*cf.* Erslev's Forfatter-Lexicon; Norðri. VIII. pp. 52–53).

Laxdæla Saga.   *In* An Icelandic Prose Reader, by G. Vigfusson and F. Y. Powell.   Oxford 1879. pp. 20–82, 346–361.

Chap. 48–78 from AM. 309. 4°, with notes.

Gudrun Osiversdatter.   *Forms pt. ii. of* Oldnordiske Læsestykker udg. af V. Levy.   Köbenhavn 1887. 8°. pp. (4)+75.

Extracts with notes.

Laxdæla saga udg. for Samfund til udgivelse af gammel nordisk litteratur ved Kr. Kålund.   Köbenhavn 1889–1891. 8°. pp. (4) +lxx+372.

Critical edition based on AM. 132 fol.   *Review:* Literaturbl. f. g. u. r. Philol. 1894. col. 328, by W. Golther

Laxdæla saga herausgg. von Kr. Kålund.   Halle a. S. 1896. (Altnordische Saga-Bibliothek. 4.) 8°. pp. (8)+xiv+276.

Annotated edition. *Reviews·* Zeitschr. f. deut. Philol. 1898. XXX. pp. 263–264, by O. L. Jiriczek;—Deut. Lit. Zeit. 1897. coll. 129–130, by F. Holthausen;—Literar. Centralbl. 1896. coll. 1114–15;—Journ. of Germanic Philol. 1899. II. pp. 547–548, by O. Brenner;—Eimreiðin. 1896. II. pp. 155–156, by V. Guðmundsson.

Laxdæla saga.   Búið hefir til prentunar Vald. Ásmundarson.   Reykjavík 1895. (Íslendinga sögur. 11.) 8°. pp. xvi+284.

Cf. Eimreiðin. 1896. II. pp. 75–76.

The Story of the Laxdale-men. *In* Origines Islandicæ, by G. Vigfusson and F. Y. Powell. Oxford 1905. II. pp. 136–187.
Extracts partly with English translation.

DANISH.—† Laxdæla-Saga, oversat af Jacob Aall. *In* Saga, et Fjerdingaars-Skrift, udg. af. J. St. Munch. Christiania 1820. III. pp. 1–306.
Previously there had appeared a portion of this translation : † Kjartan Olafssons Omvendelse, *ibid.* 1816. I. pp. 1–20.

Den Dövstumme eller Kongedatteren og hendes Æt. *In* Nordiske Fortællinger ved K. L. Rahbek. Kiöbenhavn 1821. II. pp. 196–383.

Fortælling om Laxdælerne eller Beboerne af Laxdalen. *In* Historiske Fortællinger om Islændernes Færd hjemme og ude ved N. M. Petersen. Kjöbenhavn 1840. II. pp. 47–266.—2. Udgave [*ed. by* Guðbr. Vigfússon]. Köbenhavn 1863. III. pp. 99–312 ; *also with the special title :* Eyrbyggja saga og Laxdæla saga eller Fortællinger om Eyrbyggerne og Laxdælerne *etc.*

Eyrbyggja saga og Laxdöla saga eller Fortællinger om Eyrbyggerne og Laxdölerne. Efter de islandske Grundskrifter ved N. M. Petersen. 3. Udgave ved Verner Dahlerup og F. Jónsson. Versene ved Olaf Hansen. Köbenhavn 1901. pp. 81–240.

En Kvindetype. *In* Nordahl Rolfsen's Vore Fædres Liv. Oversættelsen ved Gerhard Gran. Bergen 1888. pp. 372–413.— 2. *edition.* Kristiania 1898. pp. 389–437, 4 *illustr.*
An extract. The illustrations by A. Bloch.

ENGLISH.—Laxdæla saga translated from the Icelandic by Muriel A. C. Press. London 1899. (The Temple Classics). 8°. pp. viii+276, *map.*—2. *edition.* London 1906.
Omits the Bollaþáttr. *Review :* Saga-Book of the Viking Club. 1904. III. 2. p. 288, by A. F. Major.

The Story of the Laxdalers done into English by Robert Proctor. London (The Chiswick Press) 1903. 8°. pp. 263, *map.*
Only 250 copies printed *Review :* Saga-Book of the Viking Club. 1904. III. 3. p 489, by A. F. Major.

GERMAN.—Kjartan und Gudrun. (Laxdæla saga Kap. 28–78). Aus dem Altisländischen zum ersten Male ins Deutsche übertragen von Heinrich von Lenk. *In* Central-Organ für die Interessen des Realschulwesens. Berlin 1896. XXIV. pp. 385–422, 449–484, 513–549.

Höskuld Kolleson und Olaf Pfau. Aus der Laxdæla saga
übersetzt von F. Khull. Graz 1895. 4°. pp. 37. (*Program*).
Review: † Zeitschr. f. d. Realschulw. 1896. XXI. p. 633.

Die Geschichte des Kjartan Olafssohn und der Gudrun Osvifs-
tochter. *In* Arthur Bonus's Isländerbuch. München 1907.
I. pp. 151–246.

LATIN.—Repp's *version in the edition of* 1826 (*see above*).

NORWEGIAN.—Laksdöla elder Soga om laksdolerne. Fraa
gamallnorsk ved Stefan Frich. Kristiania 1899. (Tillegg till
Syn og Segn nr. 6. 1899). 8°. pp. 199.
Kjartan Olavsson. Eit Bilæte av Livet paa Island og i Noreg paa Tidi
hans Olav Konung Tryggvason, *an epitome in* Fraa By og Bygd.
Björgvin 1873. IV. pp. 54-82.

SWEDISH.—Sagan om Gudrun tolkad från fornisländskan af A.
U. Bååth. Göteborg 1900. 8°. pp. (4)+vii+191.

Bååth, A. U.   Studier öfver kompositionen i några isländska ättsagor.
Lund 1885. pp. 42-88.

Gíslason, Einar.   Örnefni nokkur að Helgafelli. *In* Safn til sögu Íslands.
1876. II. pp. 304-306.

Jónsson, Bryn.   Um kenningarnöfn Þórðar godda og Ólafs pá. *In* Árbók
h. ísl. Fornleifafél. 1900. pp. 32-34.

Jónsson, Finnur.   Litteratur Historie. II. pp. 440-453.

Jónsson, Jón (*of* Hlíð).   Örnefni í Snóksdalssókn. *In* Safn til sögu
Íslands. 1876. II. pp. 319-324.

Jónsson, Þorleifur.   Örnefni nokkur í Breiðafjarðardölum. *Ibid.* 1876. II.
pp. 558-577.

Kålund, Kr.   Kulturhistorisk-lexikalske småting. 2.-6.   *In* Arkiv f. nord.
filol. 1893. IX. pp. 88-91.

Magnússon, Finnur.   Disqvisitio de imaginibus in æde Olavi Pavonis
Hiardarholtensi, seculo Xmo extructa, scenas aut actiones mythologicas repræsentantibus, in Laxdæla memoratis (Cap. 29. pag. 112-
114). Havniæ 1826. 4°. pp. 11. (*Sep. repr from the ed. of* 1826).

Müller, P. E.   Sagabibliothek. I. pp. 198-224.

Nicolaysen, N.   Olaf Paa's gildestue.   *In* (Norsk) Historisk Tidsskrift.
1891. III. R. II. Bd. pp. 206-210.

Stefánsson, Jón.   Leiði Guðrúnar Ósvífrsdóttur. *In* Árbók h. ísl. Fornleifafél. 1898. pp. 39-40.

Vigfússon, Guðbr.   Um tímatal í Íslendinga sögum. pp. 340-351, 442-444,
450-456.

Vigfússon, Sig. Rannsókn í Breiðafjarðardölum og í Þórsnesþingi og um hina nyrðri strönd 1881. *In* Árbók h. ísl. Fornleifafél. 1882. pp. 60-105, 2 *pls.*

——— Rannsókn í Borgarfirði 1884. Ferð þeirra Þorgils Höllusonar um Borgarfjörð og víg Helga Harðbeinssonar. *Ibid.* 1884-85. pp. 77-97.

——— Drukknan Þorkels Eyólfssonar. *Ibid.* 1886. pp. 68-76.

——— Rannsóknir á Vestrlandi 1891. *Ibid.* 1893. pp. 61-73.

Ljósvetninga saga *or* Reykdæla saga (*or* Þorgeirs saga goða,
· Guðmundar ríka ok Þorkels háks).

C. 990-1065. Written about 1200; the saga now embodies three tales (þættir, chap. v.-xii.) which presumably were not in the original saga; imperfect at end. Vellum-fragments : AM. 561. 4° (c. 1400), AM. 162 C. fol. (15th cent.); several paper MSS. (17th cent.)

Ljósvetninga saga. *In* Íslendinga sögur. Kaupmannahöfn 1830. II. pp. 5-6, 1-112. *Also with a special t.-p.:* Ljósvetninga saga, Svarfdæla saga, Vallaljóts saga, Vemundar saga ok Víga-Skútu, Vígaglúms saga. Eptir gömlum handritum útgefnar að tilhlutun hins konúnglega norræna Fornfræða félags. Kaupmannahöfn 1830. 8°. pp. 10+410.

Edited (from AM. 485. 4°) by Þorgeir Guðmundsson and Þorsteinn Helgason.

Extracts in Antiquités Russes. 1852. fol. II. pp. 269-272; (chap. v. and xxi.) in An Icelandic Prose Reader, by G. Vigfusson and F. Y. Powell. Oxford 1879. pp. 89-94, 364-366.

Ljósvetninga saga. *In* Íslenzkar fornsögur. Kaupmannahöfn 1880. I. pp. xix-xxxii, 111-277.

Critical edition by Guðmundur Þorláksson. The text is thus divided : A. Guðmundar saga ríka : 1. Deilur Þorgeirs goða ok sona hans (chap. i.-iv.); 2. Kvánfang Sörla Brodd-Helgasonar (chap. v., c. 1000); 3. Reykdæla þáttr (chap. vi.-vii.; c. 1001-1002); 4. Vöðu-Brands þáttr (chap. viii -xii.; c. 1002-1004); 5. Þóris þáttr Helgasonar ok Þorkels háks (chap. xiii.-xx.); 6. Draumr ok dauði Guðmundar ens ríka (chap. xxi.); B. Eyjólfs saga ok Ljósvetninga (chap. xxii.-xxxii.). Appended are : 1. Brot af AM. 561 C. 4°. pp. 257-272; 2. Endir Guðmundar sögu eptir AM. 514. 4°., pp. 272-274; 3. Vísa úr Grettlu um Þorfinn Arnórsson, pp. 274-277. *Review:* Tímarit h. ísl. Bókmentafél. 1881 I. pp. 265-269, by B. M. Ólsen.

Ljósvetninga saga. Búið hefir til prentunar Vald. Ásmundarson. Reykjavík 1896. (Íslendinga sögur. 14.) 8°. pp. (4)+150.

The Story of the Men of Lightwater. *In* Origines Islandicæ, by G. Vigfusson and F. Y. Powell. Oxford 1905. II. pp. 344-430.

The Guðmundar saga only (text divided somewhat differently from the ed. of 1880) with English version.

DANISH.—Ljosavandsfolkenes Saga. *In* Billeder af Livet paa Island, ved Fr. Winkel Horn. Kjöbenhavn 1876. III. pp. 101–185.

Gudmund den mægtige. *In* Nordahl Rolfsen's Vore Fædres Liv. Oversættelsen ved Gerhard Gran. Bergen 1888. pp. 196–209.—*2. edition.* Kristiania 1898. pp. 177–198, *2 illustr.* Extracts. The illustrations by A. Bloch.

ENGLISH.—Vigfússon *and* Powell's *version in* Orig. Isl. II. (*see above*).

GERMAN.—Die kleine Geschichte von Gudmund und die Rauchtälern.—Die kleine Geschichte von Gudmund und der Brautwerbung. [*Transl. by* A. Heusler]. *In* Kunstwart. München 1907. XX. pp. 204–210.—*Reprinted in* Arthur Bonus's Isländerbuch. München 1907. III. pp. 322–340.

Bååth, A. U. Studier öfver kompositionen i några isländska ättsagor. Lund 1885. pp. 1–19.

Jónsson, Bryn. Rannsóknir á Norðurlandi sumarið 1900 *In* Árbók h. ísl. Fornleifafél. 1901. pp. 13–16.

Jónsson, Finnur. Litteratur Historie. II. pp. 498–505.

Muller, P. E. Sagabibliothek. I. pp. 130–140.

Vigfússon, Guðbr. Um tímatal í Íslendinga sögum. pp. 485–489.

Mána þáttr Íslendings *or* Mána þáttr skálds.
C. 1184. Found only in one MS. (AM. 327. 4°., vellum from c. 1300) of the Sverris saga by Karl Jónsson.

Frá Mána Íslendingi. *In* Noregs Konunga sögur curarunt B. Thorlacius et E. C. Werlauff. Havniæ 1818. fol. IV. pp. 149–150.
Text with Danish and Latin versions.

Frá Mána Íslendingi. *In* Fornmanna sögur. 1834. VIII. pp. 206–208.

Mána þáttr Íslendings. *In* Fjörutíu Íslendinga þættir. Þórleifr Jónsson gaf út. Reykjavík 1904. pp. 189–190.

DANISH.—Thorlacius *and* Werlauff's *version of* 1818 (*see above*). *In* Oldnordiske Sagaer. 1834. VIII. pp. 142–144.

ENGLISH.—*In* The Saga of King Sverri of Norway, translated by J. Sephton. London 1899. pp. 106–107.

LATIN.—Thorlacius *and* Werlauff's *version of* 1818 (*see above*).
Svb. Egilsson's *version in* Scripta historica Islandorum. 1837.
VIII. pp. 143-146.

Jónsson, Finnur. Litteratur Historie. II. pp. 75-76, 553.

Njáls saga, *or* Njála, *or* Brennu-Njáls saga (Fljótshlíðinga *or* Hlíðverja saga).

C. 960-1016. In its present shape it dates from the latter part of the 13th century, but it is compiled from various older sagas, as Gunnars saga, Njáls saga proper, Kristni saga, Brjáns saga, and possibly some þættir. Vellum-MSS. : Reykjabók (AM. 468. 4°., c. 1300, *cf.* Kålund's Palæografisk Atlas. 1905. Nr. 35), Möðruvallabók (AM. 132 fol, c. 1350) ; Kálfalækjarbók (AM. 133. 4°, c. 1300) ; Gráskinna (Gl. kgl. Saml. 2870. 4°, c. 1300) Gl. kgl. Saml. 2868. 4°. (c. 1400), and various fragments, the oldest from c 1280.

Sagan af Niáli Þórgeirssyni ok Sonvm Hans &c. útgefin efter gavmlvm Skinnbókvm med Konvnglegu Leyfi ok Prentvd i Kavpmannahavfn árid 1772. 4°. pp. (6)+282.

Edited by Ólafur Olavius. Text preceded by a royal letter, and a Latin preface.—*Cf.* Íslendingur. 1860. I. p. 151; 1861. II. p. 39, by Jón Þorkelsson.

Njáls Saga. *In* L. Chr. Müller's Islandsk Læsebog. Kjöbenhavn 1837. pp. 1-205. (Chap. 1-132).

Sagan af Njáli Þorgeirssyni og Sonum Hans &c. Prentud eptir útgáfunni í Kaupmannahöfn árid 1772. Videyar Klaustri 1844. 8°. pp. (4)+427.

Extracts with notes in Antiquités Russes. 1852. fol. II pp. 237-247.

Sagan af Njáli Þorgeirssyni ok sonum hans. Historia Njális et Filiorum. Textum scholis academicis subjiciendum edidit S. H. B. Svensson. I. Londini Gothorum 1867. 8°. pp. 112. (Chap. 1-74. *Cover-title.*)

Njála á kostnað hins konunglega norræna Fornfræðafjelags. Kaupmannahöfn 1875. 8°. pp. (2)+370.

Separate text-edition, without the variants and notes, of the critical edition of the same year.

Njála udgivet efter gamle håndskrifter af det kongelige nordiske Oldskrift-selskab. I.–II. bind. København 1875-1889. (Íslendinga sögur. III.–IV.) 8°. pp. xv+910, (6)+1021, 2 *facsims.*

Critical edition of the text (*vol. 1.*) by Konráð Gíslason and Eiríkur Jónsson. *Contents of vol. ii.* (published in three parts : 1879, 1883, 1889) : Konr. Gíslason : Njáll eller Njáll? en undersögelse om femstavelsede verslinier i sædvanlig 'dróttkvæðr háttr,' pp. 1-334; K. G.: Saganavnet Njála, pp. 335-340; K. G.: Bemærkninger til kvadene i

Njála, pp. 341-597; K G.: Tillæg og rettelser til Njála II. 1-597, pp. 598-645, Jón Þorkelsson: Om håndskrifterne af Njála, pp. 647-787; Guðmundur Þorláksson: Person- og tilnavne, pp 788-816; Kr. Kålund: Sted- og folkenavne, pp. 817-851; K. G. Bemærkninger til Njála II., pp 852-1019; Trykfeil i Njála I., pp. 1020-1021. A special index was afterwards compiled by Finnur Jónsson: Register til Njála andet bind og K. Gíslason's andre afhandlinger, udg. af det kgl. nord. Oldskriftselskab. Kobenhavn 1896. 8°. pp. 40 (*Rev.* Deut. Lit. Zeit. 1897. coll. 992-993, by A. Heusler). *Review* (of the text edition and vol. i.): Tímarit h. Ísl. Bókmentafél. 1882. III. pp. 131-136, by Janus Jónsson.—Selections from Njála were printed in Konr. Gíslason's Fire og fyrretyve Pröver. Kjobenhavn 1860. pp. 510-525.

Udvalgte stykker af Njála til skolebrug. Ved B. Hoff og J. Hoffory. Köbenhavn 1877. (Oldislandske læsestykker til skolebrug *etc.* [II.]). 8°. pp. (6)+42.

Udvalgte stykker af Njáls saga udg. af V. Levy. København 1893. 8°. pp. (4)+58.

These two works with notes for the use of schools

Njáls saga. Búið hefir til prentunar Vald. Ásmundarson. Reykjavík 1894. (Íslendinga sögur. 10.) 8°. pp. viii+484.

DANISH.—† Oversættelse af en Deel af Niala Saga, ved Jacob Aall. *In* Saga, et Fjerdingaars Skrift udg. af J. St. Munch. Christiania 1819. II. pp. 1-138.

De ulige Hustruer eller Gunnars og Nials Endeligt.—Kaare Solmundsen eller Blodhævneren. Efter Brennunials-Saga. *Forms* I. Bind *of* Nordiske Fortællinger ved K. L. Rahbek. Kiöbenhavn 1819. 8°. pp. (6)+398+(2).

Review: † Dansk Litteratur-Tidende. 1820. No. 22.

Fortælling om Njal og hans Sönner. *Forms* III. Bind *of* Historiske Fortællinger om Islændernes Færd hjemme og ude, ved N. M. Petersen. Kjöbenhavn 1841. 8°. pp. 388.

Njals Saga eller Fortællingen om Njal og hans sönner. Efter det islandske Grundskrift ved N. M. Petersen. 2. Udgave. Köbenhavn 1862. (Historiske Fortællinger . . . II. Bind). 8°. pp. (2)+360.

Nials Saga eller Fortælling om Nial og hans Sönner. Efter det isl. Grundskr. ved N. M. Petersen. 3. Udgave ved Verner Dahlerup og F. Jónsson. Versene ved Olaf Hansen. Köbenhavn 1901. 8°. pp. (2)+291.

A specimen of Petersen's version was published in Dansk Minerva. Dec. 1818 VII. pp 518-548 (Pröve af en Oversættelse af Niáls-Saga). —An extract from this translation is L. Varming's article: Christendommens Indförelse paa Island, in Folkekalender for Danmark 1860. pp. 59-71, with wdct.

6

Nials Saga, gjenfortalt af H. H. Lefolii. Odense 1863. 8°. pp. (4)+256.

Njaals Saga oversat af Karl L. Sommerfelt. Udg. af Selskabet for Folkeoplysningens Fremme. 2det Tillægshefte til Folkevennen, 20. Aarg. 1871. Kristiania 1871. 8°. pp. vi+(2)+334 +(2), 2 *maps*.

Njaal og Gunnar. Af Njaals saga (Efter K. Sommerfeldts oversættelse). *In* Nordahl Rolfsen's Vore Fædres Liv. Bergen 1888. pp. 26+-360.—*2. edition.* Kristiania 1898. pp. 266–372, 10 *illustr* (*by* A. Bloch).

ENGLISH.—The Story of Burnt Njal or Life in Iceland at the end of the tenth century. From the Icelandic of the Njals Saga. By George Webbe Dasent. I.-II. Edinburgh 1861. 8°. pp. xxx+cciv+256, xiii+507, 5 *maps*, 4 *pls*.

> Vol. i. has a preface and a long introduction; the appendix to vol. ii. contains: The Vikings, pp. 351-377, Queen Gunnhillda, pp. 377-396; Money and currency in the tenth century, pp. 396-416. The plates and plans are by Sigurður Guðmundsson. *Reviews:* Antiqu. Tidsskr. 1858-60. pp. 224-233, by Grímur Thomsen;—Ný félagsrit. 1861. XXI pp. 128-136, by Guðbr. Vigfússon;—Brit. Quart. Rev. 1861. XXXIV. pp 323-349 (reprinted in The Eclectic Mag. 1862. LV. pp. 11-20, 167-173);—The Edinb. Rev. 1861. CXIV. pp. 425-455;—Macmillan's Mag. 1861 IV. pp 294-305;—The Quart. Rev. 1861. CXI. pp. 115-147, by R. J. King (afterwards embodied in his Sketches and Studies, descriptive and historical, London 1874, pp. 147-196, with the heading: The Change of Faith in Iceland A. D. 1000);—The Athenæum. Apr. 27. 1861. pp. 556-558;—Germania. 1862. VII. pp. 242-247, by K. Maurer; —†Lond. Quart. Rev. 1871. XXXVI. pp. 35-65.

> Burnt Njal. [*An adaptation by* E. H. Jones] *In* Tales of the Teutonic Lands, by G. W. Cox and E. H. Jones. London 1872. pp. 346-388.— This was later embodied in the 2. ed. of the authors's Popular Romances of the Middle Ages, †London 1880, and in the American edition, New York 1880. pp. 474-505

The Story of Burnt Njal. From the Icelandic of the Njals Saga. By the late Sir George Webbe Dasent. With a Prefatory Note, and the Introduction, abridged, from the original edition of 1861. London 1900. 8°. pp. xlvi+333, *frontisp.*— *American edition.* New York 1900.

> Edited by E. V. Lucas. The frontispiece (Gunnar refuses to leave home) by Geo. Morrow.

Heroes of Iceland. Adapted from Dasent's translation of "The Story of Burnt Njal," the Great Icelandic Saga. With new preface, introduction and notes by Allen French. Illustrated by E. W. D. Hamilton. Boston 1905. 8°. pp. xlvi+297, 4 *pls.*, *map.*—† *English edition.* London 1905.

> *Review.* Saga-Book of the Viking Club. 1906. IV. 2. pp. 476-77, by A. F. Major.

The Story of Burnt Njal, the great Icelaudic Tribune, Jurist and Counsellor. Translated from the Njals saga by the late Sir George Webbe Dasent. With Editor's Prefatory Note and Author's [*sic*] Introduction. Rasmus B. Anderson, editor in chief. J. W. Buel, managing editor. Published by the Norræna Society, London Stockholm Copenhagen Berlin New York. 1906. 8°. pp. xl+311, 4 *pls*.

Forms a vol. of a series called : "Norræna. The History and Romance of Northern Europe. A Library of Supreme Classics printed in complete form. Viking edition. 1906." (*Cf.* The Athenæum. Oct 5. 1907. p. 405). This edition is said to be printed in numbered sets of 650 copies, but there are other sets called † "Saxo edition "—This edition is a mere reprint of Lucas's edition, even his preface is included, but his name is nowhere mentioned. The illustrations have no connection whatever with the text ; the last of them entitled "Funeral of Kol Thorstein's son, by Henry Semiradsky," is actually a reproduction of Hendrik Siemiradzky's gorgeous painting (now in Moscow) representing the cremation of a Russian chieftain in the 10th century from the description of Ibn Fadhlan (*cf.* Kunst-Chronik. 1884. XIX col. 382)

Stories from the Saga of "Burnt Njál." Part I. The Story of Gunnar. By ;Beatrice E. Clay. London 1907. 8°. pp. 187, *illustr*.

Adaptation from Dasent's version. *Review :* The Contemp. Rev. 1907. CXII. Lit. Supplem. 2 pp. 18-19.

FRENCH.—Gunnar et Nial. Scènes et mœurs de la vieille Islande par Jules Gourdault. Tours 1886. 8°. pp. 240, *illustr*. A paraphrase.

La saga de Nial traduite par Rodolphe Dareste. Paris 1896. (Annales du Musée Guimet.—Bibliothèque de Vulgarisation). 8°. pp. (4)+xiii+358+(2).

Review : Nouvelle revue histor. de droit franç. et étranger. 1897. XXI. pp. 326-338, b L. de Valroger.

GERMAN.—Die Nialssaga. Nach der dänischen Wiedergabe von H. Lefolii. Uebersetzt von J. Claussen. Leipzig 1878. 8°. pp. vii+223.

Review : Jenaer Literaturzeit. 1878. pp. 658—659, by K. Maurer.

Eine altisländische Brandlegung, von Bernhard Döring. Leipzig 1878. 4°. pp. (2)+20. (Program des Nicolaigymnasiums zu Leipzig). *Chap.* 124-132.

Die Geschichte Gunnars von Hlidarende und seines Freundes Njal. *In* Arthur Bonus's Isländerbuch. München 1907. II. pp. 27-145.

Some of these extracts had previously appeared in † Die Frau, June 1906, and in † Die Gegenwart, May 1906.

Extracts from the saga translated from Dasent's English version by A. E. Wollheim da Fonseca, in his Die National-Literatur der Skandinavier. Berlin 1875. I. pp. 299-315.

LATIN.—Nials-saga. Historia Niali et filiorum, latine reddita, cum adjecta chronologia, variis textus islandici lectionibus, earumque crisi, nec non glossario et indice rerum ac locorum. Accessere specimina scripturæ codicum membraneorum tabulis æneis incisa. Havniæ, sumtibus P. F. Suhmii et Legati Arna-Magnæani, 1809. 4°. pp. xxxii+872, 3 *facsims.*

The translation is by Jón Johnsonius. The printing was begun in 1791 at the expense of Suhm, and was nearly finished in 1796, when Johnsonius returned to Iceland ; it was then discontinued and the book was first issued in 1809 under the auspices of the Arna-Magnæan Commission. The preface is by Skúli Thorlacius (the description of the codices is by Johnsonius) ; the glossary (pp. 629-832) is by Guðmundur Magnússon and Johnsonius. *Reviews :* Kjöbenhavnske lærde Efterretn. 1810. pp. 161-169, by P. E. Müller ;—Götting. Anz. 1812. pp. 1017-27 (*cf.* Dansk Litteratur-Tid. 1812. pp. 495-496).

NORWEGIAN.—Njaala elder Soga um Njaal Torgeirsson og sönerne hans. Umsett fraa gamalnorsk av Olav Aasmundstad. Utgjevi av Det norske Samlaget. Kristiania 1896. (Tillegsbok til "Syn og Segn" Nr. 6. 1896 og 1897). 8°. pp. 340.

Published in 2 pts., the latter bearing the date of 1897.

SWEDISH.—Om Njål och hans söner. (Småskrifter för folket utg. af Arthur Hazelius. 3.) 2. upplagan. Stockholm 1879. 8°. pp. 24.—† *1. ed.* Stockholm 1870. 8°. pp. 24.

An epitome of the latter half of the saga.

Nials Saga från fornisländskan af A. U. Bååth. Med ett tillägg: Darrads-sången. Stockholm 1879. (Isländska sagor i svensk bearbetning för allmän läsning). 8°. pp. viii+356+(2).

Prof på en metrisk öfversättning till svenska af Nialssagans visor i dróttkvætt (och hrynhenda), af L. Fr. Leffler. *In* Arkiv f. nord. filol. 1882. I. pp. 192-196.

Njals saga *In* A. Ekermann's Från Nordens Forntid. Stockholm 1895. pp. 266-339 ; an abstract with 4 illustrations by Jenny Nyström-Stoopendaal.

Njals saga *In* Hedda Anderson's Nordiska sagor. Stockholm 1896. II. pp. 29-73 ; an abstract with 4 illustrations by J. Nyström-Stoopendaal.

Ur Njals saga. *In* R. Steffen's Isländsk och fornsvensk litteratur i urval. Stockholm 1905. pp. 97-117. (11 *chapters*).

The "Darraðarljóð" in chap. 158 of Njála was first published with Latin version in Th. Bartholin's Antiquit. Danic., 1689, 4°. pp. 617-624, and reprinted in Th. Torfæus's Orcades, 1697 (1715), fol. pp. 36-38. Translated into English by Thomas Gray (1761), and published under the title of "The fatal Sisters" in his poems, † Glasgow 1768 (often reprinted; Gosse's edition of Gray's works, 1884. I. pp. 51-58; *cf.* Walpole's Letters ed. by Cunningham, London 1840. VI pp. 338-339, from which it appears that William Mason (1724-97) about 1776 made a drawing illustrative of the poem); Gray's poem was translated into German by C. F. Weisse in his † Von den Barden, Leipzig 1770. Other German versions are by J. G. v Herder in his Volkslieder, Leipzig 1779, II pp. 210-212 (Die Todesgöttinnen), and by F. D. Gräter in Nordische Blumen, Leipzig 1789, pp. 271-277, reproduced in his Schriften, Heidelberg 1809, I. pp. 217-224 (Die Walkyriengesang). A Danish translation by B. C. Sandvig in his Danske Sange af det ældste Tidsrum, Kiöbenhavn 1779, pp. 98-102 (Krigs Sang). Text and English prose rendering in Corpus poeticum boreale. 1883. I pp. 281-283, 553-556.

Bååth, A. U.   Studier öfver kompositionen i några islandska ättsagor. Lund 1885. pp. 89-160.

Baden, Torkil.   Nials Saga, den bedste af alle Sagaer, dröftet. Kiöbenhavn 1821. 8°. pp. 32.   (*A polemical pamphlet*).

Bergmann, Friðrik J.   Gunnar á Hlíðarenda.   *In his* Vafurlogar. Winnipeg 1906 pp. 1-72.

Bugge, Sophus.   Norsk Sagafortælling og Sagaskrivning i Irland.   1. Hefte. Kristiania 1901. (Tillæg til [Norsk] Historisk Tidsskrift). 8°. pp. 80. The 4th section treats of Den islandske Brians Saga, pp. 52-78.

Finsen, Vilhjálmur.   Om den oprindelige Ordning af nogle af den islandske Fristats Institutioner.   Kjöbenhavn 1888 4°. pp 98-131

Friðriksson, Halldór Kr.   Skýringar yfir tvær vísur í Víga-Glúms sögu og eina í Njáls sögu. *In* Tímarit h. ísl. Bókmentafél. 1882. III. pp. 190-208.

Fritzner, Joh.   Om Anvendelsen af Jón í Formulaer til dermed at betegne en Mandsperson, som endnu ikke har faaet noget Egennavn eller som man ikke kan navngive.   *In* Arkiv f. nord. filol. 1886. III. pp. 320-329 *Cf.* Forhandl. paa det tredje nordiske Filologmode. 1886. pp. liv-lv

Geffroy, A.   Les sagas islandaises. La saga de Nial.   *In* Revue des deux mondes. 1875. XLV année. III. per. II t. pp. 112-140

Gering, Hugo   Zum Clermonter runenkästchen (Frank's casket).   *In* Zeitschr. f. deut Philol. 1901. XXXIII. pp 140-141, 287 Relating to chap 77   *Cf.* Corpus poet. boreale. II. pp. 504-505 (Gunnar and Egil the Archer).

Goetz, Wilh.   Die Nialssaga ein Epos und das germanische Heidenthum in seinen Ausklängen im Norden. Vortrag. Berlin 1885. (Samml. gemeinverständl. Vorträge hgg von Virchow und Holtzendorff. Heft 459). 8°. pp. 32. *Review:* Literaturbl. f. g u. r. Philol. 1885, col. 450, by H. S. v. Carolsfeld.

Gunnarsson, Sig.   Örnefni frá Jökulsá í Axarfirði austan að Skeiðará. 8. Njála. *In* Safn til sögu Íslands. 1876. II. pp. 474-476

Hauch, Joh. C.   Indledning til Forelæsninger over Njalssaga og flere med den beslægtede Sagaer. *In his* Afhandlinger og æsthetiske Betragtninger. Kjöbenhavn 1855. pp. 411-467.

Jónsson, Bryn.   Rannsókn í Rangárþingi sumarið 1899. *In* Árbók h. ísl. Fornleifafél. 1900. pp. 1-8.

—— Rannsókn í Rangárþingi sumarið 1901. *Ibid.* 1902. pp. 1-32.

—— Rannsókn á Þórsmörk sumarið 1906. *Ibid.* 1907. pp. 16-22.

Jónsson, Finnur.   Litteratur Historie. II. pp. 224-233, 525-547.

—— Om Njála. *In* Aarb. f. nord. Oldk. og Hist. 1904. pp. 89-166.
Treats of the juridical questions, *cf.* Lehmann and Carolsfeld's book, and Lehmann's reply. *Review:* Eimreiðin. 1907. XIII. pp. 156-157, by Einar Arnórsson.

Lehmann, Karl *and* Hans Schnorr von Carolsfeld. Die Njálssage inbesondere in ihren juristischen Bestandtheilen. Ein kritischer Beitrag zur altnordischen Rechts- und Literaturgeschichte. Berlin 1883. 8°. pp. vi + 234.
Preface by K. Maurer. *Reviews:* Anz. f. deut. Altert. 1884. X. pp. 68-73, by R. Heinzel ;—Literar. Centralbl. 1883. coll. 766-767, by K. Maurer ;—Literaturbl. f. g. u. r. Philol. 1884. coll. 129-131, by O. Brenner ;—†Deut. Lit. Zeit. 1883. Nr. 35, by Ph. Zorn ;—†Nord revy. 1883-84. Nr. 10, by J. Landtmanson ;—The Academy. 1885. XXVII. p. 13, by F. Y. Powell. *See also* S. Vigfússon's article in Árbók h. ísl. Fornleifafél. 1887. pp. 1-37 ; V. Finsen's Den isl. Fristats Institutioner. 1888. pp. 100-105 ; F. Jónsson's Litt. Hist. II. pp. 224-233, and his paper, Om Njála, 1904.

†Lehmann, Karl.   Jurisprudensen i Njála. *In* Tidsskr. f. Retsvidenskab. 1905. XVIII. pp. 183-199.
A reply to F. Jónsson's paper Om Njála, 1904.

Mogk, E.   Das angebliche Sifbild im tempel zu Guðbrandsdalir —Eine Hávamálsvísa in der Njála. *In* P. u. B. Beiträge z. Gesch. d. deut. Spr. u. Lit. 1889. XIV. pp. 90-94.

Müller, P. E.   Sagabibliothek. I. pp. 51-62.
Translated into English by E. Burritt in The American Eclectic. 1841. I. pp. 102-104.

† Ólsen, Björn M.   Et bidrag til spörgsmaalet om jurisprudensen i Njála. *In* Tidsskr. f. Retsvidenskab. 1906. XIX. pp. 245-248.

Pálsson, Pálmi.   Forn leiði fyrir ofan Búland í Skaptafellssýslu, par sem peir Kári bórðust við brennumenn. *In* Árbók h. ísl. Fornleifafél. 1895. pp. 36-42.
An abstract in German (Isländ. Gräber aus der Vorzeit) by M. Lehmann-Filhés in Verhandl. d. Berliner anthropol. Gesellsch. 1896. pp. 28-29.

Sigurðsson, Páll.   Um forn örnefni, goðorðaskipan og fornmenjar í Rangárþingi. *In* Safn til sögu Íslands. 1876. II. pp. 498-557.

Storch, Vilh.   Kemiske og mikroskopiske Undersögelser af et ejendommeligt Stof, fundet ved Udgravninger, foretagne for det islandske Oldsagsselskab (fornleifafélag) af Sigurd Vigfusson paa Bergthorshvol i Island, hvor ifölge den gamle Beretning Njal, hans Hustru og hans Sönner indebrændtes Aar 1011. Kjöbenhavn 1887. 8°. pp. 22, 2 *pls.*

Storch, Vilh. Efnafræðislegar rannsóknir með viðhöfðum sjónauka á einkennilegu efni, fundnu við útgröft þann, er Sigurður Vigfússon framkvæmdi á Bergþórshvoli fyrir hið íslenzka Fornleifafjelag, gerðar fyrir fjelagið af V. Storch. Reykjavík 1887 8° pp. (2)+18, 2 *pls.*

Vigfússon, Guðbr. Um tímatal í Íslendinga sogum. pp. 414-421, 434-436.

Vigfússon, Sig. Rannsóknir í Borgarfirði 1884 (Víg Glúms). *In* Árbók h. ísl. Fornleifafél. 1884-85, pp. 103-106.

—— Rannsókn í Rangárþingi og vestantil í Skaftafellsþingi 1883 og 1885 einkanlega í samanburði við Njáls sögu. *Ibid.* 1887. pp 1-37.

—— Rannsókn í Rangárþingi og vestantil í Skaftafellsþingi 1883 og 1885, og á alþingisstaðnum 1880, svo og í Breiðafirði (síðast rannsakað 1889), alt einkanlega viðkomandi Njálssögu. *Ibid.* 1888-92. pp. 1-34.

—— Rannsóknir sögustaða, sem gerðar voru 1883 um Rangárvöllu og þar í grend, einkanlega í samanburði við Njálssögu. *Ibid.* 1888 92. pp. 35-62.

—— Rannsóknir sögustaða, sem gerðar voru 1885 í Rangárþingi og í Skaftafellsþingi vestanverðu *Ibid* 1888-92 pp. 63-75.

—— Rannsókn í Austfirðingafjórðungi 1890. *Ibid.* 1893. pp. 28-32.

Þorkelsson, Jón. Skýringar á vísum í Njáls sögu. Reykjavík 1870. 8°. pp. 32. (*Program*).

For a few corrective notes see his Skýringar á vísum í Guðmundar sögu Arasonar 1872. p. 38.

Oddaverja þáttr *see* Þorláks saga biskups helga (hin ýngri).

Odds þáttr Ófeigssonar.

C. 1050. In Haralds saga harðráða of the Morkinskinna and Flateyjarbók. *Cf.* Bandamanna saga.

Commentarium anecdotum þáttr af Oddi Ófeigssyni dictum, Islandice et Latine edidit cum præfatione Birgerus Thorlacius. Havniæ 1821. fol. pp. (4)+8. (*University program*).

In Fornmanna sögur. 1831. VI. pp. 377-384.

Fra Oddi Ofeigs syni. *In* Morkinskinna. Christiania 1867. pp. 105-109.

Her segir fra (þui er) Oddr komz. . . *In* Flateyjarbók. Christiania 1868. III. pp. 381-386.

Odds þáttr Ófeigssonar. *In* Fjörutíu Íslendinga þættir. Þórleifr Jónsson gaf út. Reykjavík 1904. pp. 191-198.

DANISH.—Odd Ofeigssöns Thattr, udaf Thorlacii Program [ved K. L. Rahbek]. *In* Hesperus. 1821. IV. pp. 5-16.—*Reprinted in* Nordiske Fortællinger ved K. L. Rahbek. Kiöbenhavn 1821. II. pp. 188-196.

In Oldnordiske Sagaer. 1832. VI. pp. 309-315.

ENGLISH.—An adventure of Odd Úfeigsson with King Harold
Hardradi. *In* The Saga Library, by W. Morris and E.
Magnússon. London 1891. I. pp. 167–175.

LATIN.—B. Thorlacius's *version of* 1821 (*see above*).
Svb. Egilsson's *version in* Scripta historica Islandorum. 1835.
VI. pp. 349–356.

Jónsson, Finnur. Litteratur Historie II. pp. 549–550.
Müller, P. E. Sagabibliothek. III. pp. 351–356.

Ögmundar þáttr dytts ok Gunnars helmings.

C. 994-996. The original þáttr of Ögmundr dyttr was presumably
written about 1200, and is found in a fragmentary state in AM. 564 A,
4° (in the Víga-Glúms saga, among the fragments of the Vatnshyrna-
codex, from c. 1300) ; in the Flateyjarbók, however, the þáttr of Gunnar helmingr, which is of a later date, is added to it.

Pattur af Augmundi Ditt ok Gunnari Helming. *In* Saga Olafs
Tryggvasonar. Skálholt 1689. 4°. II. pp. 115–125.

Frá Ögmundi ditt ok Gunnari helming. *In* Fornmanna sögur
1826. II. pp. 62–78.

In Flateyjarbók. Christiania 1860. I. pp. 332–339.

[*The fragment* AM. 564 A, 4°. *ed. by* Guðm. Þorláksson.] *In*
Íslenzkar fornsögur. Kaupmannahöfn 1880. I. pp. 96–99.

Ögmundar þáttr dytts ok Gunnars helmings. *In* Fjörutíu Íslendinga þættir. Þórleifr Jónsson gaf út. Reykjavík 1904.
pp. 509–524.

DANISH.—Om Ögmund Ditt og Gunnar Helming [*trl. by* C. C.
Rafn]. *In* Oldnordiske Sagaer. 1827. II. pp 56–69.

Ögmund Dyt og Gunnar Helming. *In* Sagaer, fortalte af Brynjolf Snorrason og Kristian Arentzen. Kjöbenhavn 1849. II.
pp. 195–212

Fortælling om Ögmund Dyt. *In* Fortællinger og Sagaer, fortalte
for Börn af H. H. Lefolii. 3. Udg. Kjöbenhavn 1869. I. pp.
253–259.—†1. ed. 1859. †2. ed. 1862.

ENGLISH.—Story of Ogmund Dint. *In* The Saga of King
Olaf Tryggwason, translated by J. Sephton. London 1895.
pp. 251–260.

The Tale of Ogmund Dint and Gunnere Helming. *In* Origines
Islandicæ, by G. Vigfusson and F. Y. Powell. Oxford 1905.
II. pp. 480–486.

LATIN.—De Ögmundo Ditto et Gunnare Bicolore [*trl. by* Svb. Egilsson]. *In* Scripta historica Islandorum. 1828. II. pp. 59–72.

Cf. T. Torfæus's Hist. rer. Norvegic. pars II. 1711. fol. pp. 492-495.

Jónsson, Finnur. Litteratur Historie. II. p. 550.
Müller, P. E. Sagabibliothek. III. pp. 261–269.

Ölkofra þáttr (*or* saga), *or* Þórhalls þáttr ölkofra.

C. 1020. From the first half of the 13th century. In the Möðruvalla-bók (AM. 132 fol.; c. 1350).

Paattur af Aulkofra. *In* Nockrer Marg-Frooder Sögu-Pætter Islendinga, ad Forlage Biörns Marcussonar. Hólar 1756. pp. 34–37.

Krókarefssaga, Gunnars saga Keldugnúpsfífls og Ölkofra þáttr. Kaupmannahöfn 1866 pp. 65–75.

Edited by Þorvaldur Björnsson. *Reviews*. Germania. 1867. XII. pp. 480-482, by K. Maurer;—Þjóðólfur. 1867. XIX pp. 147-148, by Jón Þorkelsson

Olkofra þattr herausgg. von Hugo Gering. Halle a. S. 1880. ("Sonderabdruck aus den 'Beiträgen zur deutschen philologie' 1880." pp. 1–24). 8⁰. pp. 24.

Ölkofra þáttr. *In* Fjörutíu Íslendinga þættir. Þórleifr Jónsson gaf út. Reykjavík 1904 pp. 524–537.

Jónsson, Bryn. Ölkofrastaðir. *In* Árbók h. ísl. Fornleifafél. 1905. p. 46.
Jónsson, Finnur. Litteratur Historie. II. p. 552.
Müller, P. E. Sagabibliothek. I. pp 316–317.
Vigfússon, Guðbr. Um tímatal í Íslendinga sögum. pp. 489–490.

Önundar-brennu saga *see* Guðmundar saga dýra.

Orms þáttr Stórólfssonar *or* Orms þáttr Stórólfssonar ok Ásbjarnar prúða.

An unhistoric tale of an historical person of the 10th century. Written about 1300, found in the Flateyjarbók.

Pattr Orms Storolfs sunar. *In* Saga Olafs Tryggvasonar. Skálholt 1689. 4°. Appendix, pp. 5–19.

Þáttr Orms Stórólfssonar. *In* Fornmanna sögur. 1827. III. pp. 204–228.

Paattr Orms Storolfssunar. *In* Flateyjarbók. Christiania 1860. I. pp. 521–532.

Orms þáttr Stórólfssonar. *In* Fjörutíu Íslendinga þættir. Þórleifr Jónsson gaf út. Reykjavík 1904. pp. 199–222.

DANISH.—Fortælling om Orm Storolfsson [*trl. by* C. C. Rafn].
In Oldnordiske Sagaer. 1827. III. pp. 180–201.

LATIN.—Particula de Ormo Storolvi filio [*trl. by* Svb. Egilsson].
In Scripta historica Islandorum. 1829. III. pp. 201–223.

> The "Ásbjarnarvísur" or the Deathsong of Ásbjörn was first printed
> with Latin version in Th. Bartholin's Antiquit. Danic., Hafniæ 1689,
> 4°. pp. 158–162; translated into German by H. W. von Gerstenberg, in
> Briefe über Merkwürdigkeiten der Litteratur, I. u. 2. Samml. †Schlesw.
> u. Leipzig 1766 (new ed. by A. v. Weilen, Strassb. 1890. pp. 60–61),
> and by J. G von Herder, in Volkslieder, Leipzig 1778, I. pp. 242–246,
> into Danish by B. C. Sandvig, in Danske Sange fra det ældste Tidsrum,
> Kiöbenhavn 1779, pp. 106–109; into English by Wm. Herbert, in
> Select Icelandic Poems, London 1804, I. pp. 52–60 (repr. in his Works,
> London 1842. I. pp. 251–255).

Jónsson, Finnur. Litteratur Historie. II. pp. 763–764.
Müller, P. E. Sagabibliothek. I 353–354.

Ormssona saga.   *See* Svínfellinga saga.

Páls saga biskups.
> Life of Páll Jónsson (b. 1155), bishop of Skálholt from 1195-1211, by
> the same author as Hungrvaka, a contemporary of the bishop.
> Paper-MSS. (AM. 205 fol , etc.)

Hungurvaka . . . Páls biskups saga sive Historia Pauli Episcopi
. . . ex manuscriptis Legati Magnæani, cum interpretatione
Latina, annotationibus . . . Hafniæ 1778. pp. 142–253.
> Edited and translated by Jón Ólafsson. *See* Hungrvaka.

Extract (ch. ix.) in Grönlands hist. Mindesmærker. 1838. II. pp. 762–767.

Páls saga biskups. [*Ed. by* Guðbr. Vigfússon]. *In* Biskupa
sögur. Kaupmannahöfn 1858. I. pp. xxv–xxxiv, 125–148.

Saga Páls Skálaholts biscups oc Hungurvaka, Útgefandi :
Stefán Sveinsson. Winnipeg 1889. pp. 34.
> Reprint of the text of 1778.

Póls saga. *In* Origines Islandicæ, by G. Vigfusson and F. Y.
Powell. Oxford 1905. I. pp. 502–534.
> Icelandic text with English version.

ENGLISH.—Vigfússon *and* Powell's *version in* Orig. Isl. I.

LATIN.—J. Ólafsson's *version in the ed. of* 1778 (*see above*).

Jónsson, Finnur (*bishop*).   Historia Ecclesiastica Islandiæ.   Havniæ 1772.
4°. I. pp. 300–306.
Jónsson, Finnur. Litteratur Historie. II. pp. 567–569.
Müller, P. E. Sagabibliothek. I. p. 188

Rafns saga.   *See* Hrafns saga Sveinbjarnarsonar.

Reykdæla saga *or* Vémundar saga ok Víga-Skútu.

C. 950-990. The names of Reykdæla saga and Vemundar saga are used in the saga, although the latter only applies to the first sixteen chapters. Written about 1200 Vellum-MS., AM. 561. 4° (c. 1400) imperfect; complete in paper-MSS.

Sagan af Vemundi og Vígaskútu. *In* Íslendinga sögur. Kaupmannahöfn 1830. II. pp. 7-8, 229-320.

Edited by Þorgeir Guðmundsson and Þorsteinn Helgason. Also with a special t.-p., *see* Ljósvetninga saga.

Reykdæla saga. *In* Íslenzkar fornsögur. Kaupmannahöfn 1881. II. pp. i-xiii, 1-152.

Critical edition by Finnur Jónsson. Vémundar saga kógurs, ch. i-xvi, Víga Skútu saga, ch. xvii-xxx.

Reykdæla saga. Búið hefir til prentuuar Vald. Ásmundarson. Reykjavík 1896. (Íslendinga sögur. 16.) 8°. pp. vi+(2)+112.

Gunnarsson, Sig Örnefni frá Jökulsá í Axarfirði austan að Skeiðará. 12. Vémundar saga og Víga-Skútu. *In* Safn til sögu Íslands. 1876. II. pp. 481-482.

Jónsson, Bryn. Rannsóknir á Norðurlandi sumarið 1900. *In* Árbók h. ísl. Fornleifafél. 1901. pp. 11-13.

—— Rannsókn í Norðurlandi sumarið 1905. *In* Árbók h. ísl. Fornleifafél. 1906 pp. 8-9, 10, 17-20.

Jónsson, Finnur. Litteratur Historie. II. pp 505-511.

Lehmann-Filhés, M. Isländisches Grab aus dem 10. Jahrhundert. *In* Globus. 1901. LXXX. 4°. pp. 12-13, *illustr.*

Cf. Eimreiðin. 1902. VIII. pp. 74-75, by V. Guðmundsson.

Lotspeich, Claude. Zur Víga-Glúms- und Reykdæla-saga. Inaugural-Dissertation. Leipzig 1903. 8° pp. 45+(3).

Müller, P E Sagabibliothek. I. pp. 264-267.

Vigfússon, Guðbr. Um tímatal í Íslendinga sögum. pp. 399-401.

—— Um nokkrar Íslendingasögur. II. Reykdæla saga. *In* Ný félagsrit. 1861. XXI. pp. 121-122.

Reykdæla saga. *See* Ljósvetninga saga.

Reykdæla þáttr.

C. 1001-1002. Originally an independent þáttr (written in the 13th century), but now embodied in the Ljósvetninga saga (*q. v.*)

Sighvats þáttr skálds.

C. 1015-1045. There once existed a separate saga of Sighvatr Þórðarson, which is now lost. This þáttr consists of chapters gathered from the sagas of King Olaf the Saint: the larger saga by Snorri Sturluson (Saga Ólafs konungs ens helga. Christiania 1853), and the legendary saga of the 12th century (Ólafs saga hins helga. Christiania 1849); from Ólafs saga helga and Magnús saga góða in Snorri Sturluson's Heimskringla (see especially Finnur Jónsson's edition, Kóbenhavn 1893-1901. II.-III.), and of the Flateyjarbók (Christiania 1862-68. II.-III.). *Cf. also* Fornmanna sögur IV.-VI.; Oldnordiske Sagaer IV.-VI.; Scripta historica Islandorum IV.-VI.; Fagrskinna (Christiania 1847 and Kobenhavn 1902-03).

Sighvatz saga.   *In* An Icelandic Prose Reader, by G. Vigfusson
and F. Y. Powell.   Oxford 1897. pp. 111–114, 373–374.
Only a few selections considered by the editors to be from the original
saga.

Sighvats þáttr skálds.   *In* Fjórutíu Íslendinga þættir.   Þórleifr
Jónsson gaf út.   Reykjavík 1904. pp. 223–250.
The þáttr is followed by Sighvatr's poems, pp. 250–277.
For the poems by Sighvatr see : Corpus poeticum boreale. 1883. II. pp.
118–150 (with English prose version) ; Konr. Gíslason's Udvalg af old-
nord. Skjaldekvad, Kjöbenhavn 1893, pp 35–42, 169–213 ; Th Wisén's
Carmina norræna, Lund 1886, I. pp 38–43. Swedish version of the
Bersöglisvísur : Sighvat Tordssöns dikt "Fria ord" af A. U Bååth.
Göteborg 1898 (Särtryck ur Göteborg högskolans festskrift tillägnad
Konsul O. Ekman). 8°. pp (2)+9. For other special editions see
below (under Kyhlberg, Ternström and Vendell).

Bugge, Sophus.   Sagnet om hvorledes Sigvat Tordssón blev Skjald.   *In*
Arkiv f nord. filol. 1897. XIII. pp. 209–211.

Flo, R J.   Sigvat skald og hans samtid.   *In* Syn og segn. 1902. VIII. pp.
178–190.

Jónsson, Finnur.   Litteratur Historie.   I. pp. 590–612.

——— Sigvat skjald Tordsson   Et livsbillede.   Köbenhavn 1901. (Studier
fra Sprog- og Oldtidsforskning udg af det philol.-hist. Samfund. Nr.
49). 8°. pp 35.
Danish metrical translation of the Bersoglisvísur (Frimodighedskvadet)
by Olaf Hansen, pp. 31–35.

Kyhlberg. O.   Om skalden Sighvat Thordsson samt tolkning af hans
Vestrvíkingar- och Nesja-vísur. Academisk afhandling. Lund 1868. 8°.
pp (4)+63.
Icelandic text of the poems with Swedish version.

Lorentsen, G.   Sighvat skjald.   *In* Nordisk månedskrift for folkelig og
kristelig oplysning.   Odense 1878 pp. 249–289.

Muller, P E.   En norsk Hofdigters Levnet fra det ellevte Aarhundrede.
In Nyt Aftenblad.   Kjöbenhavn 1824. Nr. 8. 4°. pp. 57–63.

Ólsen, Bjorn M.   Ströbemærkninger til norske og islandske skjaldedigte.
V. Sighvats sidste vers.   *In* Arkiv. f. nord. filol. 1902. XVIII. pp. 203–
204

Ternström, Alfred.   Om skalden Sighvat Thordsson samt tolkning af hans
Austrfararvísur, Vestrfararvísur och Knútsdrápa Akademisk afhand-
ling Lund 1871 8°. pp. (2)+59+(3).
Icelandic text of the poems with Swedish version.

Vendell, Herman A.   Om skalden Sighvat Tordsson samt tolkning af
hans Flokkr um fall Erlings och Bersöglisvísur. Akademisk afhandling Helsingfors 1879. 8°. pp x+100
Icelandic text of the poems with Swedish version.

Skáld-Helga saga.

C. 1000–1050. A lost saga the subject of which is known from the
Skáld-Helga rímur of the 14th century (AM. 604 F, 4°., vellum of

the 16th cent) *Cf.* F. Jónsson's Litteratur Historie. I. pp. 504, III. pp. 41-42.

Skjald-Helge, Grönlands Laugmand, et historiskt Mindedigt. *In* Grönlands historiske Mindesmærker. Kjöbenhavn 1838. I. pp. 419-575

Skáldhelgarímur. *In* Rímnasafn. Samling af de ældste islandske rimer. Udg. for Samf. til udg. af gl. nord. litt. ved Finnur Jónsson. Köbenhavn 1905-1906. pp. 105-165.

Sagan af Skáld-Helga. Reykjavík 1897. 8°. pp. 41.—This saga is a recent composition from the rímur.

Sneglu-Halla þáttr *or* Grautar-Halla þáttr.

C. 1050. Written in the earlier part of the 13th century; in the Morkinskinna, and somewhat longer in the Flateyjarbók.

In Fornmanna sögur. 1831. VI. pp. 360-377.

Þáttr af Sneglu- eðr Grautar-Halla. *In* Sex sögu-þættir, sem Jón Þorkelsson hefir gefið út. Reykjavík 1855. pp. vii-xiii, 18-43.—2. prentun (*anastatic*). Kaupmannahöfn 1895. Edited from a paper-codex.

Fra Sneglohalla. *In* Morkinskinna. Christiania 1867. pp. 93-101.

(Þattr Snegluhalla). *In* Flateyjarbók. Christiania 1868. III. pp. 415-428.

Træk af livet ved kong Haralds hird. *In* Oldnordiske læsestykker udg. af V. Levy. Köbenhavn 1888. III. pp. 32-47, 74-80.

Sneglu-Halla þáttr. *In* Fjörutíu Íslendinga þættir. Þórleifr Jónsson gaf út. Reykjavík 1904. pp. 278-304.

This and the edition of 1855 give the longer recension.

DANISH.—Sneglu-Halle's Reiser og Hændelser. Oversatte af det Islandske ved Finn Magnusen. *In* Det Skandinaviske Selskabs Skrifter. Kjöbenhavn 1820. XVII. pp. 31-74.— †*Also separate reprint.*

The longer recension.

Sneglu-Halle. En Fortælling, oversat efter islandske Håndskrifter, ved Finn Magnusen. *In* Tidsskrift f. nord. Oldkyndighed. Kjöbenhavn 1829. II. pp. 27-53.—†*Also separately printed.* Kjöbenhavn 1826.

In Oldnordiske Sagaer. 1832. VI. pp. 294-304.

Snegluhalle. *In* Sagaer, fortalte af Brynjolf Snorrason og Kristian Arentzen. Kjöbenhavn 1850. III. pp. 135-154.

GERMAN.—Die Geschichte eines Skaldenverses. *In* Arthur Bonus's Isländerbuch. München 1907. II. pp. 287-296.

An extract.

LATIN.—Svb. Egilsson's *version in* Scripta historica Islandorum.
1835. VI. pp. 333-349.
Cf. T. Torfæus's Hist. rer. Norvegic. pars III. 1711. fol. 335-337.

Jónsson, Finnur. Litteratur Historie. I. p. 635-637, II. pp. 552-553.
Müller, P. E. Sagabibliothek III. pp 337-351.

Sörla þáttr Brodd-Helgasonar.
C. 1000. An independent tale which is now embodied in the Ljósvetninga saga (*q. v.*).

Spesar þáttr *or* Þorsteins þáttr drómundar.
Unhistorical; forms the last seventeen chapters (89-95) of the Grettis
saga (*q. v*); it was probably written in the 14th cent. and is possibly
by the same author as the saga.
Jónsson, Finnur. Litteratur Historie. III. pp. 82-83.

Stefnis þáttr Þorgilssonar.
C. 996-1000. In Ólafs saga Tryggvasonar of the Flateyjarbók   *Cf.*
F. Jónsson's Litteratur Historie. I. p. 480.
Pattur Stefnis Þorgils sunar.   *In* Saga Olafs Tryggvasonar.
Skálholt 1689. 4°. II. pp. 61-63, 307-308.
In Fornmanna sögur. 1825-27. I. pp. 276, 283-286, II. p. 118,
III. pp. 19-20.
Paattr Stefnis Þorgilssunar.   *In* Flateyjarbók. Christiania 1860.
I. pp. 285-287, 363, 500.
Stefnis þáttr Þorgilssonar.   *In* Fjörutíu Íslendinga þættir.
Þórleifr Jónsson gaf út.   Reykjavík 1904. pp. 305-310.

DANISH.—C. C. Rafn's *version in* Oldnordiske Sagaer. 1826-27.
I. pp. 248-249, 255-258, II. p. 105, III. p. 17.

ENGLISH.—*In* The Saga of King Olaf Tryggwason, translated
by J. Sephton. London 1895. pp. 188, 193-195, 288, 441.

LATIN.—Svb. Egilsson's *version in* Scripta historica Islandorum.
1828-1829. I. pp. 299-300, 306-309, II. p. 109, III. p. 23.

Steins þáttr Skaptasonar.
C. 1025-1030. In the Flateyjarbók, but the story is also told in
the larger Ólafs saga helga by Snorri Sturluson (Christiania 1853)
and in his Heimskringla; see also the legendary saga of King Olaf
(Christiania 1849)   *Cf.* F. Jónsson's Litteratur Historie. I. p. 579.
In Fornmanna sögur. 1829-30. IV. pp. 287, 313-314, 318-325,
V. pp. 180-181.
Paattr Steins Skaptasunar.   *In* Flateyjarbok. Christiania 1862.
II. pp. 261-267.

Steins þáttr Skaftasonar   *In* Fjörutíu Íslendinga þættir.   Þórleifr Jónsson gaf út. Reykjavík 1904. pp. 311–322.

DANISH.—*In* Oldnordiske Sagaer. 1831. IV. pp. 262, 285–287,
288–296, V. pp. 164–165.

LATIN.—Svb. Egilsson's *version in* Scripta historica Islandorum.
1833. IV. pp. 266, 288–289, 291–298, V. pp. 185–186.
Cf. T. Torfæus's Hist. rer Norveg pars III. 1711. fol pp. 132–135.

Stjörnu-Odda draumr.
A legend from the 12th century ; probably penned about 1300.
Stiörnu Odda draumr.   *In* Rymbegla, edidit Stephanus Biörn-
sen. Hafniæ 1780 (*also a title-edition of* 1801). 4°. pp. 1–32.
Text with Latin version. The second poem is omitted.
Stjörnu-Odda draumr.   *In* Bárðar saga Snæfellsáss . . . Draum-
vitranir . . . ved Guðbrandr Vigfússon.   Kjöbenhavn 1860.
pp. 106–123, 166–169.

DANISH.—G. Vigfússon's *paraphrase in the ed. of* 1860. pp.
166–169.

LATIN.—St. Björnsson's *version in the* Rímbegla (*see above*).

SWEDISH.—Stjörnu-Odda draumr.   Akademisk afhandling af
Karl Sidenbladh.   Uppsala 1866. 8°. pp. (2)+32.

Jónsson, Finnur. Litteratur Historie. II. pp. 183, 765.

Stúfs þáttr blinda *or* Stúfs þáttr skálds Kattarsonar.
C 1050. Written in the 13th century. In the Hulda (AM. 66 fol.,
vellum of the 14th cent.), the Morkinskinna and the Flateyjarbók.
In Fornmanna sögur. 1831. VI. pp. 389–393.

Af Haraldi og Stúf.   *In* Fire og fyrretyve Pröver af oldnordisk Sprog og Literatur udg. af Konr. Gíslason.   Kjöbenhavn
1860 pp. 489–491.

Fra Stuf blinda.   *In* Morkinskinna. Christiania 1867. pp. 104–
105.

Stufr h(inn blindi).   *In* Flateyjarbók. Christiania 1868. III.
pp. 379–381.

Fra Stuf blinda.   *In* Analecta norræna herausgg. von Theodor
Möbius. Leipzig 1877. pp. 68–71.

Stúfs þáttr blinda.   *In* Fjörutíu Íslendinga þættir. Þórleifr
Jónsson gaf út. Reykjavík 1904. pp. 323–327.
Followed by the fragments of Stúfsdrápa (an obituary poem on King
Haraldr), pp. 327–329.—*Cf.* Corpus poeticum boreale. 1883. II. pp. 222–
223.

DANISH.—Samtale holden i Midten af det ellevte Aarhundrede imellem den norske Konge Harald Hardraade og Skalden Stuf, oversat af det Oldskandinaviske ved P. E. Müller. *In* Athene. Febr. 1814 (Kiöbenhavn). pp. 93–102. *In* Oldnordiske Sagaer. 1832. VI. pp. 319–323.

ENGLISH.—*In* Corpus poeticum boreale, by G. Vigfusson and F. Y. Powell. Oxford 1883. II. pp. 221–222.

LATIN.—Svb. Egilsson's *version in* Scripta historica Islandorum. 1835. VI. pp. 361–364.

Jónsson, Finnur. Litteratur Historie. I. pp. 633-634, II. p 548.
Müller, P. F. Sagabibliothek. III. pp. 377-380.

Sturlu saga *or* Heiðarvígs saga.

1148-1183. Life of Sturla Þórðarson of Hvammr (d. 1183), the founder of the Sturlung family. Written shortly after 1200, and existed as an independent saga, but is now embodied in the Sturlunga saga (*q. v.*). The name Heiðarvígs saga is derived from a skirmish which took place 1171.

Jónsson, Finnur. Litteratur Historie. II. pp. 556-558.
Ólsen, Björn M. Um Sturlungu. pp 213-224.

Sturlunga saga.

A collection of sagas relating to the history of Iceland from 1117-1264, put together about 1300 by an unknown person (possibly by Þórðr Narfason, the lawman, or one of his relatives) It consists of the following parts : Geirmundar þáttr heljarskinns (850-900; has no direct connection with the other sagas), Þorgils saga ok Hafliða (1117-1121); Ættartölur ; Sturlu saga (1148-1183); Guðmundar saga biskups góða (prestssaga ; 1161-1202); Guðmundar saga dýra (1184-1200), Hrafns saga Sveinbjarnarsonar (1203-1213); Íslendinga saga Sturlu Þórðarsonar (1183-1242); Þórðar saga kakala (1242-1250); Svínfellinga saga (1248-1252); Þorgils saga skarða (1252-1258), followed by a few chapters of doubtful origin bringing the narrative down to 1264. Besides the sagas mentioned there are also, according to some critics, found in the collection some chapters from a lost saga of Gizurr Þorvaldsson (d. 1268). The principal MSS. are the vellum codices AM. 122 A, fol. (Króksfjarðarbók, from the first half of the 14th cent.), and AM. 122 B, fol. (Reykjarfjarðarbók, from c 1400).

Sturlúnga-Saga edr Islendinga saga hin mikla. Nú útgengin á prent ad tilhlutun hins íslenzka bókmentafélags eptir samanburd hinna merkilegustu handarrita, er fengist gátu. I.–II. bindini. Kaupmannahöfn 1817–1820. 4 *vols.* 4°. pp. (4)+227, (2)+260+(2), (2)+320. (2)+vii+190+(2).

Printed from paper-MSS.; no distinction is made between the sagas forming the collection, the text of vols. i-iii. is divided into 10 þættir (sections) ; vol. iv. (II. 2) contains Árna biskups saga Þorlákssonar (pp. 1-124), chronological table and index of persons (pp. 125-190) by Svb. Egilsson and Gísli Brynjúlfsson sen., who together with S. S. Thorarensen and Þ. Magnússon prepared the text for the press. The

prefaces are by Bjarni Thorsteinsson, president of the Icelandic Literary Society. *Reviews:* Dansk Litteratur-Tidende for 1820. pp. 440-447, by P. E. Müller ;—Götting. Anz. 1819. pp. 1529-30.
Extracts in Grönlands historiske Mindesmærker. 1838 II pp. 779-784 (*cf.* I. pp. 65-70), and in Antiquités Russes. 1852. fol. II. pp. 350-355.

Sturlunga Saga including the Islendinga Saga of Lawman Sturla Thordsson and other works, edited with prolegomena, appendices, tables, indices, and maps by Gudbrand Vigfusson. Vol. I.–II. Oxford 1878. 8°. pp. ccxix+(2)+409, (4)+516+ (2), 2 *maps*.

Edited from MSS. on vellum and paper, the division of the text being the editor's work. *Contents: vol i.:* preface; tbl. of contents; Prolegomena, pp. xv-ccxiv; facsimiles, pp. ccxvii-ccxix; Þáttr af Geirmundi heljarskinn, pp. 1-6; Þorgils saga ok Hafliða, pp. 7-39; Sturlu saga, pp. 40-85; the compiler's preface, p. 86; Guðmundar saga góða (Prestz-saga), pp 87-125; Guðmundar saga dýra, pp. 126-174; Hrafns saga ok Þorvaldz, pp. 175-187; Íslendinga saga by Sturla Þórðarson, pp. 189-409 (Ættartölur, pp 189-194); *vol. ii.:* Íslendinga saga (continued), pp. 1-274 (Þórðar saga kakala, pp. 1-82; Svínfellinga saga or Ormssona saga, pp. 83-103; Þorgils saga skarða, pp. 104-256); Appendices 1. Hrafns saga, pp. 275-311, 2 Árons saga, pp. 312-347; 3. Íslenzkir annálar (Annales regii), pp. 348-391; 4. Ártíðaskrá or Obituarium, pp. 392-396; 5. Sundries (From Hákonar saga, chap. 311; Máldagabréf of 1262; Oath of 1262; Snorri's genealogy; A charter of 1226-1230), pp. 397-400; Indices (of places, persons, things, families, seasons, events, literary works etc., nicknames), pp. 401-468, List of logsogumenn, archbishops, and bishops, pp. 469 471; Obituary, pp. 472-473; Fjords, p. 474; Eruptions and earthquakes in the 14th and 15th cent., pp. 475-477; Emendations, pp. 478-480; Genealogies (of the 12th and 13th cent.), pp. 481-503; List of abbots in Iceland, p. 504; On the site of the Lögberg (with map), pp. 505-512; Addenda, emendations etc., pp. 513-516, (1)-(2).—*Reviews:* Tímarit h. Ísl. Bókmentafél. 1880. I. pp. 5-32, by Ben. Gröndal,—The Academy. 1879. XV pp. 518-519, by E. Gosse, (*cf.* The Academy. 1877. XII pp 514, by A. H. Sayce);—Jahresber d. germ. Philol. 1879. pp. 82-84,—The Nation (N Y.). 1880. XXX. pp. 63-64, by W. Fiske.—*Cf.* Brim's article of 1892 noted below.

Sturlunga saga efter membranen Króksfjarðarbók udfyldt efter Reykjarfjarðarbók udg. af det kongelige nordiske Oldskrift-Selskab. I. bind. Köbenhavn og Kristiania 1906. 8°. pp. (4) +576.

Critical edition by Kr. Kålund. In progress. Covertitle given. *Reviews:* Skírnir. 1906. LXXX pp. 361-367, by B. M Ólsen ;—Literar. Centralbl. 1907. col. 1025, by E. Mogk.

DANISH.—Sturlunga saga i dansk oversættelse ved Kr. Kålund, versene ved Olaf Hansen. Udg. af det kongelige nordiske Oldskriftselskab. I.–II. bind. Köbenhavn og Kristiania 1904. 8°. pp. xv+362, (2)+365+(3), *map*.

Contents: vol. i.: preface; Fortællingen om Geirmund Helskind, pp. 1-6; Slægtregistre, pp. 6-7; Torgils og Havlides saga, pp. 8-52;

Slægtregistre, pp. 52-56; Hvam-Sturlas saga, pp. 57-115; Sagaerne om Gudmund den gode som præst og Gudmund dyre, pp. 116-209; Islændinge saga, pp. 210-512; *vol, ii.:* Tord kakales saga, pp. 1-96; Svinfellinge +aga, pp. 97-120; Gi-surs saga, pp. 121-124; Torgils skardes saga, pp. 125-304, Sturlunga saga, pp. 305-336; Navnefortegnelse, pp. 337-365; Kort over altingsstedet på Tingvold, p. (1); Stamtavle over Sturlunga-slægtens vigtigste medlemmer, pp. (2)-(3). *Review:* Arkiv. f. nord. filol. 1906. XXII. pp. 292-299, by Emil Olson.

Boesen, J. E. Snorre Sturlesön. Et nordisk tidsbillede fra det 13de hundredår. Kòbenhavn 1879. pp. (4)+154+(4).

Brím, Eggert Ó. Athuganir og leiðréttingar við Sturlunga sögu. *In* Arkiv f. nord. filol. 1892. VIII. pp 323-367.

—— Athuganir við fornættir, er koma fyrir í Sturlunga-sögu. *In* Safn til sögu Íslands. 1899. III. pp. 511-568.

Jónsson, Bryn. Rannsóknir í Norðurlandi sumarið 1900. *In* Árbók h. ísl. Fornleifafél. 1901. pp. 23-25.

Jónsson, Finnur. Litteratur Historie. II. pp. 553-558, 561-564, 572-575, 717-743, 765-768.

Jónsson, Jón (*of* Hlíð) Örnefni í Snóksdalssókn. *In* Safn til sögu Íslands. 1876. II. pp. 319-324.

Jónsson, Þorleifur. Örnefni nokkur úr Breiðafjarðardölum. *Ibid.* 1876. II pp 558-577.

Ker. W. P. Sturla the Historian. Oxford 1906. (The Romanes Lecture 1906). 8°. pp. 24. *Reviews.* The Times, Liter. Supplem., 1907. pp. 52-53 ,—Saga-Book of the Viking Club. 1907. V. 1 p 194, by A F Major

Kålund, Kr. Om håndskrifterne af Sturlunga saga og dennes enkelte bestanddele. *In* Aarb. f. nord. Oldk. og Hist. 1901. pp. 259-300

Melsteð, Bogi Th. Utanstefnur og erindisrekar útlendra þjóðhöfðingja á fyrri hluta Sturlungaaldar 1200-1239. *In* Tímarit h ísl. Bókmentafél. 1899. XX. pp. 102-155 —Síðari hlutinn 1239-1264. *Ibid.* 1900. XXI. pp. 57-131.—*Also separate reprints.* [Reykjavík 1899-1900]. 8°.

Müller, P. E. Sagabibliothek. I. pp. 243-249.

Munch, P. A. Det norske Folks Historie. Christiania 1857-58. III. pp. 781-881, IV. 1. pp. 222-376.

—— Bryllupet og Branden paa Flugumyre Et Optrin af Borgerkrigene paa Island i det 13de Aarhundrede *In* Norsk Folkekalender for 1840. pp. 111-120, wdct. (*by* Flintóe).

Ólsen, Björn M Ávellinga goðorð. *In* Tímarit h. ísl. Bókmentafél 1881. II. pp. 1-31.

—— Um Sturlungu. *In* Safn til sögu Íslands. 1897 III pp. 193-510.— *Also separate reprint.* Kaupmannahöfn [1897]. 8°. *Reviews:* Þjóðólfur 1899. LI. pp. 33-34, by Matth. Jochumsson;— Jahresber. f. germ. Philol. 1897. p. 195, by A. Gebhardt.

Pétursson, Helgi. Sturla Sighvatsson. *In* Skírnir. 1906. LXXX. pp. 262-271.

Cf. Eimreiðin. 1907. XIII. pp. 1-8, by Guðm. Friðjónsson.

Sars, J. E. Udsigt over den norske Historie. Christiania 1877. II. pp. 242-304.

Skúlason, Sveinn. Æfi Sturlu lögmanns Þórðarsonar og stutt yfirlit þess er gjörðist um hans daga. *In* Safn til sögu Íslands. 1856. I. pp. 503-639.

Vigfússon, Sig. Rannsókn í Borgarfirði 1884. (Reið Þórðar kakala um Borgarfjörð.—Reykjaholt—Hvítárbrú). *In* Árbók h. ísl. Fornleifafél. 1884-85. pp. 106-128. *Cf. ibid.* 1886. pp. 45-47.

——— Rannsóknarferð um Húnavatns- og Skagafjarðarsýslur 1886. *Ibid.* 1888-92. pp. 76-90.

† Þorkelsson, Jón. Æfisaga Gizurar Þorvaldssonar. Reykjavík 1868. 8°. pp. viii+143.
Review : Germania. 1869. XIV. p. 114, by K. Maurer.

Svaða þáttr ok Arnórs kerlingarnefs.

C. 1000. Unhistorical. In the Flateyjarbók

Pattur Svada oc Arnors Kellingarnefs. *In* Saga Olafs Tryggvasonar. Skálholt 1689. 4°. II. pp. 231-235.

In Fornmanna sögur. 1826. II. pp. 222-228.

Pattr Suada ok Arnors kellingarnefs. *In* Flateyjarbók. Christiania 1860. I. pp. 435-439.

Svaða þáttr ok Arnórs kerlingarnefs. *In* Fjórutíu Íslendinga þættir. Þórleifr Jónsson gaf út. Reykjavík 1904. pp. 330-337.

DANISH.—C. C. Rafn's *version in* Oldnordiske Sagaer. 1827. II. . pp. 197-203.

ENGLISH.—*In* The Saga of King Olaf Tryggwason, translated by J. Sephton. London 1895. pp. 358-362.

LATIN.—Svb. Egilsson's *version in* Scripta historica Islandorum. 1828. II. pp. 208-214.

Jónsson, Finnur. Litteratur Historie. II. p. 759.

Svarfdæla saga.

10th century. In its present shape it dates probably from the beginning of the 14th century, but there doubtless existed an older saga. It is of little historical value, although based upon some historical events, the continuation of which is told in the Valla-Ljóts saga (*q. v.*). Paper-MSS. only, more or less defective.

Svarfdælasaga. *In* Íslendinga sögur. Kaupmannahöfn 1830. II. pp. 6-7, 113-198.

Edited (from AM. 161 fol.) by Þorgeir Guðmundsson and Þorsteinn Helgason. Has also a special t.-p., *see* Ljósvetninga saga.

Svarfdæla saga. *In* Íslenzkar fornsögur. Kaupmannahöfn 1883. III. pp. iii–xxxviii, 1–111, 133–141.
  Critical edition (based on Icel. Lit Soc., Nat. Libr. Reykjavík, no. 226. 4°) by Finnur Jónsson. Appended are: Skinnblað úr Svarfdælu (AM. add. 20, fol.=AM. 455 C, 4°., vellum fragment of the 15th cent.), pp. 133–140; Ur Landnámu, p. 141.

Svarfdæla saga. Búið hefir til prentunar Vald. Ásmundarson. Reykjavík 1898. (Íslendinga sögur. 20.) 8° pp. x+(2)+103.

DANISH.—Fortælling om Svarfdölerne. *In* Historiske Fortællinger om Islændernes Færd hjemme og ude, ved N. M. Petersen. Kjöbenhavn 1844. IV. pp. 259–275.
  A paraphrase, omitted in the later editions of this collection.

Jónsson, Finnur. Om Svarfdæla saga. *In* Aarb. f. nord. Oldk. og Hist, 1884. pp. 120–142.—*Also separate reprint*. Kjöbenhavn 1884. 8°.
——— Litteratur Historie. II. pp. 754–756.
Müller, P. E. Sagabibliothek. I. pp. 300–307.
Vigfússon, Guðbr. Um tímatal í Íslendinga sögum. pp. 389–391.

Svínfellinga saga *or* Ormssona saga.
  1248–1252. Written probably in the seventh or eighth decade of the 13th century by an unknown ecclesiastic. Is now found only as a part of the Sturlunga saga (*q. v.*), but was originally an independent saga.
Jónsson, Finnur. Litteratur Historie. II. pp. 766–767.
Ólsen, Björn M. Um Sturlungu. pp. 469–472.

Valla-Ljóts saga.
  C. 985–1010. Forms a continuation of the Svarfdæla saga (*q. v.*). Written about 1200. Paper-MSS.
Valla-Ljóts saga. *In* Íslendinga sögur. Kaupmannahöfn 1830. II. pp. 7, 199–228.
  Edited (from AM 161 fol.) by Þorgeir Guðmundsson and Þorsteinn Helgason. For special t.-p. *see* Ljósvetninga saga.
Valla-Ljóts saga. *In* Íslenzkar fornsögur. Kaupmannahöfn 1881, II. pp. xiii–xx, 153–195.
  Critical edition (based on AM. 158 fol.) by Finnur Jónsson.
Valla-Ljóts saga. Búið hefir til prentunar Vald. Ásmundarson. Reykjavík 1898. (Íslendinga sögur. 21.) 8°. pp. (4)+32.

Jónsson, Bryn. Rannsóknir í Norðurlandi sumarið 1900. *In* Árbók h. ísl. Fornleifafél. 1901. pp. 18–19.
Jónsson, Finnur. Litteratur Historie. II. pp. 496–498.
Müller, P. E Sagabibliothek. I. pp. 94–97.
Vigfússon, Guðbr Um tímatal í Íslendinga sögum. pp. 484–485.

Vápnfirðinga saga *or* Brodd-Helga saga.

C. 980-990. Forms a continuation of Þorsteins saga hvíta (*q. v.*).
Written towards the end of the 12th century. Paper-MSS., all having a
lacuna ; vellum fragment AM. 162 C, fol. (15th cent.)

Vápnfirðinga saga, Þáttr af Þorsteini hvíta, Þáttr af Þorsteini
stangarhögg, Brandkrossa þáttr besörget og oversat af G.
Thordarson, udg. af det nordiske Literatur-Samfund. Kjöbenhavn 1848. (Nordiske Oldskrifter. V.) 8°. pp. (4)+63 +
70.

Text (AM. 513, 4°), pp. 3-32, and Danish version, pp. 3-36. Text
issued separately with Icelandic title (*cf.* Erslev's Forf Lex., Supplem.
III. 398) † Vápnfirðinga saga, útgefin á kostnað Fornritafjelags Norðr-
landa í Kaupmannahöfn af G. Þórðarsyni. Kaupmannahöfn 1847.
8° pp. 63.

A transcript of the vellum-fragment (AM. 162 C, fol.) deciphered by
Guðbr. Vigfússon was published in Nýtt félagsrit. 1861. XXI. pp. 122-
125 (Um nokkrar Íslendinga sögur. III. Vopnfirðinga saga), repr. in
Vigfússon and Powell's Icelandic Prose Reader. 1879. pp 119-121, 375.

Vápnfirðinga saga. Búið hefir til prentunar Vald. Ásmundarson.
Reykjavík 1898. (Íslendinga sögur. 22.) 8°. pp. iv+48.

Vápnfirðinga saga.   *In* Austfirðinga sögur udg. ved Jakob
Jakobsen. Köbenhavn 1902. pp. xiii-xxx, 21-72.

Critical edition (AM. 513. 4°). *Review* · Deut. Lit Zeit. 1904. coll.
1819-20, by G. Neckel.

DANISH.—Gunnl. Þórðarson's *version in the ed. of* 1848 (*see
above*).

Vopnfjordingernes Saga. *In* Billeder af Livet paa Island ved
Fr. Winkel Horn. Kjöbenhavn 1871. (I.) pp. 155-184.

Vaapnfjordingernes Saga.   Fortællingen om Brodd-Helge og
hans Sön Bjarne. Oversat af O. A. Överland. Kristiania
1897. (Norske historiske Fortællinger af O. A. Ö. Ny Serie.
I. Bind. No. 6.). 8° pp. 52, *frontisp.* (*by* A. Bloch).

Gunnarsson, Sig. Örnefni frá Jökulsá í Axarfirði austan að Skeiðará. 4.
Vopnfirðinga saga. *In* Safn til sögu Íslands. 1876. II. pp. 468-471.

Jónsson, Finnur. Litteratur Historie. II. pp. 513-516.

Müller, P E   Sagabibliothek I. pp 97-100.

Vigfússon, Guðbr. Um tímatal í Íslendinga sögum. pp. 404-406.

Vigfússon, Sig. Rannsókn í Austfirðingafjórðungi 1890. *In* Árbók h. ísl.
Fornleifafél. 1893. pp. 28-60.   .

Vatnsdæla saga.

C. 830-1013. The present saga is a recension of a comparatively late
date, not much older than 1300, and has many interpolations, but the
original saga was probably of the earlier period of sagawriting (c. 1200).
Paper-MSS , copies of the lost Vatnshyrna-codex ; vellum-fragment
AM. 445 B. 4°. (15th cent.).

Vatnsdæla saga ok saga af Finnboga hinum rama. Vatnsdölernes Historie og Finnboge hiin Stærkes Levnet. Bekostede af Jacob Aal. Udgivne af E. C. Werlauff. Kjöbenhavn 1812. 4°. pp. xxi+(3)+384.

Introduction, pp. v-xvi, text (AM. 128, fol.) with Danish version, pp. 1-205. *For review see* Finnboga saga ramma.

Vatnsdæla saga. Útgefandi: Sveinn Skúlason. Akureyri 1858. (Íslendinga sögur. 1. hepti). 8°. pp. 108.

Reprint of the text of 1812. *Reviews:* Ný félagsrit. 1859. XIX. pp. 128-131, by Guðbr. Vigfússon; *cf.* Norðri 1859. VII. pp. 132-133, by Sv. Skúlason, Þjóðólfur. 1860. XII. pp. 113-114, by G. Vigfússon;— Þjóðólfur 1859. XI. pp. 10-12, by Jón Þorkelsson.

Vatnsdæla saga. *In* Fornsögur . . . herausgg. von Guðbrandr Vigfússon und Theodor Möbius. Leipzig 1860. pp. xiv-xxi, 1-80, 162-168.

Text from AM. 559. 4°. Appended are: Membranfragment, Cod. AM. 445 B, 4°., pp. 162-168; Zu Vatnsdælasaga aus Landnámabók vergl. mit Hauksbók, pp. 185-189, aus Melabók (AM 106 fol.), pp 189-195.—For emendations of the text of this edition *see* Origines Islandicæ. 1905. II pp. 276-277.

Vatnsdæla saga. Búið hefir til prentunar Vald. Ásmundarson. Reykjavík 1893. (Íslendinga sögur. 7.) 8°. pp. viii+128.

DANISH.—Werlauff's *version in the ed. of* 1812 *(see above).*

Fortælling om Vatnsdölerne. *In* Historiske Fortællinger om Islændernes Færd hjemme og ude, ved N. M. Petersen. Kjöbenhavn 1844. IV. pp. 3-106.—2. udgave [*ed. by* G. Vigfússon]. København 1868. IV. pp. 1-102; *also with the title:* Fortællingerne om Vatnsdælerne, Gunlaug Ormetunge, Kormak og Finboge den Stærke *etc.*

Fortællinger om Vatnsdölerne, Gisle Sursen, Gunlaug Ormetunge, Grette den Stærke. Efter de islandske Grundskrifter ved N. M. Petersen. 3. Udg. ved Verner Dahlerup og F. Jónsson. Versene ved Olaf Hansen. Köbenhavn 1901. pp. 1-86.

Sagafortællinger ved H. Vexelsen. Throndhjem 1881. 8°. pp. 94+(2).

This vol. consists chiefly of a paraphrase of the Vatnsdæla, pp 5-66; it contains also some brief extracts from other sagas (Laxdæla etc.).

Ingemund i Vatnsdalen. *In* Nordahl Rolfsen's Vore Fædres Liv. Oversættelsen ved Gerhard Gran. Bergen 1888. pp. 361-366. —2. edition. Kristiania 1898. pp. 373-380, *illustr.*

An extract. The illustration by A. Bloch.

ENGLISH.—Vatzdæla saga (The Story of the Waterdalemen). *In* Origines Islandicæ, by G. Vigfusson and F. Y. Powell. Oxford 1905. II. pp. 275-314.
The Story of Hrolleifr—*a version of chap.* 22-26, *in* Iceland, by S. Baring-Gould. London 1863. pp. 138-147.

GERMAN.—Vatnsdäla saga d. i. die Geschichte der Bewohner der Vatnsdal (auf Island) um 890-1010 n. Chr. Aus dem Altisländischen zum erstenmale ins Deutsche übertragen von Heinrich v. Lenk. Leipzig [1893]. (Reclam's Universal-Bibliothek. 3035-36.) 8⁰. pp. 160.
Reviews. Literaturbl. f. g. u. r. Philol. 1894. col. 389, by B. Kahle;—Eimreiðin. 1900. VI. p. 155, by V. Guðmundsson.

SWEDISH.—Vatnsdalingarnes Saga. Från fornnordiskan of C. J. L. Lönnberg. Norrköping 1870. (Fornnordiska Sagor. I.) 8⁰. pp. (2)+146, *map*.

Bååth, A. U. Studier öfver kompositionen i några isländska attsagor. Lund 1885, pp. 20-41.

Jónsson, Bryn. Rannsókn sögustaða í vesturhluta Húnavatnssýslu sumarið 1894. II. Vatnsdæla. *In* Árbók h. ísl. Fornleifafél. 1895. pp. 3-7.

—— Rannsókn á Norðurlandi sumarið 1900. Húnavatnssýsla. *Ibid* 1901. pp. 26-27.

Jónsson, Finnur. Litteratur Historie II. pp. 477-485.

Lehmann, Alfred. Overtro og Trolddom. Kjöbenhavn 1895-96. IV. pp. 285-287.—*German translation by* Petersen : Aberglaube u. Zauberei. Stuttgart 1898. pp. 483-484.

Müller, P. E. Sagabibliothek. I. pp. 146-152.

Vigfússon, Guðbr. Um tímatal í Íslendinga sögum. pp. 377-384.

Vigfússon, Sig. Rannsóknarferð um Húnavatns- og Skagafjarðarsýslur 1886. Rannsóknir í Vatnsdal 1. og 3. sept. 1886. *In* Árbók h. ísl. Fornleifafél 1888-92. pp. 118-123,

Vémundar saga og Víga-Skútu. *See* Reykdæla saga.

Víga-Barða saga. *See* Heiðarvíga saga.

Víga-Glúms saga *or* Glúma *or* Esphælinga saga.
C. 900-1003. One of the oldest sagas, written before 1200. The principal MS. is the Möðruvallabók (AM. 132 fol.; 14th cent.)

Sagann af Vijga-Glwm. *In* Agiætar Fornmanna Sögur, ad Forlage Biörns Marcussonar. Hólar 1756. pp. 180-240.

Viga-Glums saga, sive Vita Viga-Glumi. Cujus textus ad fidem præstantissimi Codicis membranei diligenter exactus est, et collatus cum multis libris chartaceis. Cum versione latina ;

paucis notulis ad sensum pertinentibus ; varietate lectionis in latinum versa, et criticis observationibus mixta ; carminum in ordinem prosaicum redactione, et indice triplici ; uno rerum memorabilium, altero chronologico, tertio vocum et phrasium; qvi etiam commentarii vicem in loca difficiliora sustinet. E manuscriptis Legati Magnæani. Havniæ (sumptibus P. F. de Suhm) 1786. 4°. pp. xxx+242.

Edited (AM. 132 fol.) and translated by Guðmundur Pétursson (G. Petersen). A copper-plate found in some copies (*cf.* Bibl. Dan. III. 634, and Chr. Bruun's biography of Suhm, 1898, p. 231) is lacking in the two copies in the Fiske Icelandic Collection. *Review* · Götting. Anz. 1788. pp. 169-170.

Víga-Glúms saga. *In* Íslendinga sögur. Kaupmannahöfn 1830. II. pp. 8-9, 321-398.

Edited by Þorgeir Guðmundsson and Þorsteinn Helgason. For a special t.-p. *see* Ljósvetninga saga

Glúma. *In* Íslenzkar fornsögur. Kaupmannahöfn 1880. I. pp. iii-xix, 1-110.

Critical edition by Guðmundur Þorláksson. In an appendix (pp. 88-110) are printed fragments of several vellum-MSS. *Review:* Timarit h ísl. Bókmentafél. 1881. I pp. 261-265, by B. M. Ólsen

Víga-Glúms saga. Búið hefir til prentunar Vald. Ásmundarson. Reykjavík 1897. (Íslendinga sögur. 19.) 8°. pp. vii+103.

Viga Glums Saga. *In* Origines Islandicæ, by G. Vigfusson and F. Y. Powell. Oxford 1905. II. pp. 431-479.

Text with English translation (extracts)
For a few stanzas of the saga *cf.* K. Gíslason's Udvalg af oldnord. Skjaldekvad. 1892. pp. 15-16, 93-95.

DANISH.—Vigaglums Saga. *In* Billeder af Livet paa Island, ved Fr. Winkel Horn. Kjöbenhavn 1871. (I.) pp. 195-256.

ENGLISH. — Viga-Glum's Saga. The Story of Viga-Glum. Translated from the Icelandic, with notes and an introduction, by Sir Edmund Head. London 1866. 8°. pp. xvi+124, 2 *tbls.*

Reviews · Revue Britannique. 1867. Ser. 9 Tom. IV pp. 183-195, by Adolph de Circourt ;—The Spectator. 1866 XXXIX. pp. 412-413 ;— The Examiner (London). 1866. p. 196 ;—The Saturday Rev. 1866. XXI. pp. 139-140 ;—† Lond. Quart. Rev. 1871. XXXVI. pp. 35-65.

Vigfússon *and* Powell's *extracts in* Orig. Isl. II. (*see above*).

GERMAN.—Viga-Glum. Eine germanische Bauerngeschichte der Heidenzeit. Aus dem Altisländischen frei und verkürzt übertragen von Ferdinand Khull. Graz 1888. (Sonder-Abdruck aus dem Jahresberichte des II. Staats-Gymnasiums in Graz pro 1888). 8°. pp. 32.

Des Viga-Glum Aufgang. *In* Arthur Bonus's Isländerbuch. München 1907. II. pp. 9–26.

Six chapters of the saga, translated from the English, in A. E. Wollheim da Fonseca's Die National-Literatur der Skandinavier. Berlin 1875 I. pp. 172–179.

LATIN.—G. Pétursson's *version in the ed. of* 1786 *(see above).*

Benjamínsson, Kr. H. Fundið vopn. *In* Eimreiðin 1898. IV. pp. 111–112

Brím, Eggert Ó. Víg Gríms á Kálfsskinni eða Þorvalds í Haga (Land-náma 3. 13; Glúma k. 27.) *In* Tímarit h ísl. Bókmentafél. 1882. III. pp. 100–112.

Cf. Rev. Jón Jónsson's article *ibid.* 1897. XVIII. pp. 196–198: Nokkrar athuganir við Íslendinga sögur. II Um móðurætt Þórarins spaka (Langdælagoða) og Þórdísar konu Halldórs Snorrasonar.

Cederschiold, Gustaf Kalfdrápet og vänpröfningen. Ett bidrag till kritiken af de islandska sagornas trovardighet. Lund 1890. 8°. pp. 41. *Reviews:* Literar. Centralbl. 1890. coll. 667–669, by Konr. Maurer;— † Politiken (Copenhagen), June 22, 1890. (trl. into Icel. in Tímarit h ísl. Bókmentafél. 1892. XIII. pp. 104–108, by B. Gröndal),—† Finsk tidskr. 1890. VI. pp. 469–470, by Herm. Vendell,—Literaturbl. f g. u. r. Philol. 1891. coll 73–75, by W. Golther,—Tímarit h. ísl. Bókmenta-fél. 1892. XIII. pp. 60–73, by Valtýr Guðmundsson. *Cf.* F. Jónsson's Litt. Hist. II. pp. 237–242.

Friðriksson, Halldór Kr Skýringar yfir tvær vísur í Víga-Glúmssögu og eina í Njálssögu. *In* Tímarit h. ísl. Bókmentafél. 1882. III. pp. 190–208

Jónsson, Bryn Rannsóknir í Norðurlandi sumarið 1900. *In* Árbók h ísl. Fornleifafél. 1901. pp. 16–18, 1 *pl.*

—— Rannsóknir á Norðurlandi sumarið 1905 *Ibid.* 1906. pp. 16 19.

Jónsson, Finnur. Litteratur Historie I. p. 528, II. pp. 237–242, 491–496.

Jónsson, Janus. Glúma 8o. 63–70 bls. (Ísl. forns. I. Kmh. 1880). *In* Tímarit h ísl. Bókmentafél. 1882. III. pp. 113–124.

With an explanatory note on the stanza of chap. 26, by Jón Þorkelsson, pp. 123–124 (*cf. ibid.* 1883. IV. p. 273).

Lotspeich, Claude. Zur Víga-Glúms- und Reykdælasaga. Inaugural-Dissertation. Leipzig 1903 8°. pp. 45+(3).

Möbius, Theodor. Über die ältere isländische Saga. Leipzig 1852. 8°. pp. (2)+92 (*Inaug.-Diss.*) Concerning the Víga-Glúms saga see pp. 35–92.

Vigfússon, Guðbr. Um tímatal í Íslendinga sögum. pp. 394–399.

Víga-Skútu saga. *See* Reykdæla saga.

Víga-Styrs saga. *See* Heiðarvíga saga.

Víglundar saga *or* Víglundar saga væna *or* Víglundar saga ok Ketilríðar, *or* Þorgríms saga prúða ok Víglundar væna.

A fictitious saga written in the 14th century; date of events placed in the 10th century. MSS.: AM. 510 and 551 A, 4°. (15th cent. vellums).

Saga af Þorgrimi Pruda og Vijglunde Syne hanns. *In* Nockrer Marg-Frooder Sögu-Pætter Islendinga, ad Forlage Biörns Marcussonar. Hólar 1756. 4°. pp. 15–33, 187–188.

Bárðar saga Snæfellsáss, Víglundarsaga ... ved Guðbrandr Vigfússon. Udg. af det nordiske Literatur-Samfund. Kjö-'benhavn 1860. (Nordiske Oldskrifter. XXVII.) pp. 47–92, 158–166.
Text (AM. 510. 4°) with Danish paraphrase.

Víglundar saga. Búið hefir til prentunar Vald. Ásmundarson. Reykjavík 1902. (Íslendinga sögur. 38.) 8°. pp. (4)+64.

DANISH.—Thorgrim Prude og hans Sön Viglund. Biografisk Fortælling oversat af det ældre skandinaviske Sprog af [W. H. F.] Abrahamson. *In* Skandinavisk Museum. 1800. II. pp. 1–71.—*Also separate reprint.* Kiöbenhavn 1800. 8° pp. 72.

Thorgrim den Prude og hans Sön Viglund den Væne. *In* Sagaer, fortalte af Brynjolf Snorrason og Kristian Arentzen. Kjöbenhavn 1850. IV. pp. 137–188.

ENGLISH.—The Story of Viglund the Fair. *In* Three Northern Love Stories, and other Tales. Transl. by Eiríkr Magnússon and William Morris. London 1875. pp. vi, 115–186.—New edition. London 1901. pp. vi, 123–200.
For another edition of † London 1901, *see* Gunnlaugs saga ormstungu

GERMAN.—Viglund und Ketilrid. Eine altisländische Novelle. Aus dem Urtexte frei und verkürzt übertragen von Ferdinand Khull. Separat-Abdruck aus dem XXI. Jahresbericht des k. k. zweiten Staats-Gymnasiums in Graz, für das Jahr 1890. Graz 1890. 8°. pp. 22.
Review: † Zeitschr f. d. Realschulwesen. 1891. XVI. p. 187, by F. Prosch.

NORWEGIAN.—Saga um Viglund og Kjellrid. Umsett av Matias Skar. Kristiania 1874. 8°. pp. 51.

Jónsson, Finnur. Litteratur Historie. III pp. 84–85
Müller. P. E. Sagabibliothek I. pp. 349–351.
Thorlacius, Árni Skýringar yfir örnefni í Bárðar sögu og Víglundar. *In* Safn til sögu Íslands. 1876. II. pp. 299–303.

Vöðu-Brands þáttr.
C. 1002–1004. Was originally an independent þáttr, but is now embodied in the Ljósvetninga saga (*q. v.*).

Vopnfirðinga saga. *See* Vápnfirðinga saga.

Þiðranda þáttr ok Þórhalls.

A legend from c. 1000. In Ólafs saga Tryggvasonar of the Flateyjarbók and other vellums (AM. 54 and 61. fol., c. 1400).

Pattur Þiðranda oc Þorhalls. *In* Saga Olafs Tryggvasonar. Skálholt 1689. 4°. II. pp. 210–214.

In Fornmanna sögur. 1826. II. pp. 192–197.

Paattr Þiðranda ok Porhallz. *In* Flateyjarbók. Christiania 1860. I. pp. 418–421.

Þiðranda þattr [*from* AM. 61 *and* 54. 4°]. *In* An Icelandic Prose Reader, by G. Vigfusson and F. Y. Powell. Oxford 1879. pp. 102–106, 369–370.

Þiðranda þáttr ok Þórhalls. *In* Fjórutíu Íslendinga þættir. Þórleifr Jónsson gaf út. Reykjavík 1904. pp. 338–343.

DANISH —C. C Rafn's *version in* Oldnordiske Sagaer. 1827. II. pp. 171–175.

ENGLISH.—*In* The Saga of King Olaf Tryggwason, translated by J. Sephton. London 1895. pp. 338–341.

LATIN.—Svb. Egilsson's *version in* Scripta historica Islandorum. 1828. II. pp. 177–182.

Jónsson, Finnur. Litteratur Historie. II. p. 762.

Þórarins þáttr Nefjólfssonar.

An unhistoric tale found in a vellum-codex from c. 1400 (Tómasskinna, Gml. kgl. Saml. 1008 fol.). Þórarinn is an historical person often mentioned in the sagas of King Olaf the Saint, c. 1020-30 (*see* Ólafs saga ens helga, by Snorri Sturluson Christiania 1853. pp. 74-75, 117-118, 125-127; Heimskringla. Kobenhavn 1893-1901. II. pp 157-160, 254-257, 273-277,—and all other editions and translations of this work; Flateyjarbók. Christiania 1862 II. pp. 89-91, 231-232, 239-241; Fornmanna sögur. 1829. IV. pp. 174-178, 263-266, 280-284; Gronlands historiske Mindesmærker. 1838. II. pp 237-250. Danish version: Oldnordiske Sagaer. 1831. IV. pp. 159-163, 240-244, 256-260. Latin version: Scripta historica Islandorum. 1833. IV. pp. 166-170, 245-248, 260-264. German version of one chapter (Der hässliche Fuss) in Arthur Bonus's Isländerbuch. München 1907. II. pp 281-286).

Frá Þórarni Nefjúlfssyni. *In* Fornmanna sögur. 1830. V. pp. 314–320.

Þórarins þáttr Nefjólfssonar. *In* Fjörutíu Íslendinga þættir. Þórleifr Jónsson gaf út. Reykjavík 1904. pp. 344–363.

Contains the þáttr and the chapters from the Ólafs saga helga, mentioned above.

DANISH.—Om Thoraren Nefjulfsön. *In* Oldnordiske Sagaer. 1831. V. pp. 284–290.

LATIN.—De Thorarine Nevjulfi filio [*trl. by* Svb. Egilsson]. *In*
Scripta historica Islandorum. 1833. V. pp. 293–299.

Jónsson, Finnur. Litteratur Historie. II. p. 760.

Þórarins þáttr stuttfeldar.
C 1120. Is found in the Saga Sigurðar Jórsalafara, Eysteins ok Ólafs
in the Heimskringla (not in all MSS. of it) *cf.* Unger's ed. 1868 pp.
685–687; F. Jónsson's ed. 1893–1901. III. pp. 507–509; Codex Frisianus.
1869. pp. 298–300. English versions by Laing (1889. IV. pp. 157–159)
and by Morris and Magnússon (1895. IV. pp. 286–288). *See also* Fornmanna sögur. 1832. VII. pp 152–155; Oldnordiske Sagaer. 1832. VII.
pp. 129–131; Scripta historica Islandorum 1836 VII. 150–153. *Cf.*
F. Jónsson's Litteratur Historie. II. pp. 61–62.

Þórarins þáttr stuttfeldar. *In* Fjörutíu Íslendinga þættir. Þórleifr
Jónsson gaf út. Reykjavík 1904. pp. 364–367.
Followed by the fragments of the Stuttfeldar-drápa (a poem on King
Sigurðr), pp. 367–368. *Cf.* Corpus poeticum boreale 1883 II. pp. 250–
252.

Þórðar saga hreðu.
An unhistorical saga (events placed in the 10th cent.) written about
the middle of the 14th century. There are two recensions, one in the
vellums AM. 471, 551 D and 586, 4° (all of the 15th cent.), the other
defective among the fragments of the Vatnshyrna-codex (AM. 564 A,
4°, c. 1400).

Saga af Þoordi Hredu. *In* Nockrer Marg-Frooder Sögu-Þætter
Islendinga, ad Forlage Biörns Marcussonar. Hólar 1756. 4°.
pp. 59–81, 188.

Sagan af Þórði hreðu, besörget og oversat ved H. Friðriksson,
udg. af det nordiske Literatur-Samfund. Kjöbenhavn 1848.
(Nordiske Oldskrifter. VI.) 8°. pp. (6)+66+65.
Text (AM. 551 D. 4°) with Danish version.

Bárðar saga Snæfellsáss . . . Þórðar saga . . . ved Guðbrandr
Vigfússon. Udg. af det nordiske Literatur-Samfund. Kjöbenhavn 1860. (Nordiske Oldskrifter. XXVII.). pp. 93–105.
Text of the Vatnshyrna fragments. *Cf.* Sturlunga saga. 1878. II. pp.
501.

Þórðar saga hræðu. Búið hefir til prentunar Vald Ásmundarson. Reykjavík 1900. (Íslendinga sögur. 29.) 8°. pp. xii+
89.
Contains both recensions.

DANISH.—Friðriksson's *version in the ed. of* 1848 (*see above*).

ENGLISH.—The Story of Thorðr Hreða (the Terror). *In* Summer Travelling in Iceland, by John Coles. London 1882. pp.
173–204.

Jónsson, Bryn. Rannsókn sögustaða í vesturhluta Húnavatnssýslu 1894.
V. Þórðar saga hreðu. *In* Árbók h. ísl. Fornleifafél. 1895. pp. 10–12.
Jónsson, Finnur. Litteratur Historie. III. pp. 87–89.
Jónsson, *Rev.* Jón. Nokkrar athuganir við Íslendinga-sögur. Ættmenn
klyppe hersis á Íslandi. *In* Tímarit h. ísl. Bókmentafél. 1898. XIX.
pp. 93–109.
Maurer, K. Die Quellenzeugnisse über das erste Landrecht und über die
Ordnung der Bezirksverfassung des isländischen Freistaates. München
1869. 4°. pp. 29–61.
Müller, P. E. Sagabibliothek. I. pp. 270–274.
Vigfússon, Guðbr. Um tímatal í Íslendinga sögum. pp. 370–371.

Þórðar saga kakala.

1242–1250. Written shortly after Þórðr kakali's death (1256) by an
ecclesiastic. Is now found only as a part of the Sturlunga saga (*q. v.*)
Jónsson, Finnur. Litteratur Historie. II. pp. 765–766.
Ólsen, Björn M. Um Sturlungu. pp. 437–469.

Þorfinns saga karlsefnis ok Snorra Þorbrandssonar. *See* Eiríks saga rauða.

Þorgeirs saga goða, Guðmundar ríka ok Þorkels háks. *See* Ljósvetninga saga.

Þorgeirs saga Hávarssonar ok Þormóðar Kolbrúnarskálds. *See* Fóstbræðra saga.

Þorgils saga ok Hafliða.

1117–1121. Written before or about 1200, probably by an ecclesiastic
and possibly an eye-witness of the events. It is now embodied in the
Sturlunga saga (*q. v*)
Jónsson, Finnur. Litteratur Historie. II. pp. 553–555.
Ólsen, Björn M. Um Sturlungu. pp. 207–213.

Þorgils saga Örrabeinsstjúps. *See* Flóamanna saga.

Þorgils saga skarða.

1252–1258. Written shortly after Þorgils's death in 1258. It is now
embodied in the Sturlunga saga (*q. v.*).
Jónsson, Finnur. Litteratur Historie. II. pp. 767–768.
Ólsen, Björn M. Um Sturlungu. pp. 472–501.

Þorgríms saga prúða ok Víglundar væna. *See* Víglundar saga.

Þorgríms þáttr Hallasonar ok Bjarna Gullbrárskálds.

C. 1050 (the chronology of the þáttr is wrong). It is in the Magnús
saga góða of the vellum-codices Hulda (AM. 66 fol., 14th cent.), and
Hrokkinskinna (Gml. kgl. Saml. 1010 fol., 15th cent.) *Cf.* F. Jónsson's Litteratur Historie. I. pp. 619–620.
In Fornmanna sögur. 1831. VI. pp. 30–36.

Þorgríms þáttr Hallasonar ok Bjarna Gullbrárskálds.   *In*
Fjörutíu Íslendinga þættir.   Þórleifr Jónsson gaf út.   Reykja-
vík 1904.   pp. 369-375.
Followed by the fragment of Bjarni's poem Kálfsflokkr, pp. 375-377.
Cf. Corpus poeticum boreale. 1883. II. pp. 162-164.

DANISH.—*In* Oldnordiske Sagaer. 1832. VI. pp 25-29.

LATIN.—Svb. Egilsson's *version in* Scripta historica Islandorum.
1835. VI. pp. 26-30.

Þórhalls þáttr knapps.
A legend from c. 1000.   A chapter of the Ólafs saga Tryggvasonar of
the Flateyjarbók.
In Saga Olafs Tryggvasonar.   Skálholt 1689. 4°. II. pp. 235-
238.
In Fornmanna sögur.   1826. II. pp. 229-232.
In Flateyjarbók.   Christiania 1860. I. pp. 439-441.
Þórhalls þáttr knapps.   *In* Fjörutíu Íslendinga þættir.   Þórleifr
Jónsson gaf út.   Reykjavík 1904. pp. 378-382.

DANISH.—C. C. Rafn's *version in* Oldnordiske Sagaer. 1827.
II. pp. 203-206.

ENGLISH.—*In* The Saga of King Olaf Tryggwason, translated
by J. Sephton.   London 1895. pp. 362-364.

LATIN.—Svb. Egilsson's *version in* Scripta historica Islandorum.
1828. I. pp. 214-216.

Þórhalls þáttr ölkofra.   *See* Ölkofra þáttr.

Þorláks saga biskups helga.
Life of Þorlákr Þórhallason the Saint (b. 1133), bishop of Skálholt 1178-
1193.   There are three recensions : the original saga written about 1206
(Þorláks saga hin elzta. MSS.: Cod. Holm. 5 fol., from c. 1360, and
several on paper) ; the second saga (Þorláks saga hin yngri) written
about 1225-30 (MS.: AM. 382, 4°, vellum from the first half of the 14th
cent.), the third saga (Þorláks saga hin yngsta) written in the earlier
part of the 14th cent., a compilation of the two earlier recensions
adding only miracles.   The second saga is considerably longer than
the first, although based on it, containing among other matters the
Oddaverja þáttr or the story of the quarrels between the bishop and the
family of Oddi (Jón Loptsson).   A book containing the miracles of
this saint was compiled under his successor, Bishop Páll Jónsson, and
was read at the Althing in 1199, the MS of it written in that year or
shortly after being still in existence (AM. 645, 4°; *cf.* Kålund's Palæografisk Atlas. 1905. Nr. 13).
Saga Þorláks biskups hin elzta.   *In* Biskupa sögur.   Kaupmannahöfn 1858. I. pp. xxv-xxxvi, 87-124, 391-394.

Þorláks saga helga hin yngri. *Ibid.* pp. xlii–liii, 261–332.
Edited by Guðbr. Vigfússon. Appendices 1. Jarteinabók Þorláks
biskups, sú er Páll biskup lét lesa upp á alþingi 1199, pp. 333–356 ; 2.
Onnur jarteinabók Þorláks biskups (AM. 379, 4°), pp. 357-374 ; 3.
Jarteinir úr sögu Þorláks biskups hinni yngstu (AM 379, 4°), pp. 375-
391 ; 4. Brot af Þorláks sögu hinni elztu (AM. 383. 1, 4°) pp. 391-394 ;
5. Latínsk lesbókabrot um Þorlák biskup (AM. 386, 4°), pp 394-404
(these legends having been printed before in † Langebek's Scriptores
rerum Danicarum Hafniæ 1777. fol. IV. pp 624-636).—Extracts from
the youngest saga (AM. 379, 4°) in Grönlands historiske Mindesmærker. 1838. II. pp. 767-772.
Isländska handskriften No. 645 4° i den Arnamagnæanska Samlingen i
Universitetsbiblioteket i Köbenhavn i diplomatarisk aftryck utg. af
Ludvig Larsson. I. Handskriftens äldre del. Lund 1885. 8°. pp. (4)+
lxxxviii+130+(2).
The miracle-book of 1199 (beginning lacking), pp. 1-33.

Þorláks saga. *In* Origines Islandicæ, by G. Vigfusson and F.
Y. Powell. Oxford 1905. I. pp. 455–502.

Second Life of Thorlac (Oddaverja þáttr). *Ibid.* I. pp. 567–591.
The oldest saga and the þáttr with English versions.

ENGLISH.—The Story of Bishop Thorlak of Skalholt, commonly
called S. Thorlak. *In* Stories of the Bishops of Iceland.
Translated by the Author of "The Chorister Brothers"
[Mrs. Disney Leith]. London 1895. pp. 73–123.
The oldest saga with a few selections from the other.

Vigfússon *and* Powell's *version in* Orig. Isl. I. (*see above*).

Bjarnason, Þorkell. Um Þorlák Þórhallason hinn helga. Fyrirlestur.
Reykjavík 1898. 8°. pp. 46.
Jónsson, Finnur (*bishop*). Historia Ecclesiastica Islandiæ. Havniæ 1772.
4°. I. pp. 287-300
Jónsson, Finnur. Litteratur Historie. II pp. 569-572.
Müller, P. E. Sagabibliothek. I. pp. 335-338

Þorleifs þáttr jarlsskálds.
10th century (second half). Written probably in the beginning of the
14th century, found in the Flateyjarbók.

Þáttr Þorleifs jarlaskálds. *In* Fornmanna sögur. 1827. III. pp.
89–104 (*cf.* XII. pp. 69–70).

Paattr Þorleifs. *In* Flateyjarbók. Christiania 1860. I. pp. 207–
215.

Þorleifs þáttr jarlsskálds. *In* Íslenzkar fornsögur. Kaupmannahöfn 1883. III. pp. xviii–xxi, xxxviii–xlvii, 113–132,
155–161.
Critical edition by Finnur Jónsson.

Þórleifs þáttr jarlsskálds.   *In* Fjörutíu Íslendinga þættir.   Þórleifr Jónsson gaf út. Reykjavík 1904. pp. 383–399.
   Cf. Konr. Gíslason's Udvalg af oldnord. Skjaldekvad. 1892. pp. 19,
   101-102.

DANISH.—Fortælling om Thorlejf Jarleskjald [*trl. by* C. C.
Rafn]. *In* Oldnordiske Sagaer. 1827. III. pp. 80–94.

LATIN.—Particula de Thorleivo dynastarum poëta [*trl. by* Svb.
Egilsson]. *In* Scripta historica Islandorum. 1829. III. pp.
93–108.
   Cf. T. Torfæus's Hist. rer Norvegic. pars II. Havniæ 1711. fol. pp.
   356-360 (De Thorleifo jarlaskalde).

Jónsson, Finnur. Litteratur Historie. I. pp. 549-552, II. p. 760.
Müller, P. E Sagabibliothek. III. pp. 211-217.
Vigfússon, Guðbr. Um tímatal í Íslendinga sögum. pp. 391-392.

Þormóðar þáttr Kolbrúnarskálds.   *See* Fóstbræðra saga.

Þórodds þáttr Snorrasonar.
   C. 1024-1030. A tale of adventures found in the sagas of King Olaf
   the Saint. *See :* Saga Ólafs konungs ens helga, by Snorri Sturluson,
   Christiania 1853. pp. 150-154; all editions and translations of the
   Heimskringla (in F Jónsson's edition, 1893-1901, II pp. 328-337);
   Flateyjarbók. 1862. II. pp. 270-274; Fornmanna sögur. 1829 IV. pp.
   332-341, (Danish) Oldnordiske Sagaer. 1831. IV. pp. 303-311, (Latin)
   Scripta historica Islandorum. 1833. IV. pp. 304-311
Þórodds þáttr Snorrasonar. *In* Fjörutíu Íslendinga þættir.
Þórleifr Jónsson gaf út. Reykjavík 1904. pp. 400–409.

Þorskfirðinga saga.   *See* Gull-Þóris saga.

Þórsnesinga saga.   *See* Eyrbyggja saga.

Þorsteins draumr Síðu-Hallssonar.
   C. 1050. Probably written about 1300.   *Cf.* Þorsteins saga *and* þáttr
   Síðu-Hallssonar.
Draumr Þorsteins Síðuhallssonar. *In* Analecta norræna her-
ausgg. von Theodor Möbius. Leipzig 1859. pp. 184–186.—
Also separate reprint together with the saga, pp. 16–18.
Draumr Þorsteins Síðu-Hallssonar. *In* Bárðar saga Snæfells-
áss . . . Draumvitranir . . . ved Guðbr. Vigfússon. Kjöben-
havn 1860. pp. 130–132, 170.
Draumr Þorsteins Síðu-Hallssonar. *In* Þorsteins saga Síðu-
Hallssonar. Búið hefir til prentunar Vald. Ásmundarson.
Reykjavík 1902. pp. 24–29.

Draumur Þorsteins Siduhallssonar. *In* Austfirðinga sögur udg. ved Jakob Jakobsen. Köbenhavn 1903. pp. lxxxii–lxxxiv, 233–236, 240–241.
Critical edition (AM 564 C, 4°).

Jónsson, Finnur. Litteratur Historie. II. p. 765.

Þorsteins draumr Þorvarðssonar. *See* Kumlbúa þáttr.

Þorsteins saga (*or* þáttr) hvíta.
C. 900–960. Written about 1200. Continued by the Vápnfirðinga saga. Paper-MSS.

Vápnfirðinga saga, Páttr af Þorsteini hvíta . . . besörget og oversat af G. Thordarson. Kjöbenhavn 1848. pp. 35–47, 39–52.
Text (AM 144 fol) with Danish version.

Þorsteins saga hvíta. Búið hefir til prentunar Vald. Ásmundarson. Reykjavík 1902. (Íslendinga sögur. 32.) 8°. pp. (4) +19.

Þorsteins saga hvíta. *In* Austfirðinga sögur udg. ved Jakob Jakobsen. Köbenhavn 1902. pp. iii–xiii, 1–19.
Critical edition (AM. 496, 4°).

DANISH.—Gunnl. Þórðarson's *version in the ed. of* 1848 (*see above*).

Sagaen om Torstein Hvide oversat af O. A. Överland. Kristiania 1897. (Historiske Fortællinger. 28. *or* Norske historiske Fortællinger af O. A. Ö. Ny Serie. I. Bind. Nr. 5.) 8°. pp. 22, *frontisp.* (*by* A. Bloch).

Gunnarsson, Sig. Örnefni frá Jökulsá í Axarfirði austan að Skeiðará. 5. Þáttr af Þorsteini hvíta. *In* Safn til sögu Íslands. 1876. II. pp. 471–473.
Jónsson, Finnur. Litteratur Historie. II. pp. 511–513.
Müller, P. E. Sagabibliothek. III. pp. 344–345.
Vigfússon, Guðbr. Um tímatal í Íslendinga sögum. pp. 265–267.

Þorsteins saga Síðu-Hallssonar.
C. 1000–1050. Written about 1300. Defective. MS.: AM. 142 fol. (paper-copy of a lost vellum). *Cf.* Þorsteins draumr *and* þáttr Síðu-Hallssonar.

Sagan af Þorsteini Síðu-Hallssyni (ex Cod. AM. 142 fol.) ok Draumr Þorsteins Síðu-Hallssonar (ex Cod. AM. 564 C, 4°). Leipzig 1859. 8°. pp. (2)+18.—*Separate reprint from* Analecta norræna herausgg. von Theodor Möbius. 1859. pp. 169–186.
The saga fills pp. 1–16, and 169–184, respectively.

8

Saga af Þorsteini Síðu-Halls syni. *In* Fire og fyrretyve Pröver
af oldnord. Sprog og Literatur udg. af Konr. Gíslason. Kjöbenhavn 1860. pp. 42–58.

Þorsteins saga Síðu-Hallssonar. Búið hefir til prentunar Vald.
Ásmundarson. Reykjavík 1902. (Íslendinga sögur. 33.) 8°.
pp. vii + 36.

Þorsteins saga Síðu-Hallssonar. *In* Austfirðinga sögur udg.
ved Jakob Jakobsen. Köbenhavn 1903. pp. lxxvi–lxxxii,
213–232.

Bugge, Sophus.   Norsk Sagafortælling og Sagaskrivning i Irland. 1.
  Hefte. Kristiania 1901. 8°. pp. 80.
  Treats of the Icelandic Brians saga, pp. 52–78 ; *cf.* Njáls saga.
Gunnarsson, Sig   Örnefni frá Jökulsá í Axarfirði austan að Skeiðará. 11.
  Saga Þorsteins Síðu-Hallssonar. *In* Safn til sögu Íslands. 1876. II.
  pp. 479–481.
Jónsson, Finnur. Litteratur Historie. II. pp. 761–762.
Lehmann, Karl *and* H. Schnorr von Carolsfeld. Njála und Þorsteinssaga
  Síðuhallssonar. *In their* Die Njálssage. Berlin 1883. pp. 161–165.
  For reviews see Njáls saga.
Vigfússon, Guðbr. Um tímatal í Íslendinga sögum. pp. 490–491.

Þorsteins þáttr austfirðings *or* suðrfara, *or* Þáttr af Þorsteini, er
hjálpaði Styrbirni.
  C. 1040. Penned probably in the latter part of the 13th cent   Paper-
  MSS.

Þáttr af Þorsteini austfirðing. *In* Sex sögu-þættir, sem Jón
Þorkelsson hefir gefið út. Reykjavík 1855. pp. vii, 13–17.—
2. útgáfa (*anastatic*). Kaupmannahöfn 1895.

Þórsteins þáttr austfirðings. *In* Fjörutíu Íslendinga þættir.
Þórleifr Jónsson gaf út. Reykjavík 1904. pp. 410–414.

Jónsson, Finnur. Litteratur Historie. II. p. 761.
Müller, P. E. Sagabibliothek. I. p. 348.

Þorsteins þáttr drómundar. *See* Spesar þáttr *and* Grettis saga.

Þorsteins þáttr forvitna.
  Unhistorical (c. 1050), probably written in the 13th century In the
  Flateyjarbók.

Þáttr af Þorsteini forvitna. *In* Sex sögu-þættir, sem Jón
Þorkelsson hefir gefið út. Reykjavík 1855. pp. xiii, 69–71.—
2. útgáfa (*anastatic*). Kaupmannahöfn 1895.
  Edited from a paper-codex.

(Þattr Þorsteius forvitna). *In* Flateyjarbók. Christiania 1868.
III. pp. 431–432.

Þórsteins þáttr forvitna. *In* Fjörutíu Íslendinga þættir. Þórleifr Jónsson gaf út. Reykjavík 1904. pp. 415–418.

DANISH.—† En Fortælling om Thorsten den Nysgierrige.
Oversat af det Islandske (ved Th. G. Repp.) *In* Tilskueren.
1818. Nr. 60. pp. 433–436.

Jónsson, Finnur. Litteratur Historie. II. p. 764.
Müller, P. E. Sagabibliothek. III. pp. 477–479.

Þorsteins þáttr fróða, *an unwarranted name for* Íslendings þáttr
sögufróða (*q. v.*)

Þorsteins þáttr hvíta. *See* Þorsteins saga hvíta.

Þorsteins þáttr Síðu-Hallssonar.
C. 1040. In the Flateyjarbók (Magnús saga góða). *Cf.* Þorsteins
draumr *and* saga Síðu-Hallssonar.
In Fornmanna sögur. 1831. VI. pp. 97–102.

Fra Þorsteine Hallzsyne er kom . . . *In* Flateyjarbók. Christiania 1868. III. pp. 318–321.

DANISH.—*In* Oldnordiske Sagaer. 1832. VI. pp. 79–83.

LATIN.—Svb. Egilsson's *version in* Scripta historica Islandorum.
1835. VI. pp. 94–98.

Müller, P. F. Sagabibliothek. III. pp. 474–477.

Þorsteins þáttr skelks.
A legend from the end of the 10th century. In the Flateyjarbók (Ólafs
saga Tryggvasonar).
Pattur Þorsteins Skelks. *In* Saga Olafs Tryggvasonar. Skálholt 1689. 4°. II. pp. 208–210.

Þáttr Þorsteins skelks. *In* Fornmanna sögur. 1827. III. pp.
199–203.

Pattr Þorsteins skelkis. *In* Flateyjarbók. Christiania 1860. I.
pp. 416–418.

DANISH.—Fortælling om Thorstejn Skelk [*trl. by* C. C. Rafn].
In Oldnordiske Sagaer. 1827. III. pp. 176–179.

ENGLISH.—The Tale of Thorstan Shiver (Last news of
Starkad). [*Transl. by* F. Y. Powell.] *As appendix IV to*
The First Nine Books of the Danish History of Saxo Gram-
maticus, transl. by Oliver Elton. London 1894. pp. 418–421.
In the so-called Norræna Society's reprint of this work, 1905. vol. II.
pp. 603–607.

GERMAN.—Thorstein der Gruseler. *In* Arthur Bonus's Isländerbuch. München 1907. II. pp. 297–306.

LATIN.—Particula de Thorsteine Trepidulo [*trl. by* Svb. Egils-
son]. *In* Scripta historica Islandorum. 1829. III. pp. 197–
200.

Cf. T. Torfæus's Hist. rer. Norvegic. pars II. 1711. fol. pp. 496–497
(De Thorsteino skelko).

Jónsson, Finnur. Litteratur Historie. II. p. 759.

Þorsteins þáttr stangarhöggs.
C. 1000.   A continuation of Vápnfirðinga saga (in AM. 496, 4° it is
called Þáttr ur Voknfirðinga sögu).   Written in the latter part of the
13th century.   Paper-MSS.; a vellum fragment AM. 162 C fol. (15th
cent.)

Vápnfirðinga saga . . . Þáttr af Þorsteini stangarhögg . . . besörget og oversat af G. Thordarson. Kjöbenhavn 1848. pp.
48–56, 52–61.

Text (AM. 144 fol.) with Danish version.—*Cf.* Sturlunga saga. 1878.
II. p. 502 ; *and* Safn til sögu Íslands. 1876. II. p. 474.

Þórsteins saga stangarhöggs. *In* Austfirðinga sögur udg. ved
Jakob Jakobsen. København 1902. pp. xxx–xxxviii, 73–92.

Critical edition (AM. 156 fol.) with reproduction of AM. 162 C fol.

Þórsteins þáttr stangarhöggs. *In* Fjörutíu Íslendinga þættir.
Þórleifr Jónsson gaf út. Reykjavík 1904. pp. 419–430.

The Tale of Thorstan Staff-smitten. *In* Origines Islandicæ, by
G. Vigfusson and F. Y. Powell. Oxford 1905. II. pp. 576–
580.

DANISH.—Gunnl. Þórðarson's *version in the ed. of* 1848 (*see
above*).

Thorsten Stanghug. *In* Sagaer, fortalte af Brynjolf Snorrason
og Kristian Arentzen. Kjöbenhavn 1849. I. pp. 179–193.

Fortælling om Thorsten Stanghug. *In* Fortællinger og Sagaer
fortalte for Börn af H. H. Lefolii. 3. Udg. Kjöbenhavn 1869.
I. pp. 269–279.—† *1. ed.* Kbh. 1859 ; † *2. ed.* Kbh. 1862.

Fortælling om Torstejn Stanghug. *In* Billeder af Livet paa
Island, ved Fr. Winkel Horn. Kjöbenhavn 1871. (I.) pp.
185–194.

Thorstein Stanghug. *In* N. Rolfsen's Vore Fædres Liv. Oversættelsen ved Gerhard Gran. Bergen 1888. pp. 366–371.—
2. *edition*. Kristiania 1898. pp. 381–388, *illustr.*

The illustration by A. Bloch shows the reconciliation.

Sagaen om Thorstein Stanghug gjenfortalt af O. A. Överland.
Kristiania 1896. (Norske historiske Fortællinger. Nr. 19.) 8°.
pp. (2)+16, *frontisp.*
The illustration by A. Bloch represents the duel between Bjarni and
Þorsteinn.

ENGLISH.—The Tale of Thorstein Staff-smitten. *In* Three
Northern Love-Stories and other Tales. Transl. by E. Mag-
nússon and W. Morris. London 1875. pp. vii, 231–243.—
New edition. London 1901. pp. vii, 249–262.
For another edition of † London 1901 *see* Gunnlaugs saga ormstungu.—
This translation is reproduced under the heading "Saga Literature"
with some introductory remarks by Johannes H. Wisby in Poet Lore.
Boston 1894. VI. pp. 281–298.

GERMAN.—Die Geschichte von Thorstein Stangarhögg. Aus
dem Altnordischen übersetzt von Georg Herzfeld. *In* (Her-
rig's) Archiv fur das Studium der neueren Sprachen u.
Litteraturen. 1881. LXXIX. pp. 403–410.
Die Geschichte von Thorstein Staugennarbe. [*Transl. by* A.
Heusler.] *In* Kunstwart. München 1907. XX. pp. 198–204.
—*Reprinted in* Arthur Bonus's Isländerbuch. München 1907.
III. pp. 301–321.

SWEDISH.—† Thorsten Stånghugg. Berättelse från Östra Island.
Forsvenskad af O. W. Ålund. *In* Svenska illustr. familj-
journal. 1877.

Jónsson, Finnur. Litteratur Historie I. p. 761.
Müller, P. E. Sagabibliothek. I. pp. 342–343.

Þorsteins þáttr tjaldstæðings (Ásgrímssonar).

Second half of the 9th century. Written about 1200; is found in the
Flateyjarbók, and partly also in the Hauksbók recension of the Landnámabók (Köbenhavn 1899. pp. 110–112).

Páttr af Þorsteini tjaldstæðing. *In* Fire og fyrretyve Pröver af
oldnord. Sprog og Literatur udg. af Konr. Gíslason. Kjöbenhavn 1860 pp. 1–5.
(Pattr Þorsteins Asgrimssonar). *In* Flateyjarbók. Christiania
1868. III. pp. 432–435.
Þórsteins þáttr tjaldstæðings. *In* Fjörutíu Íslendinga þættir.
Þórleifr Jónsson gaf út. Reykjavík 1904. pp. 431–437.

Jónsson, Finnur. Litteratur Historie. II p. 552.

Þorsteins þáttr uxafóts.

End of the 10th century, but for the most part fabulous. Probably
written about 1300. In the Flateyjarbók.

Pattur Porsteins Vxa-Fots. *In* Saga Olafs Tryggvasonar. Skálholt 1689. 4°. II. pp. 20–36.

Páttr Porsteins Uxafóts. *In* Fornmanna sögur. 1827. III. pp. 105–134.

Paattr Porsteins vxafotz. *In* Flateyjarbók. Christiania 1860. I. pp. 249–263.

Pórsteins þáttr uxafóts. *In* Fjörutíu Íslendinga þættir. Pórleifr Jónsson gaf út. Reykjavík 1904. pp. 438–466.

DANISH.—Fortælling om Thorstejn Oxefod [*trl. by* C. C. Rafn]. *In* Oldnordiske Sagaer. 1827. III. pp. 95–120.

ENGLISH.—The Tale of Thorstan Oxfoot. *In* Origines Islandicæ, by G. Vigfusson and F. Y. Powell. Oxford 1905. II. pp. 581–587.
Chap. I.-VI. only.

LATIN.—Particula de Thorsteine Bovipede [*trl. by* Svb. Egilsson]. *In* Scripta historica Islandorum. 1829. III. pp. 109–137.
Cf. T. Torfæus's Hist. rer. Norvegic. pars II. 1711. fol. pp. 461–466 (De Thorsteino tauripede).

Gunnarsson, Sig.   Örnefni frá Jökulsá í Axarfirði austan að Skeiðará. 10. Þáttr af Þorsteini uxafæti. *In* Safn til sögu Íslands. 1876. II. pp. 478–479.

Jónsson, Finnur.   Litteratur Historie. II. pp. 762–763.

Maurer, Konrad.   Die Quellenzeugnisse über das erste Landrecht und über die Ordnung der Bezerksverfassung des islandischen Freistaats. München 1869. (Abhandl. d. philos.-philol. Cl. d. kgl. bayer. Akad. d. Wissensch. XII. 1). 4°. pp. 9–15.

Müller, P E.   Sagabibliothek. III pp. 232–237.

Þorvalds þáttr tasalda.
A legend from the end of the 10th cent.   In the Flateyjarbók.

Pattur Porvalds Tasalda Steingrímssonar. *In* Saga Olafs Tryggvasonar. Skálholt 1689. 4°. II. pp. 36–41.

In Fornmanna sögur. 1826. II. pp. 144–153.

Paattr Porvalldz tasallda. *In* Flateyjarbók. Christiania 1860. I. pp. 378–383.

Pórvalds þáttr tasalda. *In* Fjörutíu Íslendinga þættir. Pórleifr Jónsson gaf út. Reykjavík 1904. pp. 467–476.

DANISH.—Thorvald Tasaldi. En Fortælling af det Islandske [ved Th. G. Repp.] *In* Dansk Minerva. (November) 1818. pp. 385–398.

C. C. Rafn's *version in* Oldnordiske Sagaer. 1827. II. pp. 128–137.

ENGLISH.—*In* The Saga of King Olaf Tryggwason, translated by J. Sephton. London 1895. pp. 307–312.

LATIN.—Svb. Egilsson's *version in* Scripta historica Islandorum. 1828. II. pp. 133–141.

Cf. T. Torfæus's Hist. rer. Norvegic. pars II. 1711. fol. pp. 495–496 (De Thorvaldo Tasaldio).

Jónsson, Finnur. Litteratur Historie. II. p. 760.
Müller, P. E. Sagabibliothek. III. pp. 257–261.

Þorvalds þáttr víðförla.

981–986. Historical in its main features, but filled with miracle stories and other legends, and evidently written by a monk about 1300; it is, however, presumed that it originally came from the pen of Gunnlaugr Leifsson, the monk (d. 1218 or 1219). A shorter recension or extract is found in the Flateyjarbók (Christiania 1860. I. pp. 268–273; also in the Skálholt edition of Ólafs saga Tryggvasonar, 1689. 4°. II: pp. 42–47 : Þáttr af Biscupi oc Þorvaldi).

Hungrvaka ... et Þáttr af Thorvalldi Vidförla, sive Narratio de Thorvalldo Peregrinatore ... Hafniæ 1778. pp. 254–339.

Icelandic text (from paper-MSS.) ed. with Latin version and notes by Jón Ólafsson (from Grunnavík).

In Fornmanna sögur. 1825. I. pp. 255–276.

Páttr af Þorvaldi víðförla. *In* Biskupa sögur. Kaupmannahöfn 1858. I. pp. xxiv–xxv, 33–50.

Edited (from AM. 61 fol., c. 1400) by Guðbr. Vigfússon.

De Saga van Thorwald Kodransson den bereisde. Eene bladzijde uit de Geschiedenis den Christelijke Zending in de tiende eeuw, uit het Oud-Ijslandsch vertaald, en toegelicht door E. H. Lasonder. Utrecht 1886. 8°. pp. xvi+205+(2)

Contents: preface; Icelandic text with Dutch version, pp. 1–41; Thorwalds tijd, land en volk, pp. 43–137, Anteekeningen, pp. 139–199. *Reviews:* Literar. Centralbl. 1887. coll. 452–453, by E. Mogk ;— Literaturbl. f. g. u. r Philol 1888. coll. 50–51, by O. Brenner.

Pórvalds þáttr víðförla. *In* Fjörutíu Íslendinga þættir. Þórleifr Jónsson gaf út. Reykjavík 1904. pp. 477–502.

Kristni saga, Þáttr Þorvalds ens víðförla ... herausgg. von B. Kahle. Halle a. S. 1905. pp. xv–xxii, 59–81.

Annotated edition. This and the preceding edition have as an appendix the chapter from the Flateyjarbók and AM. 62 fol concerning the last years of Þorvaldr and his legendary meeting with Ólaf Tryggvason *Cf.* Kristni saga.

DANISH.—C. C. Rafn's *version in* Oldnordiske Sagaer. 1826. I. pp. 230–248.

DUTCH.—Lasonder's *version of* 1886 (*see above*).

ENGLISH.—The Stories of Thorwald the Far-farer and of Bishop Isleif. Translated from the Icelandic by the Author of "The Chorister Brothers" [Mrs. Disney Leith]. London 1894. 8°. pp. 32.—*Also in the same translator's* Stories of the Bishops of Iceland. Translated from the Icelandic "Biskupa sögur." London 1895. pp. 1–24.

In The Saga of King Olaf Tryggwason, translated by J. Sephton. London 1895. pp. 174–188.

The Tale of Thorwald the Far-farer. *In* Origines Islandicæ, by G. Vigfusson and F. Y. Powell. Oxford 1905. I. pp. 407–412.

GERMAN.—Drei Missionsreisen nach Island im zehnten Jahrhundert. Nach dem alten isländischen Quellen dem katholischen Volke erzählt von Ferdinand Khull. Graz 1900. 8°. pp. 36.

The Þorvalds þáttr, pp. 6–22, is followed by an account of the missionary journeys of Stefnir and Þangbrandr from Ólafs saga Tryggvasonar, pp. 22–33, and an extract from the Íslendingabók, pp. 34–36

LATIN.—Jón Ólafsson's *version in the ed. of* 1778 (*see above*).

Svb. Egilsson's *version in* Scripta historica Islandorum. 1828. I. pp. 281–299.

Jónsson, Finnur. Litteratur Historie. II. pp. 409, 575.

Kahle, B. Zu den handschriften des kürzeren þáttr Þorvalds ens víðförla. *In* Arkiv f. nord filol 1905. XXI. pp. 256–260

Müller, P. E. Sagabibliothek. I. pp. 319–320.

Cf. also the titles under Kristni saga.

Þorvarðs þáttr krákunefs.

C. 1050. In the Morkinskinna and the Flateyjarbók

In Fornmanna sögur. 1831. VI. pp. 356–360.

Fra jslenzkum manne. *In* Flateyjarbók. Christiania 1868. III. pp. 357–359.

Fra þvi er Þorvarþr crakonef villdi gefa segl Haralldi konvngi. *In* Morkinskinna. Christiania 1871. pp. 73–75.

Þórvalds [*sic*] þáttr krákunefns. *In* Fjorutíu Íslendinga þættir. Þórleifr Jónsson gaf út. Reykjavík 1904. pp. 503–507.

DANISH.—*In* Oldnordiske Sagaer. 1832. VI. pp. 291–294.

Thorvard Kragenæb. *In* Fortællinger og Sagaer, fortalte for Börn af H. H. Lefolii. 3. Udg. Kjöbenhavn 1869. I. pp. 155–159.—† *1. ed.* Kbh. 1859 ; † *2. ed.* Kbh. 1862.!

LATIN.—Svb. Egilsson's *version in* Scripta historica Islandorum.
1835. VI. pp. 330-333.

Jónsson, Finnur. Litteratur Historie. II. p. 759.
Müller, P. E. Sagabibliothek. III. pp. 368-371.

ADDENDA.

Egils saga. To p. 13.

Jónsson, Finnur. Kritiske studier over en del af de ældste norske og
islandske skjaldekvad Kobenhavn 1884. 8°. pp. (8)+189. (*Inaug.-
Diss.*)
Concerning the stanzas and poems of Kveldúlfr, Skallagrímr and Egill
and other verses, with normalized text of Egill's stanzas, see pp. 99-
189.

Eiríks saga rauða *and* **Grænlendinga þáttr.** To pp. 17-18 and 29.

The Danish General Staff facsimile-edition of the Grænlendinga þáttr and
Reeves's facsimile-edition of the Eiríks saga rauða (of the Hauksbók)
are reproduced (without due acknowledgment) in a vol. publ. by
the so-called Norræna Society, entitled. The Flatey Book and re-
cently discovered Vatican Manuscripts concerning America as early
as the Tenth Century . . London, Stockholm . . . New York 1906. 4°.

Gísla saga Súrssonar. To p. 27 l. 26.

The Saturday Review. 1866. XXI. pp. 139-140.

Laxdæla saga. To p. 77.

GERMAN.— Die Geschichte von den Lachstälern. Laxdæla
Saga. Eine Erzählung von nordischen Bauern und Seefahrern
die im 8. Jahrhundert aus Norwegen gefahren, und auf
Island eine neue Heimat gefunden. Aus dem Altisländischen
übertragen von Severin Rüttgers. Düsseldorf 1907. (Die
Wanderer. Acht Bücherfolge für die deutsche Jugend, hgg.
von Gust. Kneist und S. Rüttgers. VII. 1.) 8°. pp. xvii+180,
map.

APPENDIX.

A LIST OF POETICAL WRITINGS AND WORKS OF PROSE FIC-
TION ON SUBJECTS FROM THE ICELANDIC SAGAS.*

Árna saga biskups Þorlákssonar.
Barmby, B. H.   Lord Raven Oddsson.   *A poem in her:* Gísli Súrsson,
a drama, *etc.* Westminster 1900. pp. 161-165.

Auðunar þáttr vestfirzka.
Ploug, C. P.   Kong Harald og Islændingen.   *In* Folkekalender for
Danmark. 1859. (Kjöbenhavn). pp. 114-120, *wdct.*

Eiríks saga rauða.
Ballantyne, R. M.   The Norsemen in the West or America before
Columbus.   A tale. 6. edition. London 1880. 8°. pp. vi+406, 4 *pls.*
The first edition is of †London 1872 (*cf.* The Athenæum, Nov. 16, 1872);
the first American edition, †New York 1878.
Clement, Edw. Henry.   Vinland.   *A poem in* E. N. Horsford's The Dis-
covery of the ancient city of Norumbega.   Boston 1890. 4° pp. 43-55.
Hodgetts, J. Fred.   Nordmændenes Opdagelse af Amerika.   Novellistisk
fremstillet.   Kristiania 1891. (Parmann's Illustreret Familielæsning.
XVIII.-XX.).   8°. pp. (8)+170, *illustr.*
The English original appeared in †"The Boy's Own Paper."
Kellett, E. E   Bjarni.   *In his* The Passing of Scyld and other poems.
London 1902. pp 28-35.
Liljencrantz, Ottilie A.   The Thrall of Leif the Lucky.   A Story of
Viking Days.   Pictures by Troy and Margaret West Kinney.   Chicago
1902. 8°. pp. 354, 6 *pls.*
——— The Vinland Champions.   Illustr. by T. and M. W. Kinney. New
York 1904. 8°. pp. x+255, *pls.*

Eyrbyggja saga.
Kellett, E. E.   The Holy Hill.   *In his* The Passing of Scyld and other
poems.   London 1902 pp 44-49.
Otis, G. E.   Thurid and other poems   Boston 1874. pp. 1-34.
Riemann, Robert.   Björn der Wiking.   Ein germanisches Kultur-
drama in vier Akten.   Leipzig [1901]. 8° pp (4)+76.

---

*This list includes chiefly works which have been published separately in book form,
with a few poems and tales in other languages than Icelandic, which have appeared in
periodicals or other books. The list contains only titles found in the Fiske Icelandic
Collection or in Cornell University Library.

Finnboga saga ramma.

Sigurðsson, Ásmundur. Rímur af Finnboga ramma. Akureyri 1879. 8°. pp. 152.

Gísla saga Súrssonar.

Barmby, Beatrice Helen. Gísli Súrsson : a drama. Ballads and poems of the Old Norse days and some translations. Westminster 1900. 12°. pp. xxiv+206.

—— Gísli Súrsson. Sjónarleikur; einnig nokkur kvæði. Matthías Jochumsson íslenzkaði. Akureyri 1902. 8°. pp. (2)+vii+99. Breiðfjörð, Sig. Rímur af Gísla Súrssyni. Kaupmannahöfn 1857. 8°. pp. 95.

Grænlendinga þáttr.

See the titles under Eiríks saga rauða.

Grettis saga.

Grettis rímur, *see* p. 31.

Jochumsson, Matth. Grettisljóð. Ísafjörður 1897. 8°. pp. (4)+204. (*Cf.* Þjóðólfur. 1897. XLIX. p. 233).

Norris, Frank. Grettir at Thorhall-stead. *A tale in* Everybody's Magazine. (New York) 1903 VIII No. 4. pp. 311-319, *illustr.* (*by* J. J. Gould).

Sandel, Joh. Saga om Gretter den Stærkes Tvekamp dramatisk fremstillet. Kjöbenhavn 1878 8° pp. 106.

Gunnlaugs saga ormstungu.

Arentzen, Kristian. Gunlog Ormetunge, dramatisk Digtning Kjöbenhavn 1852. 8°. pp. 90.

Review : Nordisk Tidskrift (utg. af Sohlman. Stockholm.) 1852. pp. 196-200, by Geo. Stephens.

Bjarnason, Símon. Rímur af Gunnlaugi ormstungu og Helgu fögru. Akureyri 1878. 8°. pp. iv+64.—2. útgáfa. Reykjavík 1906. 8°. pp. 68. Bleibtreu, Karl. Gunnlaug Schlangenzunge. Eine Inselmär. Berlin 1879. 8°. pp. (4)+271. (*Two editions of the same year*).

Edzardi, Anton. Schön-Helga und Gunnlaug Eine Dichtung frei nach der altnordischen Gunnlaugs saga. Hannover 1875. 8° pp. vi+(2)+ 152.

First printed as a manuscript with the title : Gunnlaug. Eine Dichtung *etc.* Anklam 1875. 8°. pp. (4)+152, but afterwards a new t.-p. was printed, as given above, and a dedication to Möbius, a preface, and a list of errata were added to it.

Fouqué, F H. K. de la Motte. Die Saga von dem Gunnlaugur, genannt Drachenzunge und Rafn dem Skalden. Eine Islandskunde des eilften Jahrhunderts. In drey Bucher wiedererzählt. I.-III. Theil. Wien 1826. 8°. pp. 227+205+211, 3 *frontisp.* (*Dedicated to the Icelandic Literary Society*).

Francke, G. C. Th. Gunlaug. *A poem in his* Der Skalde. Hamburg [1839]. pp. 119-128.

Heinzen, Wilhelm. Isländisch Blut. Drama in fünf Akten. Leipzig 1903. 8°. pp. 95.

Hallfreðar saga vandræðaskálds.
Drachmann, Holger. Hallfred Vandraadeskjald. Et Drama i fem Handlinger. Kjöbenhavn 1900. 8°. pp. 174.

Harðar saga.
Bjarnason, Símon. Ríma af Hörði Hólmverjakappa og Helgu Jarlsdóttur konu hans. Akureyri 1879. 8°. pp. 24.

Hávarðar saga Ísfirðings.
Bjarnason, Símon. Rímur af Hávarði Ísfirðing. Reykjavík 1891. 8°. pp. 99.

Kjalnesinga saga.
Bjarnason, Símon. Rímur af Búa Andríðarsyni. Reykjavík 1872. 8°. pp. iv+106.
Thomsen, Grímur. Rímur af Búa Andríðarsyni og Fríði Dofradóttur. Reykjavík 1906. 8°. pp 60.

Kormáks saga.
[Leighton, William, *jr.*] Kormak, an Icelandic Romance of the tenth century. In six cantos. Boston 1861. 8°. pp. 118.

Kristni saga.
Holm, Torfhildur Þorsteinsdóttir. Elding Söguleg skáldsaga frá 10. öld. Reykjavík 1889. 8°. *portr* pp. 773.
In this novel various sagas are drawn upon, but the subject is the change of faith in Iceland.

Króka-Refs saga.
Króka-Refs rímur, *see* p. 69.

Landnámabók.
Andersen, Carl. Ingolfs og Hjörleifs Saga. Et episk Digt i to Afsnit. Kjöbenhavn 1860 8°. pp. 179 +(5).
Jochumsson, Matthias. Helgi hinn magri. Dramatiskar sýningar eða söguleikur í fjórum þáttum. Reykjavík 1890. 8°. pp. 123.
Kellett, E. E Thorkell Mani.—Storolf and Dufthak. *In his* The Passing of Scyld and other poems. London 1902. pp. 14-19, 36-42.

Laxdæla saga.
Barmby, B. H. Bolli and Gudrun *A poem in her* Gísli Súrsson, a drama *etc.* Westminster 1900. 12°. pp. 128–129. (*Translated into Icelandic by* Matth. Jochumsson *in* Barmby's Gísli Súrsson. Akureyri 1902. pp 98–99).
Bjarnason, Símon. Ríma af Kjartani Ólafssyni. Reykjavík 1871. 8°. pp. 23.—*2. edition.* Reykjavík 1890. 8°. pp. 24.
Holm, Torfhildur Þorsteinsdóttir. Kjartan og Guðrún. Skáldsaga. Reykjavík 1886. 8°. pp. 15

Howard, Newman. Kjartan the Icelander. A tragedy. London 1902.
8°. p.p vi+107.
Reviews: The Academy. 1902. LXII. pp. 501-502 ;—The Spectator.
1902. LXXXVIII. pp. 445-446 ;—The Times Literary Supplement. 1902.
pp. 51-52 ;—Saga-Book of the Viking Club. 1902. III. 1. p. 127, by
A. F. Major.

Jónsson, Brynjólfur. Guðrún Ósvífsdóttir. Söguljóð. Reykjavík 1892.
8°. *portr* ., pp. viii+109.

Morris, William. The Lovers of Gudrun. A poem. Reprinted from
"The Earthly Paradise." Boston 1870. 8°. *frontisp.* pp. (2), 249-382.
Reviews: The Athenæum, Dec. 25, 1869. pp. 868-869 ;—The Academy.
Febr. 20, 1870. pp. 121-122.—*Cf.* J. Riegel : Die Quellen von W. M.'s
Dichtung The Earthly Paradise. (Erlanger Beiträge zur engl. Philol.
hgg. von H. Varnhagen. IX.) Erlangen 1890, pp. 54-58.—There are,
of course, many other editions of this poem.

Oehlenschläger, Adam G. Kiartan og Gudrun. Tragödie. *In his*
Poetiske Skrifter. Udg. af F. L. Liebenberg. XII. Deel (Tragiske
Dramaer. III. Deel). Kjöbenhavn 1859. pp. 265-382.
Was first printed in †Kjöbenhavn 1848, and a new edition †1849.

Njáls saga.

Brandes, Edvard. Asgerd. Skuespil i 3 Akter. Kjöbenhavn 1895. 8°.
pp. 224.

Breiðfjorð, Sig. Rímur af Gunnari á Hlíðarenda. Akureyri 1860. 8°.
pp. 236.

Green, W. C. Two Sagas from Iceland. (I. Gunnar's Death. II. The
Burning of Njal). *Poems in* Blackwood's Magazine. 1890. CXLVII.
pp. 103-114.

Hole, Richard. The Tomb of Gunnar. *A poem in* The Gentleman's
Magazine. 1789. LIX. p. 937.

Oswald, Elizabeth J. The end of the feud. A true story of Iceland. A. D.
1017. *A poem in her* By Fell and Fjord. Edinburgh 1882. pp. 174-
175. (*Translated into Icelandic by* Bryn. Jónsson, *in* Iðunn. 1885. II.
pp. 190-192 : Sætt Flosa og Kára).

Sighvats þáttr skálds.

Kellett, E. E. Sighvat. *In his* The Passing of Scyld and other poems.
London 1902. pp. 20-26.

Skáld-Helga saga.

Skáld-Helgarímur, *see* p. 93.

Sturlunga saga.

Barmby, B. H. Two sonnets on Sturla's Íslendinga saga.—Sturla
in exile.—The rescue-ride.—Thórd the sheriff.—The burning of Flugu-
mýr.—The end of Sir Ingimund. *Poems in her* Gísli Súrsson, a drama
etc. Westminster 1900. 12°. pp. 107-127. (*The second and the fifth
poem transl. into Icelandic by* Matth. Jochumsson *in* Barmby's Gísli
Súrsson. Akureyri 1902. pp. 91-98).

Brím, Eggert Ó. Gizur Þorvaldsson. Leikr í fimm þáttum. *In* Draupnir. (Reykjavík) 1895-1897. III.-IV. pp. 1-206.—*Also separate reprint.* Reykjavík 1897. 8°. pp. 206.

Einarsson, Indriði. Sverð og bagall. Sjónleikur í fimm þáttum frá Sturlungaöldinni. Reykjavík 1899. 8°. pp. 143.

—— Sværd og Krumstav. Oversat fra Islandsk af Henrik Ussing. Köbenhavn 1901. 8°. pp. 136.

Hansen, Holm. Groa eller "Oldemoder." Dramatisk Skildring fra Islands Forfaldsperiode. Köbenhavn 1900. 8°. pp. 200.

Jochumsson, Matth. Víg Snorra Sturlusonar nóttina milli 22. og 23. septbr. 1241. Kvæði. 2. útgáfa. Eskifjörður 1879. 8°. pp. 24.
Was first published in Baldur. 1870 III. pp. 2-5.

Rudbeck, T. G. Qvinnoränet. Historisk berättelse från medlet af 13de århundradet. *In his* Stockholms forntid. Norrköping 1845. I. pp. 31-200.
One of the characters in this tale is Stúrla Þórðarson.

Sölvason, Sveinn. Rímur af Gissuri jarli Þorvaldssyni. Kveðnar 1769. Leirárgarðar 1800. 8°. pp. (2)+226.

Svarfdæla saga.

Zedlitz, J. C. Ingvelde Schönwang. *In his* Altnordische Bilder. Stuttgart 1860. pp. 1-123 —†*f. edition.* Stuttgart 1850.

Vatnsdæla saga.

Briem, Halldór. Ingimundur gamli. Sjónleikur í þremur þáttum. Reykjavík 1901. 8°. pp. (4)+63

Víglundar saga.

Breiðfjörð, Sigurður. Rímur af Víglundi og Ketilríði, orktar 1840. Reykjavík og Kaupmannahöfn 1857. 8°. pp. (2)+130.—2. útgáfa. Bessastaðir 1905. 8°. pp. 110.

Þórðar saga hreðu.

Jónsson, Hallgrímur. Rímur af Þórði Hreðu. Reykjavík 1852. 8°. pp. 180.—*2. edition* Reykjavík 1907. 8°. pp. 149.

Þorsteins þáttr stangarhöggs.

French, Allen. The Story of Rolf and the Viking's Bow. Illustr. by Bern. J. Rosenmeyer. Boston 1904. 8°. pp. xii+(2)+408.
"The fragment (*sic*) of Thorstein Staffsmitten has been drawn upon in the closing incidents of the story " (*preface*).

Þorsteins þáttr uxafóts.

Böðvarsson, Árni. Rímur af Þorsteini Uxafæti. Utgefnar af Ólafi Ólafssyni Kaupmannahöfn 1771. 8°. pp. 112.—2. útgáfa. Kaupmannahöfn 1858. 8°. pp. 91.

Þorvalds þáttr víðförla.

Hauch, J. Carsten. Saga om Thorvald Vidförle eller den Vidtbereiste. I.-II. Kjöbenhavn 1849. 8°. pp. viii+260; (4)+262 —2 Oplag. Kjöbenhavn 1874. 8°. pp. viii+405.